WELLES-TURNER MEMORIAL
GLASTONBURY, CT

W9-BKW-737

DISCARDED BY
WELLES-TURNER
MEMORIAL LIBRARY
GLASTONBURY, CT

A Good Place to Hide

HOW ONE FRENCH COMMUNITY SAVED THOUSANDS OF LIVES DURING WORLD WAR II

PETER GROSE

PEGASUS BOOKS

NEW YORK LONDON

A GOOD PLACE TO HIDE

Pegasus Books LLC
80 Broad Street, 5th Floor
New York, NY 10004

Copyright © 2015 by Peter Grose

First Pegasus Books hardcover edition April 2015

All rights reserved. No part of this book may be reproduced in whole or in part
without written permission from the publisher, except by reviewers who may quote
brief excerpts in connection with a review in a newspaper, magazine, or electronic
publication; nor may any part of this book be reproduced, stored in a retrieval system,
or transmitted in any form or by any means electronic, mechanical, photocopying,
recording, or other, without written permission from the publisher.

ISBN: 978-1-60598-692-0

10 9 8 7 8 6 5 4 3 2 1

Printed in the United States of America
Distributed by W. W. Norton & Company, Inc.

CONTENTS

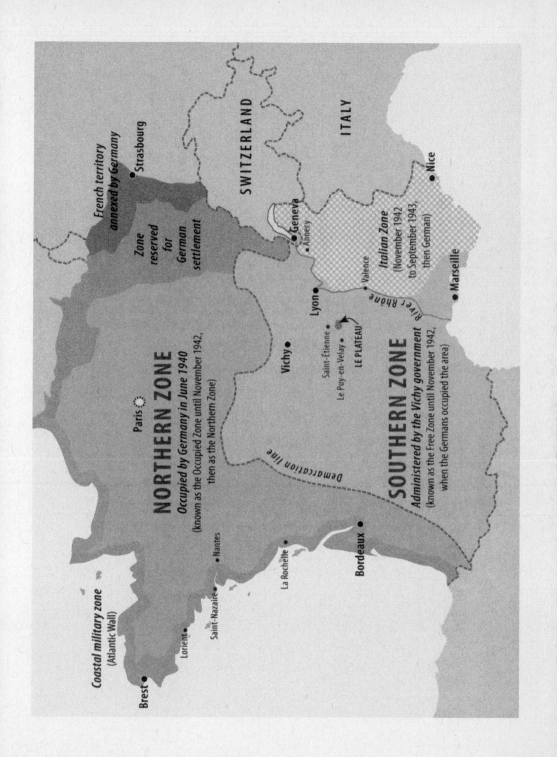

French territory annexed by Germany

Strasbourg

Zone reserved for German settlement

SWITZERLAND

ITALY

Nice

Geneva

Annecy

Italian Zone (November 1942 to September 1943, then German)

Valence

River Rhône

Marseille

Lyon

NORTHERN ZONE

Occupied by Germany in June 1940

(known as the Occupied Zone until November 1942, then as the Northern Zone)

Vichy

Saint-Étienne

Le Puy-en-Velay

LE PLATEAU

Paris

Demarcation line

SOUTHERN ZONE

Administered by the Vichy government

(known as the Free Zone until November 1942, when the Germans occupied the area)

Nantes

La Rochelle

Bordeaux

Coastal military zone (Atlantic Wall)

Lorient

Saint-Nazaire

Brest

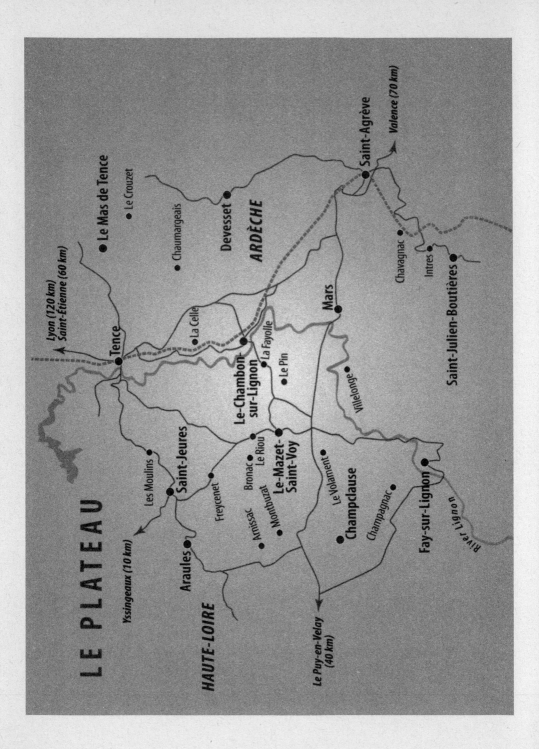

INTRODUCTION

The drive to the village of Le Chambon-sur-Lignon, in the hilly Auvergne region of central-eastern France, brings back childhood memories of those never-ending car trips peppered with the question *Are we there yet?* The 80-kilometre journey from Saint-Étienne, the nearest city of any consequence, starts on a broad national highway. The route soon narrows down to a local departmental road, the twisting and almost deserted D103, which scrambles up through hills, following the course of the River Lignon. Towards the end of this road, the trees give way to vast panoramas across green fields. These are the pastures of the plateau of Vivarais-Lignon. The joy of the drive is the scenery, which is stunningly beautiful, with towering dark forests lining the first part of the route, followed, in spring, by wild forget-me-nots along the verges, while vivid yellow Scotch broom flowers light up the fields and hillsides beyond. In winter it is a different story: the road disappears under treacherous snow, with only some slim poles to mark where the road ends and the ditch begins.

The villages of the Plateau are few, and usually far between. This is Huguenot country, and the Protestants fully live up to their French stereotype. The houses are built of grey granite supporting thick slate roofs, with none of the flashes of colour that distinguish the sunny houses of Provence or the cheerful chalets of the French skiing resorts in the mountains across the River Rhône. In the villages of the Plateau, few windows have the traditional flowerboxes with bright geraniums. These are solid, grey houses, and nothing flamboyant disturbs their serenity. They give the impression of being occupied by equally solid people, honest and hard-working, a world away from the bright lights of Paris, or the hedonistic bedlam of the Côte d'Azur. This is not wine country, or even food country. (None of the modest handful of restaurants, bars and cafés in Le Chambon is ever likely to trouble the Michelin inspectors.)

At the small village of La Fayolle, about three kilometres outside Le Chambon, there is a graceful old farmhouse close to the road. At the time of writing, it was being lovingly restored by a young couple, Philippe and Aziza Mariotte, who run part of it as a bed and breakfast (*chambre d'hôte* in French) known as L'Aulne. In the years between 1940 and 1944, the farmhouse offered a different kind of hospitality—not quite as comfortable, and a great deal more dangerous.

The buildings of L'Aulne form a U-shape. The Mariottes live in one wing and the bedrooms of the B&B occupy another. Across the courtyard from the Mariottes' home, and still part of the same U-shape, is a large stone barn. At one end there is a tiny doorway, leading to a couple of equally tiny, linked storerooms, not much bigger than two large cupboards.

Today the storerooms are piled with junk: ancient bicycles, discarded furniture, a couple of window-frames, an old metal jug. The wooden panelling on the walls has come away in places. Cobwebs festoon the beams and the ceiling. The second room looks impossibly small for someone to sleep in, let alone live in. The entry room looks even more cramped, surely too small a workspace for a pair of forgers.

Yet in these two storerooms, and in scattered barns, farmhouses, spare rooms, hostels, guesthouses, hotels and school dormitories, literally thousands of human beings survived who might otherwise have been murdered. In the years between 1940 and 1944, something extraordinary happened here and in hundreds of farmhouses like it. In those dark days of World War II, human decency was in short supply. But on the Plateau, it triumphed.

Peter Grose

March 2014

PROLOGUE

Oscar Rosowsky's childhood was nothing if not exotic. He came from a family of Russian Jews, originally from the town of Bobruysk, 600 kilometres southwest of Moscow, in Byelorussia. Oscar's grandfather had made the family fortune, building a substantial business exporting oak wood.

There was enough money to pay for graduate studies for Oscar's father, so he moved to Riga, the capital of nearby Latvia. Graduate studies were a serious privilege: higher education was not for Jews in Tsarist Russia. After the Russian revolution, Oscar's father settled in Latvia and took Latvian citizenship. In 1921 he married Oscar's mother in the Latvian beach resort town of Libau.

Oscar's grandfather had planned carefully for his three sons. The oldest son was placed in charge of one branch of the family timber business, in the port town of Danzig, then part of Germany; the youngest son managed another branch in Edinburgh, Scotland; Ruben Rosowsky, the middle son and Oscar's father, took charge in Berlin. Oscar was born in Berlin in 1923.

Oscar's family kept their Latvian citizenship, but in Berlin they led a very Russian life. They spoke nothing but Russian at home, though Oscar never learned to read or write Russian. At school, he learned to write as well as speak German. The Nazi Party was on the rise, and anti-Semitism was widespread in Germany; however, the family made no attempt to conceal their Jewish identity. It was barely visible anyway: they were liberal rather than strict or Orthodox Jews. Oscar Rosowsky remembers a visit from his grandfather to Berlin when the family observed the Passover ceremony and ate the Passover meal, but in general Oscar's father stayed away from the synagogue, doing no more than popping in occasionally for Yom Kippur.

These were golden days for the Rosowskys. Germany's Weimar Republic was breaking all records for financial catastrophe, and the German currency famously collapsed in 1923. Anyone with foreign currency was king, and the Rosowskys, whose business was exporting timber, had access to hard currency. They lived in a furnished six-room apartment in Berlin's fashionable Charlottenburg district, rented from a Prussian Army officer down on his luck (he and his wife slept behind the kitchen). Young Oscar spent his primary school years surrounded by gilt antique furniture. His parents' social life included throwing a succession of extravagant parties.

Although this was the period of Hitler's rise to power, the Rosowskys' Jewishness caused no problems. As far as their German friends and neighbours were concerned, they were Latvians, and Latvians were like brothers to Germans. The family's wealth even spared Oscar some pain at school. At the strict boys primary school he attended, one of the teachers kept two canes, which he soaked in a humidifier to inflict maximum pain on boys who irritated him. But the public beatings were reserved for poor children. Oscar's family was rich, and he emerged from primary school unscathed.

The lavish lifestyle could not last. Ruben Rosowsky had always been wayward. He was seen as the *enfant terrible* of the family, a prankster who had scandalised his parents as a child by turning up for meals wearing peasant boots with a wooden spoon tucked into the side. He was the practical joker of the family, the clown. He was also no businessman, and not even a successful business could support his extravagance. In 1933, he went bust. Hitler had already become chancellor, but it was not the threat of Nazism that chased Oscar's father out of Berlin. Instead Ruben skipped town a step ahead of his creditors and headed for the French Riviera, where there were casinos with plenty of rich players. The three Rosowskys, father, mother and Oscar, moved to a much more modest two-room apartment in Nice.

Oscar's mother, Mira, was, according to her son, vivid, attractive, resourceful and indomitable. She quickly realised that, if the family was going to eat, she would need to be the breadwinner. She trained as a milliner, and worked from home, copying designs from *Vogue* magazine and selling her hats to the Russian Jewish community on the Côte d'Azur. It was not exactly lucrative, but it paid the rent and bought the groceries. Ruben did the shopping and cooked some memorably good meals. When he could muster up the stake money from the tiny allowance his family sent him, he gambled. If he won, he bought Oscar a peach Melba. If he lost . . . well, there was always next month's allowance. One room of the apartment housed the parents' bed, a small kitchen and Mira's worktable. Oscar slept on a sofa in the other room, which doubled as a showroom for the hats.

Oscar arrived in Nice with barely two words of French. But thanks to a superb teacher, Demoiselle Soubie—'the sort of person one should fall on one's knees before,' he says—he quickly fitted in. The school building even gave him a brief aftertaste of the luxurious life he had led in Berlin: called the Imperial Park College, it was an old palace with huge rooms and a giant marble hall. Each room had two balconies, and the students could peer out and watch the King of Sweden playing tennis below them. The Côte d'Azur in the 1930s was a cosmopolitan place, packed with White Russians and other refugees, rich and poor. One of the other students, Paul Franck, taught Oscar French by sitting him down on the slope alongside the college and getting him to recite the irreverent plays and novels of Courteline. Paul Franck's Jewish father, also Paul Franck, had managed the Olympia music hall in Paris, where performers like Mistinguett basked in the spotlight. In Nice, Oscar Rosowsky was surrounded by colourful and sophisticated people, living in a pleasantly sunny and largely tolerant city.

Politics was inescapable here, too. In a world polarised between the far-left communists and the far-right fascists, there was plenty to argue about and even demonstrate against. Some teachers at the school were Pétainists, supporting the Vichy government of 'Unoccupied' France led by Marshal Philippe Pétain. Others were socialists or communists, ready to defend their beliefs with their fists. Oscar's language coach and school friend Paul Franck lost two teeth in a political brawl.

Oscar also discovered the Boy Scouts, and they became a passion. He rose to become a troop leader. The overall head of his troop was the aristocratic Jean-Claude Pluntz de Potter, a baron from his father's side, whose petite Jewish mother was born Schalit. Jean-Claude's family sympathy for the plight of Jews was soon to play a vital role in Oscar's life.

So we have a picture of young Oscar—slightly built, wearing spectacles, studious rather than one of the lads, but sharp-witted and street smart. He spoke three languages fluently: French, German and Russian. He had known rich, and he now knew poor. He says he was a lazy student, but that did not stop him passing the second and higher stage of his baccalauréat, clearing a path for him to go on to university. The Boy Scouts had taught him a degree of self-reliance, and some of the secrets of survival in the wild. He was now eighteen years old, the year was 1942, and so far life had been safe and fairly uneventful. Then the noose began to tighten.

• • •

After France's defeat in 1940, the northern half of France and the whole Atlantic coast was occupied by Germany. Under the terms of an armistice signed on 22 June 1940, the 'Unoccupied' or 'Free' southern half, including Nice, was managed from the central French town of Vichy by a government led by France's Marshal Pétain, a World War I hero. It was, by any standards, a puppet government. As well as general collaboration, military and civil, with the Germans, the Vichy government undertook to participate wholeheartedly in Hitler's persecution of Jews. This led to the passing of a swathe of vicious anti-Jewish laws, which often went beyond the anti-Jewish legislation in the German Occupied Zone to the north, or even in Germany itself. On 3 October 1940 the Vichy government passed a law that excluded Jews from jobs in the public service and parts of the private sector. The next day it passed a law authorising the immediate internment of all foreign Jews. As Latvians, the Rosowsky family were targets.

In this period, the Jewish population in the Unoccupied Zone lived in a state of quite extraordinary ignorance and denial. Although the French internment camps began to fill up with Jews from late 1940 onwards—all of them rounded up under the grotesque euphemism 'gathering the families'—news was tightly controlled, travel and communication were restricted, and people simply didn't know what was going on. This was backed up by a general sense of it-can't-happen-here. But in 1942 that all changed.

By then, Oscar Rosowsky had already lost out to the *numerus clausus*, a Vichy law which restricted Jewish entry to the professions, most notably law but also medicine. No university course could accept more than 2 per cent Jewish students. Oscar wanted to train as a doctor. He was philosophical about the missed opportunity. 'I couldn't hope to study medicine because of the *numerus clausus*,' he says. 'But in any case, I don't think my parents could have afforded to send me to study in Aix-en-Provence.' So at the end of the summer of 1941, after passing both stages of his baccalauréat, Oscar Rosowsky accepted a job with a local Nice tradesman, repairing typewriters and mimeograph machines, a form of printing press. His special beat was the local administrative district, or prefecture; he cycled there two or three times a week with his toolbox and cleaning brushes to clean the machines and sort out any problems. The various prefectures were the ultimate source of all the papers needed to function in Vichy France. Identity cards, driving licences, ration coupons, residence permits, travel permits: all originated from the prefecture. Oscar Rosowsky came to know the machines that produced these documents literally inside out.

By early 1942 the nightmare for Jews in Vichy France had well and truly begun. On 2 June 1941, the Vichy government proclaimed its oppressive *Statut des Juifs* (Jewish Statute), at the same time announcing a census requiring all Jews to declare themselves. The census created a handy list of Jews to be barred from jobs or deported, as well as a register of Jewish property to be confiscated. All French people over the age of sixteen were required to carry an identity card, including their photograph and their current address. Jews in the northern Occupied Zone had the word *Juif* (Jew) stamped on their identity card. Production of a card stamped *Juif* was a licence to officialdom to hassle the bearer in every possible way.

Food was rationed. So was tobacco. And clothing. Anyone who carried a *Juif* identity card could expect problems with all three. There were random checks. 'Your papers, *monsieur*?' Anyone who failed to produce the appropriate identity card could be arrested on the spot. A Jew—especially a non-French Jew—caught in this way could expect deportation to Germany and beyond. Most who were deported never returned.

Jews were also liable to have property confiscated, without compensation. Some old scores—or simply jealousies—were settled as neighbour denounced neighbour. *He's Jewish. She's Jewish. They're foreigners.* Next would be a raid, followed by arrest and deportation.

• • •

In August 1942 Oscar set off to a Boy Scout camp at Saint-Dalmas-Valdeblore, in the mountains a little to the north of Nice. 'It was a marvellous camp,' he recalls. 'I was "totemised" [given an animal name]. I was nicknamed Cacatoès [Cockatoo], while our troop leader Jean-Claude Pluntz became Pipistrelle [Bat].' The return to Nice, across the Gorges du Verdon, was idyllic. A beaming Oscar arrived back at his parents' apartment bursting with stories to share. He had no chance to tell his news. The nightmare had now struck at the heart of his family.

> *I walked through the front door and the first thing my mother said to me was: 'Listen to me, your father has disappeared. He's been arrested. I don't know what's happening . . . I called the lawyers, but I haven't heard anything back. And you, you've had a summons to hand yourself over to the foreign workers group at Mandelieu-la-Napoule [on the outskirts of Cannes, to the south-west of Nice].' She handed me a bit of paper. I couldn't think of what to do, so I said: 'You're kidding me. I'm heading straight back into the mountains.' It was silly of me to say it. She just said: 'No, no.' She was a clever woman, and she already had a plan. 'Definitely not. One of my clients has a husband who's a Spanish Republican. He's the under-secretary at Mandelieu-la-Napoule. We'll see if we can work something out with him.' So I said to her: 'I'll do my best.' I put on my Boy Scout uniform with all my bits and pieces, including my four-pointed hat, and I headed off to the foreign workers group at Mandelieu-la-Napoule.*
>
> *Then I had a bit of luck. When I arrived, the place seemed deserted. I found an office. There were two people behind a white*

*table: a commander from the Army Reserve wearing a uniform
with [a captain's] three bars, and his Spanish secretary standing
beside him. The commander said to me: 'What on earth are you
doing here? Everybody was brought here yesterday, and I packed
them all off to Germany.' He was outraged. I said: 'I don't want
to be worked to death like that.' He said: 'Well, listen carefully. It's
not complicated. I'll post you off to Mont Faron.' There were raids
going on in the centre of Nice at the time, but Mont Faron was on
the outskirts. It was full of Italian market gardeners. 'You can work
there,' the commander said. 'I'll give you the papers. When I've done
that, I never want to see you again.'*

*That was it. I stayed with the Italians while the raids went on in
Nice. I watered their vegetables and flowers. I didn't have a ration
card, but they gave me some bread, and I fed myself with fruit,
some delicious figs. And they made me some snails in tomato sauce,
Italian style. So I was never hungry, and I ate with them. I spent
three peaceful weeks there.*

When things had calmed down a little, Oscar slipped back to the
family apartment in central Nice. In the three weeks that had passed
since her husband's arrest, Mira had set about trying to trace him.
She had established that he had not been singled out for arrest, he
just happened to be with the wrong person in the wrong place at the
wrong time. Her natural first thought was that it was all a mistake.
He'd be released, surely? But despite her best efforts with lawyers and
contacts in the Russian and Jewish communities, she could not find
out where her husband was or what had happened to him. For three
weeks she had waited, living in hope. *We'll hear soon. We'll get some
news. He'll write.*

The truth was unimaginable. A single letter got through more
than a year later, in late 1943. He had been taken to the French

internment camp at Le Vernet, south of Toulouse, then handed over to the Germans at the notorious Drancy camp on the outskirts of Paris. He was deported from Drancy on 25 September 1942 in Convoy 37, bound for Auschwitz. There were 1004 Jews in the convoy, of whom a mere fifteen survived the war.

Mira and Oscar Rosowsky learned the rest of the story after the war. Ruben Rosowsky had been luckier than some, avoiding the immediate fate of new arrivals at Auschwitz. He was one of 175 prisoners separated from the rest of Convoy 37 and set to work. He was allocated to a slave labour camp called Blechhammer, an annexe of the Auschwitz III death camp, where he survived until 1945. However he did not survive the dreadful death march of slaves and concentration camp prisoners that marked the last days of the Third Reich. Luck finally ran out for Ruben Rosowsky, the *enfant terrible*, the family joker, the failed businessman, the talented cook, the compulsive gambler, the buyer of peach Melbas. In the dying days of the war, he finally joined the six million.

• • •

When Oscar Rosowsky returned to the family apartment in Nice after his time at the Mont Faron foreign workers site, there was still no word from his father. He knew what he had to do. 'I said to my mother: "Listen, I'm going to Switzerland, and we're going there together."'

This was easier said than done. The Swiss were turning back Jewish refugees in their tens of thousands along the whole length of the French–Swiss border. So it was not simply a matter of turning up at a border post with a valid passport and walking through. Legal entry would require visas issued by the Swiss authorities, and there were none to be had. To enter through the front door was impossible. That left an illegal border crossing, on foot, across rugged mountains. In addition, the two Rosowskys would first need to travel to the border area by train. That, too, would involve terrifying risks. In Vichy France in late 1942, a traveller faced random checks at the station and on the train from gendarmes or the *Sûreté Nationale* police, and could be asked to produce travel documents, proof of identity, and proof that the journey was authorised and legal.

There was no question of mother and son travelling under their own documents. The non-French-sounding-name Rosowsky would be enough to guarantee trouble. Oscar's Boy Scout troop leader came to the rescue, offering to lend his papers. So Oscar Rosowsky became Jean-Claude Pluntz. He simply replaced Jean-Claude's photo on the identity card with his own, using an old art pen to copy the missing quarter of the official stamp onto the edge of the new photograph. That left the question of papers for his mother. In particular, she would need a convincing identity card.

Through the Russian and Jewish communities, Mira had a vast network of contacts, which happened to include a smuggler in Saint-Gervais, near the Swiss border. Oscar leapt at this possibility. 'I'll go to Saint-Gervais,' he told his mother, 'you meet me there.' Meanwhile Mira organised some false papers for herself.

It was by now early October 1942. Oscar took the train to Saint-Gervais. No one challenged Jean-Claude Pluntz's right to travel, and he arrived without incident. He met the smuggler, handed over 100 francs[1]—a very fair price—and waited for his mother. Three days passed. No mother. It was widely believed at the time that the only targets for arrest were men, so his mother was probably okay. But as a young male Oscar was in danger, and he couldn't hang around indefinitely—better to cross the border now, and come back for her if he had to. His Boy Scout training meant the mountains held no fear for him.

The smuggler drew him a map and took him to a drop-off point at Morgins Pass, east of Geneva, about five kilometres short of the Swiss border.

The smuggler set me down in a group of little huts, telling me: 'You climb as far as the crest, and on the other side you'll see lights. That's Switzerland. Next day, don't rush. Take it easy. Don't stop at the first village. Keep going.'

I lay down in the sunshine and waited for darkness, reading Victor Hugo's book of poems The Legend of the Ages. *I had a flask of wine and some sweetened condensed milk. When it started to get dark, I got up. The smuggler stopped me: 'You must wait until it's completely dark,' he ordered. So I waited for total darkness, then I set off.*

I arrived at the crest. It was bitterly cold. [Morgins Pass is 1400 metres above sea level.] Happily, I was wearing every bit of clothing I owned. I waited for daybreak, then I literally tumbled down the other side. I knew I'd made it into Switzerland when I saw a piece of silver paper . . . a chocolate wrapper!

Then I came across a hiker, who said to me: 'Listen carefully. Don't go into the village, because they'll send you straight back.' So I went round the village. I was a bit tired by then. Having crept past the village, I found a beautiful, sunny path that led gently down the mountainside. I followed it down, but there was a bridge with a sentry. He grabbed me and marched me into the village of Morgins. I was furious. I pointed to my papers, and said to the assembled soldiers 'Listen, I'm a deserter from a group of foreign workers. You're not going to send me back.'

I didn't know anything about the laws of Switzerland. They soon put me straight. 'Look,' they said, 'it's not too difficult. If you keep on making up stories, we'll just take you back to the border and hand you over to French Customs. Otherwise, you can have an Emmental sandwich, and you can go back round the same hill that brought you here. We'll be at the bottom of the hill watching, and we'll distract them, and that's the last we'll ever hear from you.'

Oscar Rosowsky accepted the inevitable and re-crossed the border into France. At Thonon-les-Bains he caught the train and headed for Nice, expecting to be reunited with his mother.

But when he got back to the apartment, Mira was gone. He learned the full story later. She had taken the train from Nice to Saint-Gervais. On the train, the gendarmes had taken one look at her clumsily forged papers and accused her of travelling under a false name. She managed to persuade them that the papers were genuine. Then she had a terrible thought: what if they were pretending to let her go but secretly keeping an eye on her? Oscar could be waiting on the platform for her at Saint-Gervais, and the police would arrest them both. So she ran after the gendarmes, shouting that they were right, her papers were false. She was promptly arrested, taken off the train at the next stop, and sent to the French internment camp at Rivesaltes, near Perpignan.

The first news of this came to Oscar in the form of a letter from his mother, addressed to him at the apartment in Nice. It contained the bare outline of the story: she had been arrested and interned in Rivesaltes. Oscar knew he would have to act fast, before she was deported to Germany and who knew what fate. Where to start? He turned to the best network he knew, the Boy Scouts. A meeting was quickly convened at the home of a Catholic Boy Scout, Jean Boucher, totem 'Élan' (Elk). As well as Oscar, the meeting included Jean-Claude Pluntz; Anatole Dauman, a young Polish Jew with a reputation for daredevilry; and two young Protestants, Charles and Georgette Hanne, whose mother lived in a remote village in the Haute-Loire called Le Chambon-sur-Lignon.

Charles and Georgette told Oscar a little about Le Chambon. It was located on the Plateau Vivarais-Lignon, high in the mountains on the eastern side of the Massif Central, southwest of Lyon and about 200 kilometres from the Swiss border. The area was populated by farmers and small tradesmen. Most of them were Huguenot Protestants, a community whose isolation had helped them survive centuries of religious persecution in the rest of France. The Hannes had one more startling piece of information to pass on to Oscar: the people of the Plateau were willing to hide Jews.

• • •

Oscar now had somewhere to go. But first he had to get his mother out of Rivesaltes. He knew that the prefecture in Nice issued internment orders. It also issued residents' permits (*permis de séjour*). Through his old job, he was a familiar figure at the prefecture, arriving on his bicycle with his boxes of brushes and tools. He could move around unchallenged. Who cared about, or even noticed, a skinny teenage typewriter serviceman doing his rounds?

Oscar knew exactly what to do. However fast his heart was pounding, a show of calm was essential. Above all, he must not attract attention. He pedalled gently down to the prefecture, clutching his toolbox and brushes. Still outwardly calm, he strolled through the door and headed for the prefect's office. He knew what he needed, and he knew where to find it.

I was completely on my own at the back of the office, cleaning the machines. There was no one there to see what I was doing. I had no problems, none, none. I pinched some letterhead paper, and the prefect's official seal, and I made a permis de séjour *using the prefecture's Underwood typewriters.*

Ever considerate, he spared the prefect all the bother of having to sign the *permis*, which authorised a certain Madame Mira Rosowsky to leave Rivesaltes and travel to Nice. Instead, Oscar signed it on the prefect's behalf, with a nicely convincing version of the real signature. Then, apparently finished his cleaning round, he pedalled off as serenely as he had arrived, the precious paper and the prefect's stamp safely tucked away in his toolbox. It was all too easy.

Next, the burning question was how to get the paper to Mira in Rivesaltes. At this time, in early November 1942, internees in the camps were still allowed to write and receive letters, so Oscar suggested simply entrusting it to the post. Charles Hanne was adamant: no, he had connections. He would see that it got to her. To be on the safe side, Oscar arranged for two German photographers, friends of his parents', to make a good copy. Then he handed the precious original over to Charles Hanne.

Days passed. Nothing happened.

Oscar was getting desperate. Time was running out. His mother could be deported at any time. He posted the surviving copy of the permit off to the camp. Then he—and Mira—had a stroke of luck. On 8 November, 'Operation Torch' began. British and American forces struck fast and effectively, landing in the French territory of Algeria in North Africa, just across the Mediterranean from France. They quickly brushed aside Vichy resistance, and looked poised to launch an invasion of the European mainland. The Germans reacted quickly and decisively. On 11 November they ended the sham of 'Unoccupied' France by sweeping south, occupying the whole country.

With this sudden change of government, there was understandable confusion throughout the old Vichy zone. Who was in charge? Did the Vichy government's word still count for anything? Who controlled Rivesaltes? Nobody knew. It was a good moment for Mira Rosowsky to present Oscar's photocopy of her *permis de séjour* to the camp authorities. In all the chaos, they probably reasoned that one Jew less was one problem less. So they accepted the *permis* and, on 17 November 1942, they let her go. Oscar Rosowsky's career as a forger was off to a good start.

Reunited in Nice, Oscar and Mira discussed the future. They couldn't stay in Nice. They were already targets. It was clear that Switzerland was too risky. They had both already failed trying to get there. To Oscar, the only possibility was to find some way to merge unnoticed into French society, in some other part of France. The best bet looked like Le Chambon-sur-Lignon. Oscar still had Jean-Claude Pluntz's papers, so he could travel as Pluntz. He agreed with Mira that he should take a look for himself at the Plateau.

He set off alone, by train, from Nice to Le Chambon. Within hours of his arrival, he knew that this was the place. He returned to Nice to collect his mother. However, that left the problem of papers. His mother spoke French with a pronounced foreign accent. If she carried regular French papers, she would be under suspicion from the minute she opened her mouth. She needed papers that matched her accent. Again, Oscar had the answer.

Producing false papers is no simple matter. They need to be checkable against other official records, and they need to match in every possible way the person using them. Oscar searched the *Journal officiel*, the official gazette of the French republic, for a suitable history. Then, using the stolen prefect's official seal, and his newly acquired skills at forgery, he created the birth certificate and naturalisation papers of a real White Russian of a similar age to Mira, a certain Mademoiselle Grabowska, born at Samsun in Turkey. The White Russian existed, and the act of naturalisation could be verified in the *Journal officiel*. The Turkish–Russian background would explain his mother's foreign accent.

The only way to Le Chambon-sur-Lignon was by train. The fast trains were heavily policed, but the slow local trains were generally left alone by the authorities. Mother and son now caught the slow train north, travelling across lyrically beautiful countryside, to the town of La Voulte-sur-Rhône. There they boarded the narrow-gauge departmental train that wound its way up the mountain, through Le Cheylard to Le Chambon-sur-Lignon. The ancient train reminded Oscar of those he had seen in Western movies.

At this point it is worth standing back and considering the enormity of the decisions the pair had made. Ruben Rosowsky had been arrested, and neither his wife nor his son knew where he was. Mira and Oscar were foreign Jews, subject to instant deportation under Vichy law. They had already come to the attention of the authorities in Nice, so they could expect arrest at any moment. Now, on the say-so of a Boy Scout friend of Oscar's, they were travelling to a place where they had no family or friends, trusting that the strangers at their destination would risk their lives by giving the Rosowskys shelter. The countryside may have looked peaceful as it slipped past the train window, but the journey must have been a nightmare of fear and uncertainty. Would the gendarmes or anybody else on the journey spot Jean-Claude Pluntz's altered papers? Would Mira's fake papers, produced by a typewriter repairman barely out of school, pass scrutiny by experienced and suspicious policemen? The journey lasted seven hours. Throughout that time they had to remain calm, despite their fears. Someone wants to see your papers? Look them in the eye and hand over the forgeries. Don't let your hand shake. Then wait. And hope.

Finally they arrived at the tiny railway station at Le Chambon-sur-Lignon. They went straight to the apartment of Marcelle Hanne, the mother of Charles and Georgette, and spent their first few days there. However, the apartment was tiny, and they couldn't stay there for long. There was a woman who waited regularly at the station for refugees, Marcelle said. Perhaps she could help.

Sure enough, the woman at the railway station knew exactly what to do. Mademoiselle Grabowska could stay with Pastor Daniel Curtet in the village of Fay-sur-Lignon, about sixteen kilometres from Le Chambon. Jean-Claude could move into a guesthouse called Beau-Soleil

(Lovely Sunshine), which served as a dormitory for students at the New Cévenole School in Le Chambon. Nobody asked the two Rosowskys who they were, or why they had chosen Le Chambon-sur-Lignon. Clearly, they needed help; that was enough. Later, Oscar would move to a little farmhouse at La Fayolle, where the farmer Henri Héritier and his wife, Emma, had a couple of tiny spare rooms in a barn.

• • •

There is an irresistible thought at this point in the narrative. Whoever devised the Vichy *numerus clausus* law, which kept Oscar Rosowsky out of medical school and diverted him into the world of printing, can't have foreseen the consequences of his vindictiveness. France may have (temporarily) lost a good doctor, but the Vichy law had just launched the career of one of the finest—and most spectacularly successful—forgers in World War II history.

Part I

...

PREPARATION

1

Pastors

In 1935, the then French foreign minister Pierre Laval famously sought help from Russia's Stalin. He wanted Stalin to join him in persuading Pope Pius XI to take a stand against Hitler and the Nazis. Stalin couldn't believe what he was hearing. 'The Pope!' he roared. 'How many divisions has he got?'

It was a fair question, and it might have been equally well asked of the pastors of the Protestant churches[2] of the Plateau Vivarais-Lignon.

• • •

Charles Guillon was born in Paris on 15 August 1883, in humble circumstances. He came from a family of *concierges*, that unique French combination of receptionist, porter and nightwatchman without which no French apartment building could function. His family was poor, but his parents believed in education, so Charles stayed in high school until he was seventeen. He was a bright student and wanted to become an architect. However, university was out of the question for someone from such a poor family, so architecture was put on hold while he looked for a job. Though he was an agnostic at the time, he nevertheless made a beeline for the UCJG building in the Rue de Trévise, near Montmartre in Paris. UCJG stands for Union Chrétienne de Jeunes Gens, or Christian Union of Young People; in other words, he headed for what we call in English the YMCA (Young Men's Christian Association), Paris branch.

The YMCA was founded in Britain in 1844 to help young men who had recently moved from the countryside to the city as a consequence of the industrial revolution. The organisation quickly spread to Canada, the United States and Europe. Today it is seen mostly as an international chain of youth hostels, offering cheap and very basic accommodation to backpackers. But in 1900, when Charles started working for the organisation, the YMCA's Christian, Protestant and puritan roots still ran deep. In the 50 years since its foundation it had grown into a large and genuinely international organisation, and it held camps and conferences, both national and international, where Christian topics were discussed and promoted. It was also hugely influential in the ecumenical movement, which sought to unite the Christian churches. For the young Charles Guillon, though, none of this mattered: the big attraction for him was the UCJG's gymnasium and, even better, its indoor swimming pool, the only one in Paris at the time. The UCJG was his first port of call on his job hunt, and they offered him a job straight away, as a secretary.

The UCJG had a profound impact on Guillon. Within a year he had given up his agnosticism and converted to Christianity. He also gave up his ambition to become an architect. Instead he chose to study at the Paris Faculty of Theology in Boulevard Arago, in effect the University of Protestantism in France. He kept his strong connection with the UCJG, and attended the odd national and international conference on behalf of the Paris branch. Here he got to know key people in the international organisation, including its founder, Sir George Williams, by then a very old man.

After completing his theology studies, Guillon became a key figure in the running of the Paris UCJG. It was no small task. There was a boarding school to manage, plus endless conferences, meetings and sporting events to organise, Bible study groups to attend and run, even the launch of the first-ever French Boy Scout troop. By then Guillon had married, and he seemed set for a spectacular rise in the world YMCA organisation, and particularly within the European UCJG, with its headquarters in Geneva.

In 1914, war broke out. Guillon abandoned the Paris UCJG (and his young wife), and for four years served as chaplain to the French 13th Army Corps. When war ended, Guillon returned to his wife, but not to the UCJG. He decided instead to look for a parish that would accept him as pastor. He arrived with his wife at Saint-Agrève, on the Plateau, in the spring of 1919.

It was a tough first assignment—the area was listless, with an ageing population, and with 60 very recent widows, their husbands killed in the war. With furious energy, Guillon set about reviving the parish. He personally visited every family. He restored the church, galvanised the parishioners into action, and within four years had things humming. He still found time to take part in international conferences associated with the UCJG, so he remained in touch with his old contacts. Soon, though, the cold, hard winters on the Plateau got the better of him, and in 1923 he resigned from Saint-Agrève. His next move could hardly have been predicted: the parish council of Le Chambon-sur-Lignon, a mere eleven kilometres away, invited him to become their pastor, and he accepted, despite the identical climate. He moved to Le Chambon in the autumn of 1923.

If Saint-Agrève was difficult, Le Chambon was a nightmare. In May 1922 the General Assembly (the ruling body of the Protestant Church) had singled it out for harsh criticism. The parish had money problems. It was accused of neglecting the thousands of Protestant holidaymakers who arrived in the summer, and of allowing the local UCJGs to drift and lose support. Again, Guillon turned things round. Within four years the money problems had been addressed, and the congregation had swollen to something of its former glory. Guillon's sermons were widely admired, and conferences and fairs organised by the church took place throughout the summer. Charles Guillon had won the confidence of the entire parish.

In 1927, Guillon was 44 years old, married, with two young children. Contemporary photographs show a neatly dressed, rather avuncular figure, almost entirely bald, with strong, dark eyebrows; his round face bears a small, carefully trimmed moustache and a ready smile. He was affectionately known as 'Uncle Charles' to one and all. There must have been some vanity lurking somewhere: in addition to the immaculately tended moustache, Guillon famously wore rather lurid purple church robes, which people forgave. He never lost sight of his humble beginnings, and remained determinedly left-wing in a rather old-fashioned, workers-of-the-world-unite way.

Guillon's spectacular success in turning around two run-down parishes did not go unnoticed, particularly by his old employer, the Y. In 1927 the world secretariat contacted him and offered him the job of assistant secretary of the world committee of the UCJG. Guillon accepted, and resigned as pastor of Le Chambon. The scholarly Roger Casalis replaced him. (Casalis is nearly always referred to in books as a pastor-historian.)

Guillon now moved to Geneva with his wife and children. However, if the UCJG was determined to have him back, the people of Le Chambon were equally determined not to lose him. On 1 December 1929 they elected him to serve on their municipal council, and on 10 May 1931 he was elected mayor of Le Chambon.

One of Guillon's conditions for accepting the role of mayor was that he be allowed to continue his work with the UCJG. He now divided his time between Geneva and the Plateau. Despite this, he seems to have been a remarkably effective mayor. During his time in office, he presided over the electrification of the village and surrounding countryside, and the installation of a municipal water supply and sanitation system. He added 80 kilometres of new roads, and set up a clinic for mothers and babies that led to a spectacular fall in the infant mortality rate. Tourist facilities expanded with the creation of walking paths, sports grounds and the district's first tennis court. He also found time for political activity, becoming vice-president of the Federation of Christian Socialists of the Haute-Loire, and joint organiser in September 1933 of the 6th National Congress of the Federation of Christian Socialists. The conference was dedicated to 'the world economic recovery, with the double aim of a managed economy and the restructuring of agriculture'.

Wearing his UCJG hat, he also began a manic bout of world travel. In his first year in the new job in Geneva, he visited existing branches of the YMCA in Greece, Turkey, Syria, Palestine, Egypt and, as a bit of an afterthought, France. Next he travelled to Africa, starting in Senegal and visiting the Gold Coast, Togo, Cameroon and the Congo, setting up new branches in each country as he went. Then it was the turn of Latin America, where he spent four months, and Algeria, where he twice toured the Kabylie region in the north.

By 1933, after six years of globe-trotting on behalf of the UCJG, the mayor was able to write in a newsletter distributed on the Plateau: 'I have now visited 44 countries and I sense already rising perils and the march towards war.'

• • •

It is not the function of this book to give a detailed account of the origins of World War II. For readers wanting to know more, I would strongly recommend Andrew Roberts' superb book *The Storm of War* (2009), which is both highly readable and thoroughly researched. Roberts gives a wonderfully detailed and insightful account of the lead-up to war and of the war itself. Here we need only the broadest outline.

Most historians would agree that World War II in Europe was really a continuation of World War I. The Great War, as it is still sometimes called, was the first total war, the first mechanised war, and one of the deadliest tragedies in all human history. The most accurate figures available suggest there were over 37 million casualties, including 8.5 million killed, 21.2 million wounded and 7.7 million missing or taken prisoner. The bitterest fighting took place on French and Belgian soil, around the River Somme in the north of France, and in Flanders in Belgium.

The catastrophic cost of the war itself was compounded by the peace terms, which set out to put an end forever to German militarism. Clause 231 of the Treaty of Versailles declared that Germany and its allies were wholly responsible for 'loss and damage' suffered by the victors of World War I, and they would have to pay for the lot. The price was set at 269 billion gold marks, the equivalent of 100,000 tons of gold, which was slightly more than half of all the gold mined in the entire history of the world. (At today's gold prices the value would be something like US$5.8 trillion) Clearly the Germans couldn't pay. Germany's currency collapsed, leading to hyperinflation and great hardship.

This hardship was compounded by the Great Depression, which began with the Wall Street stock market crash of 1929 and spread throughout the developed world. (If what follows has horrible echoes of the world today, then be warned: last time we went through this sequence of events, it led to World War II.) The world now polarised. There were siren voices from the far right of politics offering simplistic solutions guaranteeing a return to prosperity and strength, and similar siren voices from the far left promising a sunny future in a workers' paradise. What both sides delivered in practice was a string of murderous dictatorships.

The world of the 1930s was a perfect breeding ground for demagogues, and demagogues naturally sprang up to take advantage. In

Germany there was a further problem: in the eyes of the German people—and particularly the German Army—they had not lost World War I at all. As far as the German high command was concerned, they had not been defeated in the field, and Germany had not been invaded or occupied. Their country was the victim of a jealous and vindictive international cartel, which had bankrupted them. If they *had* lost the war, it was because the politicians and other treacherous elements—the communists, the socialists and the Jews—had betrayed them. This is known as the *Dolchstosslegende*, the myth of the stab in the back, and without it we might never have heard of an ambitious World War I corporal called Adolf Hitler.

• • •

After seven years, Roger Casalis, pastor of Le Chambon-sur-Lignon since Charles Guillon's departure in 1927, had grown tired of the isolated life on the Plateau. He felt let down: he needed a car or a motorcycle to get around the huge parish, but the parish council refused to provide him with either. Time to move on. But who would take over? He had a young, firebrand pastor friend whom he knew was looking for a parish, and so he invited him to preach in the Le Chambon church one Sunday in 1934. The parish council looked on: it was very much an audition. As everybody left the church, the parish councillors were stony-faced. That, after all, was the Huguenot way. But the audition was clearly a success. On 22 June 1934 the council unanimously elected as their new pastor a 33-year-old pacifist from northern France. It was done on a 'temporary' basis so that the appointment would not have to be approved by the Regional Council in Paris. The new pastor's name was André Trocmé.

Trocmé was born on 7 April 1901 in Saint-Quentin in northern France, not far from the Belgian border. His background was so vastly different from Charles Guillon's that it is hard to imagine two such contrasting characters occupying the same position. Quite simply, the Trocmé family was rich. The patriarch, André's father, Paul, owned a flourishing cotton-weaving business, and André started life in a large house well staffed with servants. He was the youngest of eleven children from his father's two marriages: six brothers and three sisters from the first marriage, and an older brother from the second. Paul Trocmé's first wife had died, as did two girls from the first marriage.

André's father was austere, strict and a little overbearing. 'Duty' was a key theme in the Trocmé household, as was maintaining the long Trocmé tradition of leadership and success. André's mother, Paula, was German, the daughter of a Lutheran pastor from Petzen, near Hanover. To André she was a distant figure; however, they made a few visits together to Petzen, and with her help, André came to speak fluent German as well as French.

In the way of rich families at the beginning of the twentieth century, André was largely brought up by governesses, maids and servants. His daily schedule offers a fair measure of the rigidity of his life and the distance his parents maintained. Every minute of the day was accounted for, from 7 am rise-and-shine to 9 pm lights out. It included, at 7 pm: 'Two bells for dinner, followed by 15 minutes visiting with the grownups in the living room.' That was the only planned contact with his parents in the entire day. It hardly made for a warm and intimate relationship.

Two traumatic events helped to shape the future pacifist. The first took place when André was ten years old: he witnessed the dreadful death of his mother. Because they were wealthy, the family could afford not just a car but a powerful Panhard-Levasseur, famous for its race-winning qualities. Paul was driving, with his wife beside him. André, his older brother Pierre and their cousin Étienne sat behind. Another car overtook them. That couldn't be allowed, and Paul charged into the clouds of dust thrown up by the other car, intent on regaining the lead. His car smashed into a pile of stones at the side of the road, throwing the occupants onto the road. André's mother suffered the worst injuries. She was immediately knocked unconscious, and was taken home by ambulance. She died at home a few days later. André, who occupied the room next to hers, could hear only too clearly her agonised moans as her life drained away.

The family funeral service was held at home. Paul was racked by guilt and remorse, calling out: 'I killed her. I killed her.' From that point onwards, André Trocmé knew the appalling impact of even a single death. He resolved never to be the knowing cause of one.

The second traumatic event was the arrival of World War I on the Trocmé doorstep. Over the centuries, wars have not been kind to the town of Saint-Quentin. History records no fewer than six Battles of Saint-Quentin, going back to Humfrid's victory over Louis the German on 15 January 859. All of them tended to leave the town scarred, and sometimes pulverised.

In September 1914, a month after Germany had declared war on France, the city was smashed, overrun and brutally occupied by the rampaging German Army. The River Somme, scene of the most terrible trench warfare of World War I, flows through the middle of Saint-Quentin, so the worst of the carnage took place nearby. The first evacuation of civilians did not take place until March 1916, leaving the citizens of Saint-Quentin to get on as best they could for eighteen months under German occupation. The Trocmé family stayed on even longer: for two and a half years André witnessed at first hand the streams of bodies being brought back through the town from the front line. He could smell the gangrenous flesh, and see for himself the bitter consequences of war.

Then came an extraordinary encounter. A young German corporal called Kindler was billeted in the Trocmé home. André's brother Robert was a captain in the French Army and something of a war hero. André was struck by the thought that one day Kindler might be called upon to kill his brother. 'Not possible,' Kindler replied. 'I am a Christian, and Christians don't kill.' Kindler was a telegraph operator, and he explained that he had made an arrangement with his captain not to carry a revolver or dagger or any other weapon. If he came under attack, God would decide whether he lived or died. André was impressed, and invited Kindler to join him at a Sunday afternoon UCJG meeting with some young friends. Kindler attended in full German Army uniform. After a nervous start, the other UCJG members quickly accepted the young enemy in their midst. Humanity, and reconciliation, had triumphed. This first encounter with a practising pacifist was an important lesson for young André. He already knew that war was terrible. He now knew that it was possible, even when wearing a military uniform, to have nothing to do with the killing.

Towards the end of 1916, the town of Saint-Quentin came under attack from both sides, German and French. The Germans decided that the last of the civilians should be evacuated, and in February 1917 the Trocmé family joined the exodus. They were packed in cattle cars on trains, with a German sentry standing guard over them, and deposited in Belgium. The trip should have taken no more than three hours, but with the railway lines jammed with military traffic, it took closer to 24 hours, with no food, no water and no toilet facilities.

André and his brother Pierre were billeted with a poor Belgian farming family, the Demulders. Fifteen-year-old André now learned for himself what it was like to be a penniless refugee. The Demulders gave the two young Trocmés another lesson in humility: they simply shared what little they had with the two young strangers, asking for nothing in return. André could hardly avoid the comparison between his own privileged life and the humiliating poverty of the Demulders and their neighbours. Wasn't this an injustice that cried out to be put right? Pacifism was simply the opposite of making war. But weren't the Demulders victims of another kind of war, one in which the poor felt the pain? For a clever and observant teenager, whose overriding sense was one of duty, the experience of being a refugee offered plenty to think about.

André's suffering was briefer than most. The Trocmé family had relations and influential contacts all over northern France and Belgium, and André's father quickly found four people who could help—a distant cousin, an old customer of the weaving business, a neighbour from Saint-Quentin and a member of the Belgian Royal Court. The customer lent him money, the cousin and the neighbour found André a good school, and the courtier found the Trocmés a fine house in Brussels, owned by a banker who had fled with his family to Paris. All four introduced them to the well-to-do of Brussels society. Within six months of their ignominious departure from Saint-Quentin, the Trocmé family were again leading a comfortable, middle-class life.

The war ended on 11 November 1918. The Armistice was another huge lesson for André. German soldiers stripped off their medals and military decorations and danced in the streets alongside their former enemies. For the teenage André it was further evidence of the futility of war. What was the point of it all, if men who had been willing to kill each other yesterday were dancing together in the street today? World War I was sometimes referred to as 'the war to end all wars'. For André, that was the answer. There must be an end to all war.

• • •

After the Armistice, the Trocmés could not simply return to Saint-Quentin and resume their old lives. The family home had been left in ruins, along with 80 per cent of the buildings in their home city. On top of that, the Germans had systematically looted the town, dismantling factory machinery and shipping it off to Germany. The Trocmé weaving business had suffered this fate and would have to be rebuilt. While that rebuilding was going on, the family also needed to find somewhere to live. So, exactly a month after the war ended, on 11 December, the Trocmés moved from Brussels to Paris.

Paul Trocmé had previously been a major lay figure in the Evangelical Reformed Church, and his seventeen-year-old son was now beginning to develop strong religious feelings. In Paris, André embarked on a prodigious two-year course of study that included university-level Hebrew, Greek and church history at the Sorbonne, university-level philosophy at the Faculty of Theology on Boulevard Arago (Charles Guillon's alma mater), and high school German, English, geography and literature at home. He completed it all with distinction. He was now determined to become a Protestant minister.

André paints a picture of himself at the time as stiff-necked and afraid of girls. He was living in the gloriously vibrant city of Paris in the 1920s, which appeared to his puritan Protestant soul to be Sodom, Gomorrah, Babylon and the Garden of Earthly Delights all rolled into one. 'I was,' he wrote, 'unable to see the difference between sin and innocent amusement. Life was white in church, at the Christian Union meetings, [and] when we strolled through the Meudon Forest . . . and black at the movie theatre, the circus and the brothels.' He was certainly prudish. In 1919, aged eighteen, he went off to a Boy Scout camp at Domino on the Île d'Oléron, an island off the Atlantic coast of France near the port of La Rochelle. He recalled afterwards: 'The conical *marabout*-style tents were pitched in a little pine forest, and we walked around half naked (so it seemed to me) . . . here I was, wearing only a bathing suit and exposing my body to the burning sun for the first time.'[3] So prudish, yes. Tempted, yes. But give in to temptation? Never!

This puritanism stayed with him throughout his life. He never drank or smoked; sex outside marriage was beyond contemplation; and he vowed to tell the truth at all times, whatever the inconvenience.

André's life now took an unexpected turn. His next decision can be seen as wilful, or eccentric, or another example of his clear-headed originality. At theology college the young student had come into contact with a strong circle of pacifists, and he became increasingly impressed by their ideas. There were, in the world of the 1920s, two strong threads running through the pacifist ideal. On the one hand there were those, like André and his friends, who saw pacifism as a moral issue. Christians should obey the sixth commandment: 'Thou shalt not kill.' There was no ambiguity. The words meant exactly what they said. And that meant pacifism was the only choice for a believing Christian. (This was not, to put it mildly, a view shared by the established churches, Catholic and Protestant.)

The second thread was political. Essentially, the socialist left believed that wars were part of a capitalist conspiracy: the rich and powerful tricked the poor and gullible into dying on their behalf. Instead, the poor of all nations should stick together and refuse to fight in support of their kings and bosses. This was quite a different line of thought, since it allowed men to kill for what they saw as a just cause. After all, bumping off the odd tsar and tsarina never seemed to trouble the Russian revolutionaries. Although his experience as a penniless refugee had given him some inkling of the meaning of the phrase 'class warfare', this left-wing form of pacifism was never André's line. His position was always based on Christian morality.

However, we know from his (unpublished) memoirs that young André increasingly felt that his wealthy upbringing and now his cloistered life at theology college were somehow keeping him away from the real world, which included girls and other temptations. To know himself properly, he would have to enter that real world and try to make his way in it. How? All young Frenchmen were liable for military service. As a theology student, André's had been deferred. Against the universal advice of family, friends, fellow students, teachers and professors, André Trocmé knew what he must do next. The young pacifist put his theology course on hold, and joined the army.

• • •

André was remarkably tall, particularly for a French man of the time, at six feet two inches (188 centimetres). In all photographs, he towers over those around him. His confident style, middle-class accent and obvious intelligence gave him an air of real authority. Although his round spectacles lent him a slightly bookish appearance, the rest of him proclaimed a natural leader. Contemporary photographs show a young man with film-star good looks. Here, the army decided, was officer material. He was quickly promoted to corporal, and assigned to a disciplinary platoon.

He was an odd soldier: he didn't swear, and in his free time he read books while his fellow soldiers headed for the brothels and bars. (If André ever went into a bar, he drank coffee.) Above all, he made it very clear that he would not fight and kill. On arrival at the unit, he had been issued with a rifle and 250 rounds of ammunition. He never made them ready for use.

A sympathetic friend arranged his transfer to a geodesic brigade (an army map-making group), which sounded like a good refuge for a pacifist soldier. So Corporal Trocmé, his rifle and his ammunition joined the cartographic unit of the 54th Field Regiment and headed for the Bled,[4] in Morocco.

The rifle now became a problem. In France, there was no chance he would be called on to use it. But the Bled was a different proposition. The Berber tribesmen there were not too fond of the French occupying army, and the unit might be called on to shoot back, if not to shoot first. For a pacifist corporal, there was only one way forward. French Army regulations allowed soldiers to deposit unused weapons with the armoury. So Corporal Trocmé's rifle, suitably greased and wrapped, found a new home in the arms store at Rabat, Morocco, and the reluctant corporal headed off into the wild Bled armed only with a paper receipt for his weapon, signed by the armourer.

Inevitably, trouble threatened. The platoon's officer, Lieutenant Tardy, ordered an inspection of the group's arms. Corporal Trocmé explained that his rifle was back in the armoury at Rabat, adding that, as a pacifist, he would refuse to use it anyway. In his memoirs, Trocmé recorded the following dialogue.

LT TARDY: If we are attacked tomorrow, the absence of a single rifle could make a big difference in the end result of the battle.

CORP TROCMÉ: I understand, Lieutenant.

TARDY: A refusal of obedience in front of the enemy means an instantaneous court martial and an immediate execution by firing squad . . . do you understand that, too?

TROCMÉ: Yes, sir, I do.

TARDY: I should condemn you to a long prison sentence and send you back to Rabat in handcuffs. I can't do that because I need all of my men.

The lieutenant paused for a moment, and then went on.

TARDY: I'll tell you what. I'll ignore your case for the time being. I don't give a damn whether you have a rifle or not as long as we are not attacked. But, if we are ambushed and if I order my men to fire their weapons in self-defence, and you don't carry out my order for any reason, then you will be court-martialled and only God knows what will happen to you after that. Is this understood?

TROCMÉ: Yes, sir.

Happily, none of this eventuated. The Berbers fired a few shots one night, but the platoon sheltered behind a stone wall and waited for the attackers to lose interest, which they eventually did. No one was ordered to fire his weapon in self-defence, so there was no court martial and no God-knew-what to follow.

Shortly afterwards, the unit returned to Paris, to find that the whole 54th Regiment had been dissolved. Corporal Trocmé's rather unpromising military career could now end, as long as he could come up with the appropriate discharge papers. Perhaps not surprisingly, it turned out that all his military papers had been lost, and he could not find his old commanding officer or anyone else to release him. As far as the army was concerned, he didn't exist. A unit of air force balloonists had taken over his old barracks, and the phantom corporal managed to persuade an air force sergeant there to issue him with a stamped paper that declared for all the world to see that TROCMÉ, André Pascal, had been lawfully discharged from the air force, not the army, and was now a civilian. He never heard from the army again, nor they from him, undoubtedly to the relief of both.

• • •

By then it was 1923, the year Adolf Hitler made his first bid for power in Munich with the so-called Beer Hall Putsch. The attempted revolution may have failed (and led to Hitler's trial for treason) but the civil unrest that drove it seemed ever more ominous. Throughout Europe people sensed that the Great War, the war to end all wars, was far from over.

André Trocmé returned to his studies at the Faculty of Theology in Paris, this time in slightly reduced circumstances. The family home in Saint-Quentin had finally been restored, so his father and family gave up their apartment in Rue Jacob in the Latin Quarter and moved back home, while André shifted into student accommodation at the college. This was another turning point: he was now much more exposed to persuasive individuals at the college who were already taking public stands in the cause of pacifism. Jacques Martin went to prison three times for refusing conscription. Henri Roser was thrown out of the Missionary Society after returning his military papers, and had to end his studies at the college. Édouard Theis, another pacifist, became an important ally and lifelong friend and colleague of Trocmé's. Arnold Brémond mingled anti-war militancy with support for workers' causes. Surrounded by these powerful voices, André Trocmé now made up his mind: in 1924 he joined the MIR (Mouvement International de la Réconciliation), an international pacifist organisation, and became a member of its European Council. He was now a publicly declared pacifist, at a time when refusal to serve in the military was a criminal offence. The public saw pacifists as cowards and traitors, and this view was supported by the established churches, Catholic and Protestant, and by just about every government in the world. Pacifism could be a lonely business.

Two ideas now dominated André's thoughts. His experience in the army left him in no doubt about the rightness and practicality of pacifism. The mounting tension in Europe gave fresh urgency to the cause. At the same time, he grew increasingly conscious of the cruel contrast between his own comfortable, middle-class life and the lives of the poor. His Christian duty, he was convinced, was to help them.

In September 1925 he moved to New York after winning a scholarship to the Union Theological Seminary there. His father disapproved. He thought it was about time André found a parish for himself and launched a career in the Church. However, André knew his mind, and crossed the Atlantic.

If his intention had been to get away from comfortable middle-class life, that ambition fell apart in the most bizarre way. He was wanted on the phone. A strange voice said: 'I am Mr John D. Rockefeller junior, 10 West 54th Street, and I need a French tutor for my sons.' Édouard Theis had taken the job earlier, and the Rockefellers had come to trust French theology students. So André became tutor to Winthrop and David. He collected them from school each day, shared their afternoon tea and evening meal, even travelled with them to Florida for Christmas. Every Friday evening, he went to the Rockefeller country estate at Tarrytown, on the Hudson River, and returned to Manhattan on Saturday evening. On Sunday, he was free to do as he chose. The pay—$175 a month—was generous. He might even be able to save enough money to make a long-standing dream come true: to go to India to meet that great advocate of non-violence, Mahatma Gandhi. Less practically, John D. Rockefeller senior gave him a ten-cent coin and made him promise to invest it. 'It's the way I started, and I became rich,' the great man told him. Sadly, the ten cents never quite became the cornerstone of a new Standard Oil Company, but it was a kindly thought.

In 1926 the Rockefellers asked André to stay on for an extra year, or even two, but he now believed the time had come to go to work. That meant returning to France and looking for a parish of his own. He was 25 years old, and he could not remain a student forever. This resolve was strengthened in the Easter of 1926. André was sitting with some friends in the cafeteria of International House. One of the friends left. The empty chair was taken by an aristocratic and strikingly attractive Italian social work student, Magda Elisa Larissa Grilli di Cortona. It would be nice to say it was love at first sight, but the truth is it was more like love at second sight. They met again, and this time the attraction was strong.

Magda came from a radical intellectual Russian family that traced its roots back to and beyond the Decembrist uprising of 1815. The Decembrists had aimed to topple the tsar and bring democracy to Russia. They failed miserably, leading to 289 arrests, five executions and 31 imprisonments. All the other conspirators were exiled to Siberia, including Magda's great-grandfather, Alexei Poggio. Magda was proud of this radical history. She was determined to lead her own life, live by her own standards, and break from her stifling middle-class background of minor Florentine nobility and the expectations of Italian married and family life. She was forthright, clever, and a bit of a rebel. She was not religious: in particular, after five years' residence in the convent school of Le Mantellate she found the Italian Catholic Church repellent. Like André, she had grown up motherless. Her natural mother had died a month after Magda's birth, and she never got on with her stepmother.

André proposed, Magda accepted, and they married in Saint-Quentin, France, in the autumn of 1926.

André now set to work looking for a suitable parish. He was determined to work among the poor in an industrial town, and his wish was soon fulfilled. At the beginning of 1927 he was sent to the picturesque-sounding Sous-le-Bois (Under the Trees), part of the parish of Maubeuge near the Belgian border. The shady trees turned out to be a distant dream: they had long ago given way to smokestacks, steel mills and industrial grime, while the people of the town were poor, brutalised and downtrodden. Alcohol abuse was a major problem, often leading to domestic and other violence.

As pacifism was contrary to church policy, the young pastor had given an undertaking not to preach about it from the pulpit. However, he felt free to preach it elsewhere, including at a meeting of the local Socialist Party. His powerful speech pointing out that pacifism was the only logical consequence of Christian belief was reported in the local paper. That led to an angry letter of condemnation from the Regional Council of the Evangelical Reformed Church. Trocmé the troublemaker was born. Worse, his name was now on the Regional Council's watch list.

The following year, after the birth of their first child, Nelly, the Trocmés moved on to another parish, Sin-le-Noble, a suburb of the heavily industrial northern city of Douai and not far from Sous-le-Bois.

Again, there was not much nobility in evidence. Sin-le-Noble existed to dig coal for the steel mills. It was a single-company town, and that company was determinedly Catholic. Miners who skipped mass were warned they could lose their homes. The company subsidised housing, and what the company giveth, so the miners were told, the company also taketh away. It was hardly promising territory for a young Protestant pastor, but André stuck with it for seven long years, from 1928 to 1934. During this period Magda gave birth to three more children, Jean-Pierre, Jacques and Daniel. André honoured his pledge not to preach pacifism from the pulpit. But the storm clouds were now building over Europe, and the need to prevent another tragic war seemed ever more urgent. He would have to take his message elsewhere.

Using his fluent German, Pastor Trocmé even took the argument across the border into Germany itself. He spoke in Heidelberg to a meeting packed with communists and Nazis, each spoiling for a fight with the other but all vaguely agreeing on a single point: pacifism was out. At the end of the meeting, one of the Nazi Brownshirts pulled a gun and threatened Trocmé with it. 'I suggested to him in German that he should kill me right there in front of everybody,' Trocmé recalled in his memoirs. 'My proposal seemed to calm him down, because he disappeared into the crowd.'

At another meeting, this time in Reutlingen, near Stuttgart, Trocmé got a hearing from a hostile audience by springing out from behind the curtains and barking: *'Deutschland erwache!'* ('Germany awake!') As this was a favourite line of Hitler's, the Brownshirts lapsed into startled silence, and listened respectfully while André called for equal and fair treatment for both German and French former World War I soldiers. This led to cheering and general applause. Why? As one of the Brownshirts explained afterwards: 'You have precisely expressed what our Führer tells us every day—justice for all, fairness for all, and peace for all.' It was not exactly the kind of endorsement André Trocmé had in mind.

• • •

The Trocmé family now had a pressing personal problem: the children's health. The foul industrial air of Sin-le-Noble was starting to affect them all, Nelly in particular. So André began to look for a new parish. The first invitation came from Clamart, one of a group of three parishes on the southern edge of Paris. In early 1933 he met the church council of Montrouge–Malakoff–Clamart, who liked what they saw and voted unanimously to accept him. The appointment then had to be approved in Paris by the Regional Council of the Evangelical Reformed Church, the same council that had rebuked André for his pacifist views at Sous-le-Bois. André managed to persuade the Regional Council to allow him to present his case to them in person. But the council asked him only one question: 'In case of war, would you put on a uniform and defend the Fatherland? Answer yes or no.' The answer could only be no. That ended his candidacy.

With the help of a friend, André now found a vacancy for a pastor at Thonon-les-Bains, near the Swiss border and not far from Geneva. As with Clamart, André met the church council and they approved of him. But one dissident member of the council tipped off the Regional Council in Paris. This time there was no need for André to go to Paris and speak for himself. The Regional Council had already made up its mind. No, again.

In 1934 Roger Casalis wrote to André asking if he would be interested in taking over from Casalis in Le Chambon-sur-Lignon. As we've seen, this third church council also liked what they saw, and they voted unanimously to accept him. But this time they were forewarned: stay clear of the Regional Council in Paris. If they called the appointment 'temporary' there would be no need to seek approval. So on 22 June

1934, the church council of Le Chambon-sur-Lignon, an isolated village high up on the Plateau Vivarais-Lignon in the Haute-Loire department of France, appointed as their new pastor—temporarily, of course—a restless, charismatic, multilingual, troublemaking, notorious pacifist called André Trocmé.

• • •

Charles Guillon left behind no memoirs. André Trocmé did, as did Magda Trocmé. It is quite striking that neither Trocmé makes much reference to Guillon. There is no evidence that the two men did not get on, but they clearly did not have much to do with each other. However, Guillon and the Trocmés combined to play a key part in one of the most influential developments on the Plateau.

Guillon wanted to build a UCJG camp at Le Chambon, along the lines of American summer camps. It would be primarily set up as a holiday camp, but it could be used as a school during term time. The two Trocmés had a much more ambitious idea. Le Chambon had long needed a secondary school, and the Trocmés would be delighted to set it up. So began the École Nouvelle Cévenole, the New Cévenole School.[5] It would be unique in that it would be privately owned, coeducational, Protestant, and international in character, with a strong thread of pacifism. The school would be open to boarding students from all over Europe—indeed from all over the world—as well as from the Plateau. The teachers, too, would be drawn from around the world. Guillon had a suggestion. The school would need a headmaster (in French, a *directeur*). How about Édouard Theis? Theis could also act as Trocmé's assistant at the church. André jumped at the idea.

So both projects went ahead. Charles Guillon built his UCJG camp, known as Camp de Joubert, and André and Magda set up the New Cévenole School. The school opened its doors to its first eighteen pupils in October 1938. Three languages were included in the curriculum:

Édouard Theis's American-born wife, Mildred, taught English, Magda Trocmé taught Italian, and Hilde Hoefert taught German. Hilde was an Austrian Jewish schoolteacher who had fled Vienna in the wake of the Anschluss (Hitler's annexation of Austria in March 1938). In Vienna she had taught Latin. When she arrived on the Plateau, sometime in the summer of 1938, there was no work for Latin teachers. So she took a job as an au pair at the Salvation Army refuge *Les Genets*. She continued to work there even after accepting the German teaching job at Cévenole, because the first teachers at the school were unpaid.

Hilde Hoefert has some claim to being Le Chambon's first specifically Jewish refugee. She would not be alone for long.

2

War

By 1936 the Plateau Vivarais-Lignon was almost perfectly poised for its future role as a refuge. It had two things going for it: people and position. The Plateau itself spread across two French departments, the Haute-Loire and the Ardèche, in the French region known as the Auvergne. There were seventeen *communes*,[6] thirteen in the Haute-Loire and four in the Ardèche, with a total population across both departments of about 24,000. It was largely a rural community, with the population scattered widely in isolated farmhouses and small villages rather than concentrated in large towns. In the Haute-Loire the key communes were Le Chambon-sur-Lignon, population 2721, of whom 2600 were Protestant; Le Mazet-Saint-Voy, population 2221, with 2087 Protestants; and Tence, population 3662, of whom only 300 were Protestant. The figures for the key communes of the Ardèche are less precise: suffice to say that more than half the Ardèche's Plateau dwellers lived in the commune of Saint-Agrève, around 3000 in all, of whom about 1500 were Protestant. The total Protestant population of the Plateau came to around 9000, heavily concentrated in the communes of Le Chambon, Le Mazet and Saint-Agrève. The Protestants were mostly Huguenots, fundamentalist followers of John Calvin, the austere French priest who carried forward the teachings of Martin Luther. Some were Darbyists, a splinter Protestant group, who believed, among other things, that Jews were indeed God's chosen people. Thus the Plateau came well stocked with determined people, hardened by centuries of religious persecution, and all of them armed with a profound tradition of frugality, silence and sticking together.[7] The persecuted Huguenots had also developed a tradition of sheltering other victims, whatever their background. After the French Revolution of 1789 and the establishment of a determinedly secular society in France, Catholic priests came to be seen as part of the Old Order, to be hunted down where possible. The Protestants of the Plateau took them in.

Geographically, too, the Plateau was an ideal sanctuary. It was totally isolated. It straddled no strategic route from anywhere to anywhere. It housed rural communities with no heavy industry worth grabbing, and no natural resources like coal or precious metals to interest an invader. Anyone who set about conquering the Plateau would not have much to show for his efforts when the job was done. So, in general, people left the Plateau alone.

Last but not least, it had a strong tradition of hospitality. Since the late nineteenth century, the Plateau had played host to huge numbers of tourists and visitors, particularly children. Farmers took in poor children from the cities and offered them a healthy summer in the clean mountain air. The farmers received a nominal subsidy from an organisation called *Les enfants à la Montagne* (The Children on the Mountain), while the children did small chores around the farm to earn their keep. Special holiday homes catered for unaccompanied children. In 1935 some 3500 children spent their summer holidays in and around Le Chambon. The whole Plateau was littered with houses and apartments to let, guesthouses, B&Bs and even a few hotels.

Miraculously for a small and isolated rural community, Le Chambon-sur-Lignon also enjoyed the leadership of some remarkable men and women. Charles Guillon, the mayor, had at his disposal an international network of political, religious and youth organisations. André Trocmé brought with him a separate group of international contacts, as well as an unshakeable vision, huge charisma and a powerful intellect. Trocmé's efforts were rendered all the more effective by the tirelessly unsentimental, practical, sceptical Magda, who made sure her husband's feet made regular contact with the ground, and who attended to many of the details. Édouard Theis provided enormous intellectual and practical support, as well as doing his own independent work both as headmaster of the New Cévenole School and as a protector of refugees. He also turned out to be a dab hand at forgery.

The pastors of the surrounding villages would also play a vital role: encouraging, organising, sheltering, planning, conspiring. It is all too easy to write the Plateau's story as though it all happened in Le Chambon, and that André Trocmé alone carried the burden. That is far from the truth. Pastors like Daniel Curtet in Fay-sur-Lignon, Roland Leenhardt in Tence, André Bettex in Le Riou, and Marc Donadille, who worked for the Cimade refugee organisation, were all important, and all showed great courage during the testing times ahead. Dr Roger Le Forestier, who had worked with Albert Schweitzer in Africa, arrived in Le Chambon in 1936 and became a hard-working and much-loved presence. Roger Darcissac, the headmaster of the primary school, turned out to be a talented forger (which is beginning to shape up as a previously unremarked skill that goes with teaching), as well as a resourceful prevaricator when it came to telling the police who was and who wasn't on the school roll. Other outstanding figures—like Oscar Rosowsky, the Resistance leader Pierre Fayol, the extraordinary American agent Virginia Hall, or the Nobel Prize–winning novelist Albert Camus—were still to arrive.

• • •

Despite all this promise and potential, the Plateau's career in international rescue got off to a pretty shaky start.

Just as World War II can be seen as a continuation of World War I, so the Spanish Civil War can be seen as the full dress rehearsal for World War II. In brief, on 17 July 1936 war broke out between the elected Spanish government of (left-wing, often communist) Republicans and the rebel (right-wing, often fascist) Nationalists, who were led by the Spanish military. Civil wars are generally noted for their viciousness and cruelty, and the Spanish Civil War set new standards in horror. The upshot was a defeat for the Republicans, by 1 April 1939, and the imposition of the military dictatorship of General Francisco Franco, which lasted in Spain until the old brute died on 20 November 1975.

The war produced a flood of refugees, mostly Republicans, who headed for what they believed would be a sympathetic reception in neighbouring France. The bulk of the refugees congregated on the French side of the Spanish border, just across the Pyrenees, or in the French Basque Country around Biarritz, or along the Mediterranean coast near Perpignan. The numbers were enormous: perhaps as many as 500,000 Spanish Republicans fled to France. The French didn't want them, and certainly couldn't cope with them.

The department of the Haute-Loire was instructed by the French government to do its bit to help out. Three waves of refugees were allocated to them: 200 in October 1936, 500 in the summer of 1937, and a massive 1115 in the spring of 1939, when the Republicans had lost the war. The prefecture had the task of finding refuge for them.

The Spanish were not exactly greeted with open arms. The gendarmes spoke up early. They didn't want any more 'anarchists' and 'dangerous men' on their patch. In the largely Catholic and conservative town of Tence, the local council simply barred the Spanish from entry. On 25 October 1936 the eighteen Tence councillors voted unanimously to keep them out, prompted no doubt by the thought that the Republicans were both left-wing and anti-clerical. There was the usual hand-wringing explanation of the 'we'd like to help, but . . .' variety. 'The householders and hoteliers are refusing the refugees,' the council informed the prefecture, going on to say what amounted to: 'The council itself can't help either, because we don't have enough pots and pans, and bed linen. What's more, there's no work for the refugees. And in any case, the council's first duty is to its own people' (and not, by implication, to a lot of godless anarchists and troublemakers). The headline in the local Plateau newspaper, *Yssingeaux Gazette*, on 1 November 1936 gives some measure of the hostility. 'Does the Spanish invasion threaten our region?' the paper demanded. The answer seemed to be yes. So no refugees, thank you very much.

Things weren't much better in Le Chambon-sur-Lignon. Unlike the councillors of Tence, mayor Charles Guillon did not try to block the refugees. However, he made it clear that the council would do nothing official to help them. If they wanted to use their eight-francs-a-day allowance from the prefecture to pay for vacant holiday accommodation in and around Le Chambon, that was their business. Even this tepid response proved locally unpopular. Although the community could certainly use the money the refugees brought in, particularly in winter, they did not want them filling up the holiday accommodation in summer. They preferred their regular customers.

All was not lost. As early as 1936, the first glimmer appeared of the Plateau's role as a refugee shelter. Marguerite de Félice, a Swiss resident of Le Chambon, joined forces with Juliette Usach, a Spanish refugee, to set up La Pouponnière (The Creche). She followed this up with 'a call to the people of Le Chambon' to create an orphanage. The local population responded well, and the orphanage opened its doors in 1939. Meanwhile, the Salvation Army opened one refuge, Les Genêts d'Or (The Golden Brooms),[8] then a second, Les Barandons,[9] in the hills to the northeast of Le Chambon. There was also a youth hostel opened at La Bruyère, and another hostel, named rather mysteriously Fraternité d'Hommes (Men's Brotherhood).

The Spanish did themselves no favours. Some 90 per cent of the refugees were women and children, and little was expected of them. But the men were not exactly dynamic in their search for work. They preferred to live on their allowance, and were generally regarded as useless layabouts. Nor did the children endear themselves to the local population. On 18 February 1939 three young Spanish boys aged between nine and eleven, all of them residents of The Golden Broom, went to the small village of Le Crouzet, less than two kilometres from Le Chambon, and set about trying to derail the train. Happily, they failed, but they all finished up in court anyway, and there was no shortage of volunteers to keep a close eye on them afterwards. A local newspaper reported, more in sorrow than in anger: 'This attempt has produced a strong response in Le Chambon, where the refugees had all recently been given a warm welcome.'

By September 1939, most of the Spanish had left the Plateau, either returning to Spain or moving elsewhere. The few that remained now played a memorable if unexpected role. First, the prefecture in Le Puy-en-Velay, the capital of the Haute-Loire, decided that about twenty 'undesirables' should be moved to their own camp, about two kilometres from Tence. The prefect commandeered an old paper mill known as La Papeterie,[10] and the Spanish were rounded up, housed there, and told to stop idling and do some work. Some moved on, but a few of them organised work permits and moved to Le Chambon. As we have seen, Charles Guillon had long wanted to build a UCJG camp on the Plateau. He now gave free rein to his old ambition to become an architect, and designed it himself. Called Camp de Joubert, it was built about two kilometres outside Le Chambon-sur-Lignon, with Spanish refugee labour. Now at last the Spanish had some useful work, and the Plateau had a purpose-built UCJG camp (which could also come in handy if unexpected visitors arrived). The camp had nine wooden chalets, seven of them identified only by number, and two of them given names: Williams, after Sir George Williams, the founder of the YMCA; and Espérance (Hope), the name of the newspaper of the French UCJG.

At the end of 1939, the Papeterie camp, which had briefly housed Spanish 'undesirables', stood empty. Not for long: it would shortly have a vastly more sinister job to do.

• • •

While the refugees from the Spanish Civil War were on the hunt for somewhere to stay, ever more menacing storm clouds were gathering over the rest of Europe. The sense of impending calamity was strong, and there was justified fear that a rerun of the horrors of World War I was both unstoppable and imminent. On 29 September 1938, the British prime minister Neville Chamberlain and the French prime minister Édouard Daladier met Germany's Adolf Hitler and Italy's Benito Mussolini in Munich to see if they could reach a deal and avert war. The result was the Munich Agreement, signed on 30 September 1938, which cynically abandoned Czechoslovakia and gave Hitler what he wanted, all in the hope that he was a man of his word and would make no further territorial demands. Neville Chamberlain flew back to Britain and, on his arrival at Heston aerodrome, brandished aloft the piece of paper signed by himself and Hitler setting out 'the desire of our two peoples never to go to war with one another again'. The crowd there to greet him roared its approval. Later that day, from 10 Downing Street, he went further, saying the Munich Agreement had delivered 'peace for our time'.

Hitler may have fooled the prime ministers of Britain and France, but he did not fool the mayor of Le Chambon. Two weeks later, Charles

Guillon wrote in the Plateau newsletter: 'Keep your spare rooms free, stock up with provisions, we are going to have a flood of refugees.'

More cynicism was in evidence on 24 August 1939, when Germany and the Soviet Union, despite their mutual animosity, signed a non-aggression pact. Hitler was now safe from attack from the east, and he lost no time pressing his advantage. World War II duly began eight days later, on 1 September, when Hitler invaded Poland. Britain and France had warned that if Poland came under attack, both countries would declare war on Germany. This they both did, on 3 September.

The two community leaders in Le Chambon-sur-Lignon reacted in very different ways to the declaration of war. As we have seen, Charles Guillon had been clear from Munich onwards that the Plateau would soon find itself playing host to refugees. The minutes of the municipal council of Le Chambon, which met four days after the declaration, on 7 September, record that the population of the Plateau had been considerably augmented 'because the majority of the tourist population has decided to remain in Le Chambon for the duration of hostilities, some refugees have arrived, and the holiday homes and refuges for children have decided to keep their children from the city and from the department of Haute-Loire'. With the war only four days old, the Plateau was already hard at work offering people shelter, with Guillon and his council playing a part in feeding and housing them.

The French families who regularly took their summer holidays on the Plateau were due to return home by the end of September. As the minutes of the council meeting record, many of them decided to stay on. After all, it wouldn't be forever, they thought. The war would be over in a few weeks; while it lasted, they would be safe on the Plateau.

The Cambessédès were typical, a 'comfortable' middle-class Protestant family from Paris who regularly spent their summer months in La Fayolle, where they rented a substantial nine-bedroom house. They would arrive in June and leave at the end of September. The father was a successful doctor, and the mother came from an old Cévenole family. Dr Cambessédès had given money to help set up the New Cévenole School.

Madame Cambessédès quickly came to a decision: now that war had been declared, she and two sons and two daughters would stay on in the holiday house. The children could go to school in Le Chambon, not Paris. For one of the daughters, Catherine, it was a relief and a revelation. School in Paris had been an unpleasant experience; her teachers used intimidation and public humiliation to get their way. At the New Cévenole School, however, the teachers treated the students as friends. Catherine was a good pupil, but she remembers struggling with an aspect of algebra. Her maths teacher offered to walk two and a half kilometres to her house after school to help her with it. That would never have happened in Paris.

So, in 1939, teenage Catherine was well content to stay where she was. The house was cold that first winter (she remembers having to crack the ice in the water pitcher to get water to brush her teeth), but she was happily established in a pleasant school, with the war far away. Her parents could congratulate themselves on a wise decision.

If Dr and Madame Cambessédès had known then that their daughter would soon be asked to run some long and highly illegal errands carrying suitcases full of money and other supplies for the Resistance, they might have had second thoughts.

• • •

André Trocmé responded to the declaration of war in typically thoughtful fashion. It happened that 3 September 1939 was a Sunday. Traditionally, Monday was the pastor's day off so, if they could get away, he and Magda would aim to take a picnic, go for a walk or find some other escape. That Monday, 4 September, they discussed the war. What could they do? What *should* he do? His first thought was that he should serve as a pastor, yes, but possibly also as an ambulance man or nurse, in a city or village that had suffered bombardment.

The next day, Trocmé set about clarifying all this by putting his ideas down on paper. Happily, those thoughts were preserved, and can be read today. It is a curious document. It was not intended for eyes other than his own. In it he recalled his childhood and his memories of World War I, and considered his German and Italian connections. What if he abandoned his pacifism and joined the fight? He had six aunts in Germany, all married to pastors, whose religion led them to prefer prison or death to bowing down before Hitler. André's wife was Italian, the daughter of an Italian engineer and army colonel, and he had a brother-in-law in Italy. If he fought, André might be asked to kill them. He couldn't face that possibility. However, he could not simply sit tight in Le Chambon, away from danger. The final paragraph reads:

> *I have no wish to shelter in security, behind the lines. I ask only that I am given the strength to serve, in the midst of danger, the most tragic victims of war: the women and children of bombed cities. I insist that this service must be as a civilian only. I will be happy to give my life alongside others, but without abandoning faith in my Lord Jesus Christ. May God help me.*

The most immediate threat he faced was military service. He was liable to be called up at any moment. If the call-up came, he would refuse to serve, and that meant prison. And if the call-up did not come, he wanted to work among women, children and old people in a village caught up in the war. Either way, how could he continue as pastor of Le Chambon? That afternoon, Trocmé called the parish council together and offered his resignation. It must have been an odd meeting. Trocmé called in only the church elders, all laymen. The council pondered. They didn't always agree with him, the councillors told Trocmé, but he had always delivered everything he promised. So, as far as they were concerned, he should stay on in Le Chambon. They refused to accept his resignation.

Trocmé then wrote to Marc Boegner, the head of the Reformed Church in France and head of the Protestant Federation of France, setting out his position. He told Boegner he was liable to be called up for military service. The papers could be served on him at any time. He would refuse. He had offered his resignation to the parish council, but they had rejected it. He hinted strongly that he would welcome a move to another parish, one that had suffered in the war. He wrote: 'I devoutly wish to be able to serve *as a civilian* [Trocmé's emphasis] the women, the children, the elderly of a city or village which has been bombed, as a civilian stretcher-bearer or nurse.' He ended the letter: 'My only wish is to serve my brothers in their suffering, to give my life to them, without ever going against the will of God.'

Trocmé had addressed his letter formally and respectfully to 'Monsieur le Président'. Boegner's reply opened warmly with 'my dear colleague', but his message was cold and terse. After first saying that Trocmé's letter had moved him deeply, Boegner went straight to the point. He did not agree with Trocmé's interpretation of the scriptures, and nor did most of Trocmé's colleagues. Trocmé had done the right thing by offering to resign. He, Boegner, always did his best for 'those who share your convictions'. The subtext of the letter was clear: Boegner was telling Trocmé there had been enough trouble getting him into a parish and there was no possibility of finding him another one, even one closer to the heat of battle. Trocmé's pigheadedness would bring suffering on his whole family. Boegner concluded with one of the more formal French signing-off formulae: 'Please accept, my dear colleague, my cordially devoted sentiments.' So, goodbye, then.

• • •

The so-called Phoney War, when nothing much happened on land (other than a fairly disastrous campaign by Russia to conquer Finland), lasted seven months, until 9 April 1940. Then Hitler struck again. He attacked Norway and Denmark simultaneously. Danish resistance lasted four hours. Norway, with support from Britain, proved slightly tougher. However, by 7 June, Norway, too, had fallen.

Meanwhile, on 10 May, Hitler launched his major assault to the west, spearing his way into neutral Holland and Belgium. The Dutch lasted five days, surrendering on 15 May. The Belgians lasted a little longer: they surrendered on 28 May. There was still some hope that the Germans could be stopped there. In mid-September 1939, with the war only two weeks old, the British government had prepared for just such an eventuality by stationing a First Expeditionary Force in France, mostly along the northern border with Belgium but also reinforcing the so-called Maginot Line. The Maginot Line was an elaborate French defence installation further east and strung along the French–German border. Its sole purpose was to keep the Germans out of France. To do its job, the Germans would have to attack obligingly from Germany and not from elsewhere. However, they chose to bypass the Maginot Line and attack from Belgium. The combined resources of the British First Expeditionary Force and the French Army in the north were no match for Hitler's blitzkrieg, and the two Allied armies fell back to the port of Dunkirk, in northern France.

Between 26 May and 2 June some 338,000 men—198,000 British and 140,000 French—were evacuated from the Dunkirk beaches to Britain. It is called a miracle to this day, but in reality it was a massive and humiliating defeat for the Allies. The triumphant Germans, having neatly bypassed the Maginot Line, now wheeled south through France. On 10 June, exactly a month after Hitler made his move, the French government abandoned Paris and moved to Bordeaux. That same day, the fascist government of Benito Mussolini in Italy decided that it had better join the winning side quickly, while there were still spoils to be had, and declared war on the retreating Allies. France was squeezed from both sides.

Trocmé's dilemma was now acute. Having failed to persuade Boegner to clear a path to a new parish in the war zone, he had decided to volunteer to work with the Red Cross. On 22 May he wrote (in English) to the American Red Cross offices in the Champs-Élysées in Paris, offering his services as a nurse or driver, stressing that he wanted to work with the civilian population in the combat zones, where danger was most pressing, and that he required no salary. He gave as references John D. Rockefeller junior and Marc Boegner.

He followed up by going with Édouard Theis to the Red Cross offices in Lyon. There they were told that the French government had limited Red Cross recruitment to volunteers from neutral countries, which in practice meant volunteers from Sweden and Switzerland. Trocmé and Theis trudged back to Le Chambon, defeated.

• • •

Rapid-fire events now engulfed France, to the point where it was almost impossible to keep track. On 14 June the Germans occupied Paris, and continued southwards. There was still some possibility of slowing their progress: not all British troops had left France at Dunkirk. Instead huge numbers had retreated south, forming what came to be known as the Second Expeditionary Force. But by 18 June the British had evacuated this Force as well, which meant all British troops had abandoned France, leaving the French alone and at Hitler's mercy. Some 192,000 men returned by sea from eight major ports on the Atlantic coast.

On 18 June the Germans captured Brest, one of the ports used as an escape route by the Second Expeditionary Force. On 19 June they captured Nantes, close to Saint Nazaire, another of the escape ports. So the British got out in the nick of time. On 20 June the Germans took Lyon in the southeast. They now controlled a huge swathe of France. The French had lost, and everybody could see it. Meanwhile, on 17 June the French premier Paul Reynaud had resigned in favour of his 84-year-old deputy, Marshal Pétain. On 18 June, with the British gone, Pétain asked the Germans for an armistice.

He was not the only Frenchman making dramatic moves that day. A certain Brigadier-General Charles de Gaulle, a cabinet minister in the Reynaud government, had fled to England on 15 June after bitterly opposing the idea of an armistice. On 18 June, speaking on the BBC, he launched what is still widely regarded as the most influential radio broadcast of all time, telling the French people all was not lost. 'Honour, common sense, and the interests of the country require that all free Frenchmen, wherever they be, should continue the fight as best they can,' de Gaulle declared. His message was broadcast (in French) on the English language service of the BBC, and very few French people heard it. By all accounts, most of those who did thought de Gaulle was mad. The broadcast was not recorded, and might have been lost for all time and missed its place in history if de Gaulle had not asked to be allowed to repeat it. On 22 June he did so, this time to a larger and more responsive audience. The seeds of a French Resistance had been sown.

On the day of de Gaulle's second broadcast, the Armistice was duly signed by Hitler and Pétain. As we've already seen, under the terms of the Armistice, France was divided up. The Northern, or Occupied, Zone—occupied by the German Army, in other words—spread over three-fifths of France down as far as the River Loire, taking in Paris and all the vital northern industrial areas, together with a huge triangle of land along the Atlantic coast as far south as the Spanish border. The Germans wanted to control the major Atlantic ports in the west—Brest, Lorient, Saint-Nazaire, La Rochelle—as well as France's major factories and mills in the north. In what was left—the Southern, or Unoccupied, Zone—a government led by Marshal Pétain held sway from a base in the central town of Vichy. The terms of the Armistice were crippling. Marshal Pétain led a government committed to help the Germans industrially and militarily. Although technically 'free', the Vichy government would run its part of France in accordance with German principles. In particular, Jews were to be excluded and hunted down. Those who were caught could then be shipped off to work as slave labourers in German factories. As we shall shortly see, Pétain was personally and directly involved in the persecution of Jews.

It is important to be clear on two points. First, Pétain enjoyed widespread support in France after the Armistice. He was hailed as the saviour of the nation: although France had been defeated, a nominally French government still controlled a large part of the country. Pétain already enjoyed hero status dating back to his military leadership during World War I and his historic victory at Verdun. Now, in the eyes of most of the French population, he had rescued France again. Second, the Vichy government was a willing rather than a reluctant partner with the Germans in proclaiming a series of repressive laws. Far from championing French independence and traditions of liberty, equality and fraternity, Pétain was full of contrition, almost apologetic. There must be something rotten about the way France had been operating in the recent past, he told his fellow countrymen, otherwise these humiliations could not have been inflicted on their great nation. The Jews, the foreigners, the communists and the politicians had let France down. The only way for France to recover its pride and power was by cleansing itself: in the marshal's words, by *rénovation*, along German lines.

Not everyone was convinced. On 10 July some 80 deputies from the exiled French government in Bordeaux, almost without exception from the political left, refused to support Pétain. They voted against Petain's proposed rewriting of the French constitution to enshrine the terms of the Armistice. One of the leading mutinous deputies, André Philip from the socialist SFIO (Section Française de l'Internationale Ouvrière, or *French Branch of Workers International*), gathered up his feisty wife, Mireille, and their five children, and left town. They chose to move to a remote village in the Haute-Loire, Le Chambon-sur-Lignon. André Philip did not stay long. Two weeks later, on 26 July, he joined General de Gaulle in London.

Although Marshal Pétain remained popular on the Plateau until well into 1941, André Philip later wrote that the people of the Plateau were quick to show where their loyalties lay. For their first month in Le Chambon, his family ate for free: the local farmers thought it was an honour to give them food because he had voted *non*. The same farmers refused to sell anything to the Pétainists.

• • •

With the fighting now spread across most of Western Europe, André Trocmé's worst fears had been realised. The war he had argued so hard to prevent had now arrived on his doorstep. So how should he respond? And, in particular, how should a Christian pacifist respond?

The answer was little short of electrifying. The Armistice was signed on 22 June, a Saturday. The following day, André Trocmé and Édouard Theis issued a joint declaration. Trocmé read it as a sermon in the regular Sunday service in the church of Le Chambon-sur-Lignon, while Theis sat below the pulpit in full pastor's robes. At the end of the service, the two men walked side by side out of the church. No one who was present would ever forget their declaration.[11] In it, the pastors addressed themselves to their congregation, to the people of the Plateau, and to the wide world. It was an intellectual tour de force and it set the tone for the Plateau for the next four years.

Trocmé and Theis began by quoting a radio broadcast made the previous day by Marc Boegner, who had called on the French Protestant Church to humble itself for the mistakes it had made in helping to bring the French people to their present unhappy state.[12] Trocmé's rhetoric soared above Boegner's. What everybody now faced, said Trocmé, was a test comparable with the biblical sufferings of the Israelites.

First, he told the congregation, everyone should keep hope alive. All was not lost. Second, people should be honest about their own failings, and not blame others for their problems. But, third, people should remain true to their own beliefs. Totalitarian violence seemed to have won the day, but that was no reason to accept it. The power of the totalitarians was comparable to the power of the Beast of the Apocalypse. And like that diabolical power, it should be furiously resisted. The task of Christians was to stay united, whatever their politics and whatever their place in society. They should trust each other, stay close to each other, welcome each other, and remind themselves that, like the earliest persecuted Christians, they were brothers and sisters together. Then came the most striking phrase in the entire declaration:

> The duty of Christians is to resist the violence directed at our consciences with the weapons of the spirit [emphasis added]. We appeal to all our brothers in Christ to refuse to agree with or cooperate in violence, especially in the coming days when that violence is directed against the English people.
>
> To love, to forgive, to show kindness to our enemies, that is our duty. But we must do our duty without conceding defeat, without servility, without cowardice. We will resist when our enemies demand that we act in ways that go against the teachings of the Gospel. We will resist without fear, without pride, and without hatred. But this moral resistance is not possible without a clean break from

the selfishness that, for a long time, has ruled our lives. We face a period of suffering, perhaps even shortages of food. We have all more or less worshipped Mammon; we have all basked in the selfish comforts of our close family, in easy pleasure, in idle drinking. We will now be made to do without many things. We will be tempted to play our own selfish game, to cling on to what we have, to be better off than our brothers. Let us abandon, brothers and sisters, our pride and our egotism, our love of money and our faith in material possessions, and learn to trust God in Heaven, both today and tomorrow, to bring us our daily bread, and to share that bread with our brothers and sisters.

Catherine Cambessédès attended the church service on that Sunday morning. The memory of it is still vivid, as she shows in this account written in an email to me more than 70 years later.

In the church you could have heard a pin drop. I was only fifteen, yet I clearly remember my mood going from lost and frightened to safe and calm. Can you imagine what a sermon like that meant to us at a time of fear and despair? To be told, in church, that if the military situation had changed, our source of inspiration had not: it was still to follow in the steps of Jesus and the New Testament. We were not lost. We still had a direction. The day remains one of the most illuminating of my life, similar in feel to when I heard De Gaulle speak his message that we'd lost a battle, not the war. When everything seemed lost, there was one man who refused to give up.

In the fevered atmosphere of France in the days immediately following the Armistice, it was the kind of rallying cry that the country needed, and which it certainly wasn't hearing from inside its borders. As Catherine recalled, five days before Trocmé and Theis's declaration, on 18 June, de Gaulle had called on all Frenchmen not to be demoralised, and to continue the fight. De Gaulle repeated his message the day before the pastors' joint declaration. The two pastors and de Gaulle may have chosen different weapons for the forthcoming battle, but their message was the same: Resist, don't give up. Resist. Resist. Resist.

There is any amount of evidence that Trocmé's views were widely sought, and respected, in and around Le Chambon-sur-Lignon. Olivier Hatzfeld, who taught history at the New Cévenole School, later wrote that whenever an issue arose on the Plateau, the first response was: 'Does Trocmé know about it? What does he say?' or 'Trocmé will have to be informed.' Now Trocmé and Theis had spoken, with all the considerable force of personality at their command. The message was simple and direct: Stick to your moral principles, stick together and share what you've got. But, above all, resist, resist, resist.

• • •

The next day, Charles Guillon resigned as mayor of Le Chambon. He, too, was entirely clear-headed about it. In his letter of resignation to the council he wrote that after the Armistice there were two possibilities. The new Vichy government could find the terms unbearable and decide to resume fighting. Or they could surrender. In the first case, continuing the fight:

I have a mission which has been conferred on me by the organisation of which I am secretary general, the agreement with the French government concerning prisoners of war and refugees. I simply can't manage two jobs at once. But I can easily be replaced as the head of the commune. Because with you, municipal councillors, and in spite of the swelling population, the material wellbeing of the community is assured for the days to come. All the refugees have a roof, the whole population knows where its next loaf of bread is coming from, and they know where to find enough food to get by.

In the second case, surrender: 'The running of the community passes officially to other hands, or the council stays in place and carries out orders. In that second case, I do not believe I have the right to remain at the head of your council.' He would remain a council member, but not mayor. Mayors were required to swear an oath of allegiance to the new Vichy government, and Guillon would have none of it. The truth is that Guillon hated the Armistice, and thought it shameful and probably illegal. However, he realised that as mayor of a small village on a remote plateau in France he could make little difference. From Geneva he could carry on the fight far more effectively. He would have a ready-made network in the Church, among his political contacts, in the UCJG, even in the Boy Scouts, plus access to money and contacts, particularly American contacts.

He stayed in Le Chambon for three weeks, expecting a visit from Boegner, with whom he could 'set up a coordinated plan of action for the reorganisation of work in the unoccupied zone'. When Boegner failed to turn up, Guillon left for Geneva, arriving on 1 August. He then wrote a long 'Letter from France to her friends'. It was not intended for publication, being more of a private meditation. It was written at the suggestion of Tracy Strong, secretary general of the Universal Alliance of the YMCA, who was about to set off for the United States. The letter was addressed to Willem Visser 't Hooft, secretary general of the provisional committee of the newly created World Council of Churches in Geneva.

'If people saw Munich [in 1938] as an act of wise diplomacy,' Guillon wrote,

then it was a fateful date in the moral history of France. Diplomatic victories are not necessarily moral victories. Here is the question we must ask ourselves. What part can we still play? Our duty is to be ready for anything: our duty is to save the soul of our country and to work to the limit of our ability to save the Christian church. We [in France] appear in the eyes of others to have shown weakness of character, but we still have a soul and we will defend it [Guillon's emphasis]. If you ask me now what we are going to do, I tell you we will make ourselves something to be reckoned with. This means we should not only draw up a list of those who have survived, but also draw up a list of those on whom we can count in the future to carry out a clearly defined mission. We are French, and we intend to stay that way.

• • •

The first big wave of refugees came from Alsace-Lorraine, on the border with Germany. Some were evacuated by the French government and placed in refugee camps in southwest France. Others left under their own steam, and some of these found their way to the Plateau. The pace quickened with Hitler's strike against the Low Countries on 10 May. French, Belgian, Dutch and Luxembourgeois civilians fled south. Some, of course, were Jews, but the Jews were not a distinct group: most of the refugees were simply civilians trying to get away from the fighting. Again, some found their way to the Plateau. As will be maddeningly true for the rest of this narrative, there is no trustworthy record of numbers. In his letter of resignation as mayor, Charles Guillon had written to the councillors of Le Chambon about the 'swelling population', adding that 'all the refugees have a roof'. So there must have been a significant number of refugees settled in Le Chambon by that date, 24 June 1940. On 14 July, Guillon wrote to Visser 't Hooft:

I have had to take care of many thousands of refugees, and right now I am still full of Belgians, people from Luxembourg, some Dutch refugees and, naturally, French refugees. I have an entire refugee camp of Protestant Belgians. In spite of the bad times, there is not too much disease among the crowd of refugees.

Not to put too fine a point on it, Guillon seems to be exaggerating the refugee numbers, though not the overall problem. There is no evidence that 'many thousands' of refugees had arrived in Le Chambon by July 1940. Among other things, it is hard to see how they could have got there in the first place, or where they could be accommodated after they arrived. However, given that Guillon's role, agreed between the international YMCA and the French government, included looking after refugees, it is highly likely that he began steering some of them towards the Plateau as early as the summer of 1940. So sometime before July the Plateau's role as a World War II refuge had begun. At the time, the village of Le Chambon had a population of about 900. With the arrival of the tourists in summer, this number usually swelled to around 4500. If, as we have heard, the 'majority of the tourist population' stayed on, that would add perhaps 2000 extra people. They were now being joined by a trickle of refugees, which would soon become a flood. In July 1940 the combination of overstaying tourists and new refugees could indeed have run to 'thousands'. So although Guillon's claim might have benefited from rewording, it was probably grounded in reality. At various times, Guillon named seven national groups in this first wave: French, Spanish, Dutch, Belgian, Austrian, Luxembourgeois and German. He made no mention of Jews.

3

Camps

The word 'camp' has an appalling resonance in any story of the Holocaust. Yet without the internment camps set up by the Vichy government, events on the Plateau might never have taken the direction they did.

As we have seen, well before the outbreak of World War II, the French had set up camps to accommodate Spanish refugees from the civil war. The Papeterie camp near Tence on the Plateau was one example. By the end of 1939 it was empty again, and sometime around May 1940 the French government decided to use it as an internment camp for enemy aliens. On 22 June some 70 German civilians were locked up there. This was the day Pétain signed the Armistice, and in the general confusion the commandant of the camp decided to look the other way while all 70 escaped. The local gendarmes from Freycenet, Tence and Yssingeaux quickly nabbed 43 of them, but the remaining 27 were still on the loose eight days later.

A representative of the German embassy inspected the camp on 29 July 1940 and asked the non-Jewish Germans if they would like to be repatriated; a few said yes and were packed off on trains home. On 25 August another 132 German civilians arrived at the Papeterie. They were mostly anti-Nazis who had fled from Germany to France, and they were predominantly Jews. So the non-Jewish numbers shrank while the Jewish numbers swelled, until the camp was almost entirely filled with German Jews.

Conditions in the Papeterie camp were generally benign, but the same could not be said of the camps elsewhere in France. In 1939 the French had built one of their largest camps at Gurs, in the foothills of the Pyrenees, about 40 kilometres from the Spanish border. It was created to hold refugees from the Spanish Civil War. The Gurs camp may have begun its life as a well-intentioned rudimentary shelter for desperate refugees, but it quickly became little better than a concentration camp. It was already filled to bursting with Spanish refugees when, in early 1940, well before the German invasion, the French government rounded up 7000 'enemy aliens', many of whom were German Jews who had fled from Nazi persecution, and locked them up in Gurs along with the Spanish.

After the German invasion of France, the German Schutzstaffel (popularly known as the SS) added to the problem with one of their nuttier schemes. SS-Obersturmbannführer (lieutenant-colonel) Adolf Eichmann, who was in charge of the logistics of dealing with the 'Jewish problem', got it into his head that all the Jews of Europe could be rounded up and packed off to the French colony of Madagascar, where they could presumably be counted on to die of a combination of starvation and tropical disease. So between 6500 and 7500 Jews from the Baden area of Germany were crammed into trains that set off through Occupied France, then through Vichy France, to Gurs, next stop Madagascar. It is the only known example in the Nazi era of Jews being deported en masse from Germany and sent west, not east. Nineteen-year-old Max Liebmann was better prepared than most for what happened. He worked in the Immigration Office of the Jewish Community in Mannheim, Germany. He also spoke a little French.

The director of this office was the contact between the community and the Gestapo. The telephone rang the day before. 'Come down!' So he went over to the Gestapo and he was told: 'Look, tomorrow you will be arrested and deported to France.' He came back and said: 'Now we are going to close our offices, because tomorrow we will be deported.' So I went home and said to my mother: 'We're going to pack now, because we are going to France tomorrow.' She didn't believe me. Then she saw me pull out two suitcases, and it dawned on her that I wasn't kidding.

On October 22nd 1940 every Jew in the Palatinate, Baden and the Saar [German regions along the border with France] was arrested, and given one hour to pack. They were very polite. My mother had to sign over to the German government everything that was in the apartment, including the house that belonged to my grandmother. It all had to be legal. Then they picked us up, took us to train stations and put us on the train. Fortunately the train went towards France. My father was already working in France, in Nice. First stop was Lyon. The French had no idea we were coming. The Germans never notified them. The fellow who was designated transport chief—this was his first train—didn't speak French, so I came out with him. It turned out that the French had no idea who we were and what this was all about. So the train continued, and we ended up in Gurs.

Conditions in the camp were horrendous. There were 382 flimsy huts, each 25 metres square, packed into a barbed-wire-fenced compound 1400 metres long and 200 metres wide. Each cabin had to accommodate up to 60 people—so in a full cabin each person had a space 64 by 64 centimetres in which to live, sleep and store his or her possessions. The thin tar and fabric walls and roof leaked rain, wind and snow, and offered no protection from the cold. The sanitary arrangements don't bear thinking about. Food was scarce, and of poor quality. In the compound, the mud was ankle deep. Rats thrived, and disease was rife. In the first year more than 1000 cases of typhus and dysentery were reported. This was all glossed over with some breathtaking euphemisms. Camps like Gurs were referred to as Centres d'Hébergement Surveillés (Supervised Accommodation Centres).

Conditions in Gurs were a great deal worse than those in the Tence camp. However, overcrowding appeared not to bother the French authorities. On 22 October, the Vichy government closed the Papeterie camp and moved its remaining inmates to Gurs. By the end of the first week of November, Tence had been cleared.

While conditions in camps like Gurs were appalling, these were not extermination camps. The food and accommodation may have been dreadful, but there were no executions and no sadistic treatment of prisoners by the guards. The inmates were even allowed visits from aid organisations.

• • •

Towards the end of 1940, André Trocmé had twice offered his services beyond Le Chambon, and been rebuffed both times. Now he had a third proposal: he would do relief work in the camps.

By 1940 there were about 50,000 internees living in the camps at Gurs, Rivesaltes, Les Milles, Agde, Argelès-sur-Mer, Le Vernet, Brens and others. The internees were a mixed bunch: they included a smattering of Spanish refugees still stuck there from the civil war, plus communists, and anti-Nazi Germans and Austrians who had fled to the supposed safety of France (including a large proportion of German and Austrian Jews). There were also 'foreign' Jews who had been residing in France, and anybody unlucky enough to be considered an 'enemy alien'. They all faced 'deportation'. In 1940, in the early days of the Vichy government, everybody assumed 'deportation' meant slave labour in Germany. It was not until 1942 that 'deportation' and 'murder' became the same word, and while there were rumours as early as 1942, it was not until 1944 that the true fate of the 'deportees' became known.

Around the end of 1940, Trocmé called a meeting of the parish council. 'I pointed out to them how fortunate we were,' he wrote in his memoir.

I could easily spend time away from the parish because we had Édouard Theis as part-time pastor, as well as Henri Braemer, a teacher at the high school, and Noël Poivre, a retired pastor. I put it to the council that they should send me on a mission into an internment camp as 'ambassador', to distribute food and other aid, which would be collected by us from within the parish.

With the council's approval, Trocmé headed for Marseille, on the southern Mediterranean coast. At the time, several relief organisations with Christian connections were based in Marseille or had offices there. Marseille was central to the camps, which were strung out across the south of the Unoccupied Zone, several of them on the Mediterranean coast.

There were four key organisations doing relief work, but for Trocmé the American Quakers were the most important, as they combined pacifism with Christian humanitarian principles. They also had access to the camps—indeed, they had permission to live inside them—but most important of all, they had access to money. It came from America, and until America entered the war in December 1941, money could still be sent directly to France.

Another powerful group was the CIMADE (Comité Inter-Mouvements auprès des Évacués, roughly 'Inter-Denominational Commission for Evacuees', and usually referred to as 'the Cimade').

The Cimade was an almost entirely Protestant organisation, though it included some secular supporters. It was set up in 1939 specifically to carry out relief work in the camps. The Cimade's workers also had permission to live inside the camps. A third organisation, the OSE (Oeuvre de Secours aux Enfants, roughly 'Child Rescue Service'), was a Jewish organisation that focused on children rather than adults, as did the CRS–SAE (Croix-Rouge Suisse—Secours aux Enfants, or the Swiss Red Cross—Child Rescue). The American vice-consul in Marseille, Hiram Bingham IV, was another important source of aid; for ten months, from the summer of 1940 until he was summarily forced aside by his bosses in the State Department, Bingham operated a generous visa system that is credited with making possible the escape of anywhere between 1200 and 2500 refugees,[13] mostly Jewish. The American former journalist Varian Fry ran his own rescue network, based in Marseille, which worked closely with Bingham.

However, it was the Quakers who made the proposal that gave the Plateau its mission. In Marseille, Trocmé began by meeting Burns Chalmers, an American and one of the leading Quakers. Chalmers got straight down to business. He told Trocmé there was no point in his moving into a camp. They had plenty of people doing such work already. Trocmé, he said, was offering something far more valuable. As Trocmé recalled in his memoir, Chalmers went on:

You've told me you come from a mountain village where things are still pretty safe. Our problem is this: we work with doctors and the French officials who manage the camps, and we try to issue medical certificates to as many adults as we can, declaring them unfit for work. If we can't save the father, we switch to the mother. If the two parents are deported despite all this, we then take the children into our care. Next we get permission for those who are declared unfit to be lodged outside the camps. However, it's very difficult to find a

French community that is willing to run the risk of taking in hordes
of adults, teenagers and children who are all compromised in some
way. Could you be that community?

For Trocmé it was a bolt from the blue. 'These children, will we have to house them, feed them, educate them?' he asked Chalmers. 'Who will be in charge of them?' Chalmers was blunt. 'Find the houses, and the carers,' he told Trocmé. 'The Quakers and the Fellowship of Reconciliation[14] will find the money.'

• • •

Every month the twelve Protestant pastors from the parishes of the Plateau met. The meetings were known as *pastorales*, and they were pretty informal—the pastors would discuss the events of the world, any problems they had, and any issues they felt like sharing. Nobody kept minutes, so it is an educated guess that at the next meeting Trocmé reported to his fellow pastors the reaction of the Quakers to the possibility of using the Plateau as a place of refuge. He would surely have told the assembled pastors that here was something they could all do to help, and subsequent events suggest that they were unanimous in their support.

For the devout Huguenots of the Plateau, there was a startling precedent. In the Bible, Numbers 35:9–34, God gives Moses a very specific set of instructions, which Moses is told to pass on to the children of Israel. The Israelites are to set up six cities of refuge which would offer protection to people in trouble. Later, God spelled out the details to Joshua, the leader of the Israelites: 'And when he that doth flee unto one of these cities shall stand at the entering of the gate, and shall declare his cause in the ears of the elders of that city, they shall take him into the city unto them and give him a place, that he may dwell among them' (Joshua 20:4).

So the Plateau had its marching orders. There would be more than six cities—or, rather, villages—of refuge, but that was all to the good. In each of those cities, according to the rules, someone in danger must be automatically taken in and looked after. It was all in the Bible.

Part II
...
REFUGE

4

Jews

There is simply no reliable way of knowing when Jews first began arriving on the Plateau in significant numbers. No records were kept, official or unofficial; nobody asked questions; nobody gossiped; nobody was in charge; nobody had a policy, or a plan, or a piece of paper laying down the rules. The process was haphazard, spontaneous, clandestine, burgeoning and unstoppable.

Looking at likely dates, we know with some certainty that Jews came to shelter on the Plateau soon after the Armistice of 22 June 1940. We even have quite a detailed account of the arrival of the first Jew on the Trocmés' doorstep. In her unpublished memoir, Magda Trocmé says the first Jew was a German woman who simply rang their doorbell unannounced one evening. Magda gives no date for this unexpected arrival. Other elements of the story demonstrate that it was winter, and that the Armistice had already been signed. So that locates the event somewhere in the winter of 1940–41. It is clear from what follows that, although she may have been the first Jewish refugee to ring the Trocmés' doorbell, by the time she arrived other Jews were already sheltering in the village. Nelly Trocmé knew of at least one other Jew, Elizabeth Kaufmann, who had arrived in Le Chambon, encouraged by Hilde Hoefert, the German teacher at New Cévenole School. Certainly

Magda Trocmé's account suggests that the new arrival had some clue that the Plateau was already acting as a shelter for Jews.

Magda's story is both touching and revealing. The Jewish woman told her that she had made her way from Germany, that she had wandered all over France, first in the Occupied Zone and then in the Unoccupied Zone, not knowing where to go. Then she had heard that in Le Chambon there was a pastor who might be able to take her in. So there she stood, soaking wet and frozen on the doorstep of the presbytery, wearing only summer sandals on her feet, with snow pouring down outside.

Magda invited her in. There was a fire in the kitchen. She could warm up, dry her sandals, have something to eat. Magda would make up a bed for her. Then, tragedy. The woman was so tired and distressed that she put her sandals too close to the fire. They suddenly burst into flames. Like everybody else, the Trocmés were rationed to one pair of shoes each a year, so they had no shoes to spare. Magda began a frantic search in the village, knocking on doors and asking if anybody could spare shoes about the right size. Finally a Madame Monnier came to the rescue with a spare pair.

However, Magda now had a serious problem. What should she do with her refugee? She usually had a bit of extra food on hand, so she could feed an extra mouth for a day or two. But food was rationed, and two or three days were her limit. She went to the town hall for advice. The official she spoke to was totally unhelpful.[15] 'He told me it was impossible,' Magda recalled. 'He already had French Jews [in the village] and if I was going to bring in German Jews, the whole village would be in danger. He insisted that I send her back to wherever she came from. Send her back? Where? I was desperate.'

Magda knew there was a prominent Parisian Jewish woman staying in the village, sheltering there because the cities were too dangerous. She tracked her down. 'I explained to her that I had this Jew at the house, that I didn't know what to do, and that I needed her help. She was exactly like the man at the town hall. Not only did she refuse to help me, but she grabbed hold of me and told me that a flood of foreign Jews would endanger the French Jews already in place! So I was pretty discouraged.'

She discussed the problem with her husband. The conversation led the two Trocmés to cross a tiny but important line. As pacifists, they were determined to remain neutral, to love their enemies, to avoid the entanglements of war. But the imperatives of saving this refugee's life took top priority. They told her in detail how to get in touch with a group of Catholic priests in Annecy, near the Swiss border. They might be able to help. So the woman moved on alone, leaving behind a troubled Magda.

That was a turning point. As Magda wrote in her memoir: 'This is what pushed us into the clandestine world; now it would be up to us to come up with forged photo identity cards made by Monsieur Darcissac, give false names to people, and tell lies. But they were "legitimate" lies, told to save the persecuted.'

• • •

In fairness to the town hall official (and to Magda's unnamed 'prominent Parisian Jew'), it is worth looking in more detail at the law as it stood in France at the time. The new Vichy government had wasted no time in passing anti-Jewish laws. Since 1789 and the French Revolution, the Declaration of the Rights of Man had guaranteed French citizens equal rights under the law. Not anymore. Within a month of the Armistice, the Vichy government passed 'denaturalisation' laws, granting the right to strip naturalised 'foreigners' of citizenship. The law may have talked about foreigners, but it was aimed most pointedly at Jews. So who or what was a Jew? On 3 October 1940 the Vichy government passed a law requiring all Jews to register with the police or the prefecture, and defining a Jew as either someone with three grandparents 'of the Jewish race', or someone with two grandparents 'of the Jewish race' and married to someone 'of the Jewish race'. This was a wider definition than the one used in Hitler's Germany. The 3 October law then went on to bar Jews from serving as officers in the army, navy and air force, and from the press, the public service, the teaching professions and private sector management. The same law excluded Jews from practising the liberal professions like medicine, dentistry, law, architecture, and even veterinary science. The Mémorial de la Shoah (Holocaust Memorial) in Paris holds a draft copy of the law. It is covered with handwritten scribbled amendments, all of them making the various anti-Jewish provisions even harsher. For instance, the clause granting an exception for Jews born in France or Jews who had been naturalised in France before 1860 is crossed out. Handwriting experts are in no doubt about the identity of the scribbler: Pétain himself wrote all the notes and toughened up the legislation.

On 4 October, the Vichy government piled on a particularly vicious new law. 'Foreign nationals of the Jewish race' could be interned in special camps on the say-so of the prefect of the department. No charge, no trial: just a nod from the prefect and off you go. They could also 'at any time be assigned a forced residence'. So by early October 1940 all Jews were, in effect, outlaws. These Vichy laws were harsher than anything passed by the Germans in Germany or proclaimed in the Occupied Zone up to this time.

Although the Vichy law did not spell this out, those Jews rounded up into camps could be and were then deported to Germany, where the German government would know how to handle them. The first train, packed with Jews, left France for Auschwitz on 27 March 1942. The Germans 'noted the rapidity and scope of French legislation with bemusement, opportunistic glee and even occasional annoyance'.[16]

At this point the most ferocious Vichy laws were still aimed at 'foreign' Jews. While there was any amount of legislation directed at Jews generally—some 28 laws and nineteen regulatory orders over the years—in the early days of the Vichy regime, Jews in the Unoccupied Zone with no 'foreign' connection were marginally less vulnerable. So French Jews who made their way to the Plateau were less likely than foreign Jews to trigger raids and reprisals. It is for the reader to decide where his or her sympathies lie: with the town hall official and the unnamed 'prominent Parisian Jew', who were already quietly sheltering French Jews in Le Chambon and who feared this program might be derailed by the arrival of foreign Jews; or with Magda Trocmé, unconcerned by whether the refugee was French or foreign, simply concerned to help someone in trouble.

• • •

The Vichy government's treatment of Jews was well reported to the outside world. On 24 November the *New York Post* published a news item datelined Lyon and setting out the facts. The report quoted a 'particularly qualified high personality' who had reviewed the part played by Jews in the professions in France and then decided to lock them out. 'It is better to prevent than to suppress,' the particularly qualified source opined.

The report is interesting, but its author even more so. Virginia Hall is one of the most remarkable characters in this entire story. She was born in Baltimore, Maryland, and studied French, German and Italian at Columbia University. Tall and slim, with classical features and an aristocratic manner, she seems to have totally bewitched everybody who knew her. Late in 1926, she moved from New York to Europe to continue her studies in France, Germany and Austria, before landing a job as a consular clerk in the American embassy in Warsaw. She might have stayed in the American diplomatic service but for an accident:

she shot herself in the leg while hunting in Turkey, with the result that her left leg had to be amputated just below the knee. The missing part was replaced by a wooden leg, which she named 'Cuthbert'.

Thanks to Cuthbert, she was no longer eligible for a full career in the diplomatic service, so she moved to Paris and worked as a foreign correspondent for the *Washington Post*. When war broke out she briefly volunteered for the French Army ambulance service, and found herself in the Unoccupied Zone after the Armistice. She managed to escape to England. Winston Churchill had just created the Special Operations Executive (SOE), a clandestine organisation with orders to 'set Europe ablaze'. She didn't hesitate when they approached her. The so-called Baker Street Irregulars could see solid talent straight away, and put her on a 'fast track'. She hardly needed any training in clandestine work, and in August 1941, they sent her back to the Unoccupied Zone, with a cover job as the *New York Post*'s correspondent in Lyon. America was not yet at war with Germany so, as an American citizen, she was able to enter the country legally and operate under her own name.

Hall's orders were straightforward. She was to report on the situation in France, military and political. She was also to seek out likely recruits for a future resistance movement. At the same time, she was to act as a courier, passing on instructions from the SOE in London to agents in the field, and she was to assist those agents to obtain the correct false papers and whatever else they needed to allow them to function. She did all this with remarkable zeal and proficiency, while keeping up a steady flow of perceptive, whimsical and occasionally sarcastic reports for the *New York Post* on life in the Unoccupied Zone. Within the SOE it was said: 'Whenever we need a new operator, or a new station, we ask Virginia Hall.' Her base in Lyon was about 120 kilometres northeast of Le Puy, and she visited the town several times in 1941, presumably to look at the possibilities of the mountains of the

Haute-Loire as a hideout for resistance fighters, as well as to carry out her usual work as a foreign correspondent. Subsequent events suggest that she liked what she saw.

• • •

During the winter of 1940–41 the number of Jews and other refugees finding their way to the Plateau went from a trickle to a gentle stream. Many of them arrived in the village of Le Chambon knowing only one thing: the pastor could help.

Magda Trocmé recalls her next arrival—Berthe Grünhut, known only as Madame Berthe—who offered to do the cooking and housework in exchange for lodgings. This slightly threw the normally unflappable Magda: the cooking wasn't complicated, and in general there wasn't much food to cook anyway. Furthermore, Madame Berthe proved to be a lousy cook. Magda still took her in, and she stayed with them throughout the war. She was given her own hiding place in the basement.

Madame Berthe's story is a remarkable illustration of the level of secrecy that prevailed on the Plateau. In her memoir, Magda wrote of Berthe: 'She was often very upset because she didn't know where her husband and children were.' In fact, as the Trocmés discovered after the war, Berthe's son Egon was also living in Le Chambon, something she never told them. *That* was how closely secrets were guarded on the Plateau.

A Dr and Madame Mautner arrived, refugees from Vienna. As a foreign Jew, Dr Mautner had no chance of being allowed to practise medicine, so he became a househusband. For the rest of the war he did the cooking and housework at home while his wife worked as a dressmaker in Le Chambon. Magda Trocmé loaned her a sewing machine, which stayed busy throughout the war. Dr Mautner spoke in a thick Austrian accent, and he came to the presbytery regularly to borrow the Trocmés' laundry boiler. His heavily accented request—the French equivalent of: 'Can ve haf der boil-vasher, pliz?'[17]—provided the Trocmé children with endless amusement.

A desperate French woman fled to Le Chambon from the Occupied Zone to escape a possible death sentence. She had been caught giving help to English soldiers. From 24 August 1940, three months after Dunkirk, the Germans posted notices all over the Pas-de-Calais region announcing: 'Any person who protects, hides or assists in any manner a soldier of the English or French army risks the death penalty or forced labour.' Notices plastered all over the Paris Métro in October 1940 were even starker: people who sheltered anyone English without declaring them risked being shot. There were rewards for handing in or denouncing such people. The young woman stayed with the Trocmés a few days before moving on.

A certain 'Monsieur Colin' moved in. He had been in the furniture business in Berlin, and had prudently abandoned his real name, Cohn. He arrived in Le Chambon alone: he had no family left. He was understandably jumpy, and whenever anyone a bit suspicious arrived at the presbytery, Monsieur Colin always did a better than average job of hiding himself. This in itself was not without risk. When the Vichy police arrived to search the house one day, he hid in a notoriously rickety part of the attic, which miraculously held together while the police thudded about impotently below.

Monsieur Colin proved to be a major asset to the household. Because he had been in the business, he was an expert furniture maker and repairman. A fair bit of the Trocmé household was, according to Nelly, falling apart. She recalls:

Monsieur Colin could take a bunch of sticks and repair a desk, or create a new desk with some planks, or a folding desk. We were crowded and in our bedrooms we had folding desks against the wall so we could do our homework and then go to bed. Monsieur Colin did everything that needed to be done. He was silent and non-communicative, and rarely smiled. He was not a happy man.

Simone Mairesse arrived in Le Mazet with her mother and her sister Gabrielle and stayed with relatives. She was amazed to discover that the Trocmés lived a few kilometres away in Le Chambon, as she had known the family since before the birth of Nelly fourteen years earlier, and had been Nelly's first babysitter. Simone was pregnant, and her husband had gone off to war, so she knew he was in danger. She learned of his fate in the most terrible way. Sometime after her arrival at Le Mazet, someone wrote to the Trocmé family, enclosing a press cutting about a charming officer, Maurice Mairesse, who had taken a bullet wound to the thigh that had cut an artery. He was dead. It fell to Magda to break the news to Simone of her husband's death. Devastated, she looked to the Trocmés for comfort and support. Then devastation turned to quiet fury. What could she do? The Trocmés had an answer: she could work with them saving refugees, most of them Jews. Simone was persuaded. She came to the presbytery with her sister every week to do some sewing. But she also took on a vastly more important role: she scoured the Plateau looking for safe houses. It would become a full-time job.

Not all of the new arrivals endeared themselves to their protectors. Magda recalls:

One day, a lady from Paris and her family were due to arrive. I said to Simone: 'See if you can find somewhere.' She found a place between Fay-sur-Lignon and Le Chambon, very high up on the mountain, near a water mill, very well hidden. That day the weather was bad, with drizzling rain. I went up to the railway station to meet the lady, who arrived with her son: her husband would come later. Imagine my surprise, after I'd given her all the directions to find the farm, when she became angry. 'But Madame Trocmé,' she said, 'how do you expect me to go on foot in this weather?' I said: 'Madame, are you trying to tell me that it's raining? My friend Simone spends her nights running up and down the mountain trying to find these houses for people like you. Do you think she does it only when the weather is nice?' Happily, not all the Jews were like this one.

By June of 1941 the Plateau was ready for a serious influx of refugees. It was just in time. On 2 June the Vichy government passed a new law to replace the statutes of 3 and 4 October. This time they really piled on the pressure. As well as all the previous restrictions, Jews were now barred from banking, stockbroking, money lending, gambling, real estate, advertising, radio, publishing, art dealing, the movie business (including, bizarrely, working in cinemas), show business, even forestry. Any Jew who attempted to earn a living in any of these professions could be imprisoned for six months to two years and faced a hefty fine. If he or she lied or used false papers to get a job in the forbidden areas, the prison sentence rose to between a year and five years, and the fine doubled to between 1000 and 20,000 francs.

Almost two months later, on 22 July, the Vichy government passed its 'Aryanisation' law. This allowed for the confiscation of all Jewish property, most notably Jewish-owned businesses, but also private property. Jews now found life and work next to impossible. That was the whole idea.

• • •

From May 1941 onwards, the refugees arriving on the Plateau were made up of two groups. The first consisted of people (mostly Jewish) who made their own way there. For some it was only a staging post on the way to what they hoped would be total security in neutral Switzerland or Spain, or less dangerous parts of France like the Cévennes. Others were happy to sit out the war in the comparative safety of the Plateau Vivarais-Lignon. Some chose to retain their real names and identities. Others felt more secure with false names, false papers and false backgrounds—non-Jewish backgrounds, naturally. In one way or another, all of these arrivals were outside the law, so they all needed to be kept hidden. Those who needed false papers turned mostly to headmaster and forger-in-chief Roger Darcissac. The illegals were not all Jews. Some were French men and women who had fallen foul of the authorities in one way or another. Later, they were joined by members of the Resistance on the run.

The second group consisted of people (mostly children) freed from the camps by the Cimade, the Quakers, the Red Cross or the OSE. They were almost all Jews, but they came to the Plateau with the full knowledge of the Vichy authorities. They only became illegals if they assumed a false identity or tried to leave the Plateau, for instance to escape to Switzerland. In the language of the day, they were 'transferred' to the Plateau, mostly to Le Chambon. They did not need to be quite so hidden, and they provided good cover for the illegals.

From the point of view of those doing the hiding there was some danger, but things could have been worse. In Germany, and in the occupied countries, the Germans regarded as criminals those networks that organised 'pipelines' and forged papers to help Jews or Allied airmen escape, and there were dire penalties. In the Unoccupied Zone of France, under the Vichy authorities, things were different. A pre-war French law, passed on 2 May 1938, required everybody to inform the prefecture if they had 'foreigners' staying with them, and it was an offence to fail to declare them; however, this law was rarely used against foreign Jews, or anybody else.[18] In general, Vichy law took a dim view of people who made or carried forged papers, but it was not nearly so ferocious when it came to hiding Jews or even Allied airmen. In theory, the penalty for 'harbouring an escapee from an internment camp' was three months to a year in prison, but it was a threat that was very seldom carried out—possibly never. If you were caught with false papers, or could be accused of making them, you were in big trouble. If you were caught sheltering Jews, particularly Jews with false papers, then the Jews were certainly in trouble, but nobody much bothered the shelterers. As we shall see, this all changed at the end of 1942. But for the time being, sheltering Jews on the Plateau, even Jews who arrived illegally and had false papers, was not a high-risk occupation.

• • •

When the Jews of the Palatinate in Germany—including Max Liebmann and his mother—were rounded up and deported on 22 October 1940, it took more than one train to hold them. There were between 6500 and 7500 of them to be transported in a single day, so no fewer than seven trains formed a convoy headed for Gurs in southern France; in theory, next stop Madagascar. Also among them was fifteen-year-old Hanne Hirsch. She travelled with her mother, three aunts, an uncle, a few cousins and her 91-year-old grandmother. They went three days without food or water, but at least they were in proper passenger cars, with seats. Later, Jews were transported in cattle cars.

The winter in Gurs proved too much for Hanne's grandmother, who died in January, three months after their arrival. Hanne's oldest aunt was over 70 and almost blind. She died the next month, in February. Conditions were terrible for Hanne and her surviving family, as she describes.

You vegetated. The food was no different from what they got in concentration camps. We got maybe half a pound of bread for 24 hours, and something that looked like coffee in the morning. For lunch we got some watery vegetable soup, mostly root vegetables, some stuff that you feed to animals but not to humans. We had some chickpeas and sometimes a tiny bit of meat in the evening.

However, there was some relief. A worker from the Swiss Red Cross, Elspeth Kassé, had talked her way into the camp and actually lived there. She was assigned one of the barracks, and she fed the teenage inmates in rotation.

Hanne continues:

I had a job in the office. I was the mail person. I went around the barracks. One morning I was waiting at the gate, and this slightly older boy was there, someone from the camp. We walked together up to breakfast, and back down. People thought we were brother and sister. They would ask him, after I left: 'Where's your sister?' We were very good, very good teenagers.

Thus did Max Liebmann first meet Hanne Hirsch. Despite their chaste behaviour, not everyone was convinced of their virtue. People react to malnutrition in different ways. Some people become skeletal. Others swell up with an excess of fluid in the body. Hanne suffered from this condition, known as oedema.

I was really blown up. One day my mother was in the latrine and she overhead this lady, Frau Stein, saying: 'I don't understand Frau Hirsch's daughter Hanne. She's pregnant! She's pregnant from this Liebmann guy.' Frau Stein was in charge of some sort of social service thing that we'd invented for ourselves, and she would sometimes

71

ask me in the office would I do this or that for her. After that, I did
exactly nothing for her.

Nevertheless, Hanne Hirsch was in a nearly unique position in the camp. She was fifteen years old and she had a boyfriend. And Max Liebmann had a girlfriend.

• • •

Just as the word 'camp' has a sinister association in any story of the Holocaust, so does the word 'train'. Jews were deported by train, they were taken to the concentration camps by train and they went to their deaths by train.

The train onto the Plateau Vivarais-Lignon was quite a different matter. It was a narrow-gauge local railway, not part of the French national rail network, and it ran from Dunières at the foot of the Plateau, through Tence and Le Chambon to Saint-Agrève on the Plateau itself, then on to La Voulte-sur-Rhône in the Rhône Valley. The national rail network connected Dunières with the major cities of Saint-Étienne and Lyon, and from there to the rest of France. The Plateau railway line was originally built with two purposes in mind: it could carry loads of timber from the forests of the Plateau to be used as pit props in the mines around Saint-Étienne, and it could bring tourists from the industrial cities of the plain up to the clean air of the Plateau. The train, known affectionately to the locals as La Galoche (The Clog[19]), chuffed its way up the mountainside with some difficulty. Sometimes it would stop halfway, having literally run out of steam. Passengers would step down from the train to the side of the track while it built up steam again. Then the whistle would toot, everybody would climb back on board, and The Clog would gamely resume its daily battle with gravity.

Now it had an additional source of passengers. Refugees, mostly Jews, made their way from all over Europe to Dunières, then gratefully clambered on to the little train headed for the Plateau. The refugees also came by bus: two buses a day arrived from Saint-Étienne. Sometimes the refugees were expected. Mostly they arrived unannounced. In general, they knew only two things: shelter was available on the Plateau; and the Protestant pastors were the people to see.

5

Fun

In 1941 the rescue operation on the Plateau began to assume its final shape. There was still no formal organisation. No one was ever in charge, there was still no plan and there was still no reward. Yet every day at least one person, usually a woman, waited at the railway station, or at the bus stop, in case refugees appeared. The person might be Magda Trocmé. Or Simone Mairesse. Or Alphonse Dreyer, husband of the maths teacher at New Cévenole School. The train could arrive any time between eight o'clock at night and two in the morning, depending on the state of the track and, in winter, the depth of the snow. If it came late, new arrivals were put up temporarily in guesthouses like Beau-Soleil or Les Airelles (The Blueberries), or else taken straight to a farmhouse where the farmer had let it be known that there was a spare room going. There were no fewer than 38 guesthouses, eleven children's hostels and seven hotels around Le Chambon that could be called into service.

In these early days of the war, the mood on the Plateau was far from hostile to the Vichy government. On 2 May 1941 Marshal Pétain visited Le Puy, where he was well received. There was even a grudging respect from the puritanical Huguenots of the Plateau for the marshal's program of *rénovation*. If the marshal was going to rid France of sin, as he promised, then who could object to that? For their part, the

Vichy government even looked kindly on the New Cévenole School. Previous French governments had allowed the virus of secularism and anti-religion to spread its evil influence throughout France. If New Cévenole could bring the youth of France back to God-fearing religion, the Vichy government was all in favour of it.

There was a further factor at play. The new government's repeated calls for a 'return to the soil' suggested that these were men after the hearts of the farming community, and this went down well on the largely rural Plateau. In May 1941 the UCJG magazine ran a whole issue dedicated to rural youth, which noted 'the promises of Marshal Pétain for the land, farm work and the peasantry'. The issue contained an article by Charles Guillon.

• • •

From the arrival of the Germans in France in May 1940 until the end of 1942, there was no serious armed resistance in France, no *clandestines* hiding in the forests and planning sabotage, and hardly any Free French Army fighting under the command of Charles de Gaulle. Of the 140,000 French troops rescued from Dunkirk and taken to England in 1940, a mere 3000 agreed to join de Gaulle and continue the war. The rest opted to be repatriated to France and its Unoccupied Zone. The deeply unpopular *Service de Travail Obligatoire* (STO) forced labour laws, whereby young Frenchmen were sent off to Germany to work in the factories, did not arrive on the Vichy statute book until 16 February 1943. The plain fact is that in 1941 and for most of 1942 the French population was understandably preoccupied with getting enough food to eat and with continuing to earn a living, in an economy dominated by rationing, shortages, black markets and disruption. Persecution of Jews had begun in 1940 and was getting worse, but for non-Jewish, non-communist, non-resistant French men and women in the Unoccupied Zone, the government of Pétain and his Vichy ministers was not savagely oppressive. Above all, although the war continued throughout this period, including the London Blitz and the Battle of Britain, for the French of the Unoccupied Zone the sound of gunfire was a far distant and inaudible rumble.

Nevertheless, the various pastors of the Plateau scented trouble ahead. At a meeting of the regional synod on 12 and 13 November 1940, André Trocmé warned of the danger of the Church losing its independence by getting too close to the state, although the problem 'seems to be a long way off at the moment'. Trocmé was already worried about the authoritarian streak now apparent in the government's methods. In October 1941, Édouard Theis wrote in the local journal *Echo of the Mountain*:

> *We must put an end to every man for himself. It's up to us as Christians to lead by example, in accordance with the word of our Lord. We must be concerned for our parents, our neighbours, our brothers in faith, our compatriots, but also for total strangers, all of whom require that we care about them.*

In other words, we'll have to raise our game.

• • •

In May 1941 the Plateau's role as rescue service finally came out into the open. The Quakers in Marseille had secured the release of nine Jewish children from the Gurs camp. All nine were delivered to Le Chambon. On 16 May 1941 the Swiss Red Cross had opened La Guespy (The Wasps' Nest), a hostel specifically for children released from the camps. Located on the edge of the town, it had space for twenty children. It was soon full, with the arrival of seven girls and thirteen boys, eleven of them Jews released from Gurs. So the first nine released children almost certainly went straight to The Wasps' Nest. The great rescue had begun.

It is almost impossible to put oneself into the shoes of parents, particularly Jewish parents, asked to make such heartbreaking decisions. At this stage, adults who ran foul of the authorities faced 'deportation', which they took to be a code word for slave labour in Germany. They could expect to be literally worked to death there; at this point, however, names like Auschwitz and Bergen-Belsen meant nothing. The mass murder of Jews did not really get under way until 1942, so while the fear of 'deportation' was widespread and well justified, the full horror of the fate of those packed onto trains and sent east was not yet known. Nevertheless, the proposition being put to Jewish parents by representatives of the Quakers, the Cimade, the OSE and the Swiss Red Cross was stark and devastating. There was very little the rescue organisations could do to save healthy adults in an internment camp, they were told; however, they had a good chance of saving the children.

One of the rescuers was a Catholic priest, Abbé Alexandre Glasberg, a portly and avuncular figure wearing trademark horn-rimmed glasses. He would say with great gentleness to a parent in a camp: 'Entrust your child to me.' Then he would turn to the child and say: 'If you come with me, you'll have a good breakfast tomorrow.' However slight that may sound to today's ears, it had a different resonance for starving and frightened children, and they largely said yes. The unstated consequence was unbearable: the parents knew they would almost certainly never see their child again. Still, parents generally seized the chance to save part of their family. They might not survive personally, but at least the next generation would be spared.

So the setting up of hostels, mostly for children, became an urgent task. The Wasps' Nest proved to be the first of many. In January 1942 the Maison des Roches (House of Rocks) opened its doors. This was more than a mere hostel. The Geneva-based European Student Assistance Fund paid for it, and it had the status of a mini-university.

It could take in up to 50 residential students aged between seventeen and 35, housed in 32 rooms. The first principal was a Monsieur Pantet (nobody seems to have recorded his first name), but in August 1942 the role of principal was taken over by Daniel Trocmé, André's cousin.

Next came Le Coteau Fleuri (The Flowery Hill), opened in the spring of 1942 and supported with money from the Quakers and the Cimade. It had room for 50 people between the ages of five and 87. Then came L'Abric (roughly 'The Shelter'), with room for 30 children, funded by the Child Rescue Service of the Swiss Red Cross. The main body of the Swiss Red Cross then opened Faïdoli,[20] with space for 23 children over the age of twelve. Finally, the pacifist MIR (Mouvement International de la Réconciliation) opened Les Grillons (The Crickets), with space for twenty children aged ten to seventeen. Eugène Munch and Daniel Trocmé managed it jointly.

Why Le Chambon and the Plateau? Madeleine Barot, who founded the Cimade, shed some interesting light in a 1982 interview with the documentary maker Pierre Sauvage. She told him:

We had to find a place where people would be safe. In Le Chambon we felt quite secure about the population. We were very scared of a 'fifth column'—people who could be bought off by the Vichy paramilitary or by the Germans. In Le Chambon we felt that a fifth column would be spotted immediately.

• • •

In the archives of Gurs camp there is a note dated 21 August 1942. One of Hanne Hirsch's uncles, who lived in New York, had written to the camp authorities demanding the release of the uncle's mother (Hanne's grandmother, who had died in January), his sister-in-law (Hanne's mother), and his niece, Hanne. The camp commander replied on 8 September 1942 that Hanne had been transferred to a

Protestant children's home in Le Chambon-sur-Lignon. These simple words conceal an agonising decision. In fact Hanne had moved to Le Chambon in March 1942. She takes up the narrative.

It was the OSE with the help of the Swiss Red Cross who got us through the gate. They had to get permission from our parents. It was a precondition that the parents allow us to leave. We were all minors, so no way could we have made a decision. Yes, the parent had to agree—and probably sign a paper—that said they would let us go, that it is okay to leave the camp and go to Le Chambon. Did we know about Le Chambon? No. We didn't know anything. All we knew was that nothing good could come out of Gurs. So the parents said okay, maybe we will perish, or whatever's going to happen to us, but the children might be safe. And we will try to save our children.

I don't know whether the main idea was to save us, or to make sure we lived under more normal conditions and had better food. When you're sixteen or seventeen, you start to move away from your parents, slowly but surely. My mother asked me if I wanted to go, and I said yes. Who wouldn't? The OSE took us physically to Le Chambon. They accompanied us the whole way. There were seven of us—four boys and three girls. We stopped in Toulouse for lunch. I remember that we were walking in the old part of Toulouse and there was a kosher restaurant that was one flight up. After so many carrots in the camp, what did we get? Carrots!

Things took a turn for the better when they arrived in Le Chambon. They were taken to a large house just outside the centre of the village, located in the street called Côte de Molle (roughly 'Molle Way').

We had dinner there. I remember we had beef broth, or whatever it was. But it was definitely with noodles, and they poured milk into it.

Heaven! I don't know what the rest of the meal was, but I remember that soup! I'd never seen that before. It tasted wonderful! After dinner they took us to La Guespy [The Wasps' Nest], our new home.

Hanne's boyfriend Max was still stuck back in Gurs. His turn would come soon.

• • •

While I was researching this book, I interviewed as many survivors from the Plateau as I could find. There was an extraordinary and recurring plea. These were people who had spent their childhood on the Plateau, either because that was their home or because they went there as refugees. They all made the same point. Don't make it all sound terrible. A lot of the time, we had *fun*.

The first time I heard this, it sounded preposterous. These were adolescents living on so-called J3 rations, which meant 350 grams of bread a day, 180 grams of meat per week, and 500 grams of sugar per month. The bread was grey and hard, and rumour had it that it was bulked up with sawdust. They wore loden capes made from greasy mountain wool, which never fully dried and made them smell like wet dogs. They were restricted to one pair of shoes a year, so they wore wooden clogs. None of this sounded like the ideal conditions for *fun*. But as I got deeper into the research, I realised that this was almost the masterstroke of those involved in the rescue operation. Their avowed intention was to give the children now on the Plateau as normal an upbringing as possible, and they went a long way towards succeeding.

Nonetheless, the pain of those days lingers. Many of the refugees were teenagers, an age group not noted for its easy ways. These were young people just beginning to discover their sexuality, and learning the painful process of living in an adult world. Refugees from the camps had been torn from their parents, whom they might never see again. 'You were just children,' I said to one of the interviewees after hearing some particularly awful story. 'We were never children,' she responded flatly—not angrily, just correcting me.

• • •

Helping the neighbours is one of the great traditions of rural communities. At harvest time in particular, everyone pitches in. Hanne Hirsch remembers a certain Madame de Félice who owned the Wasps' Nest building and lived nearby. She visited the hostel in the autumn of 1941, only a few months after Hanne arrived in Le Chambon. Madame de Félice wanted to know if the young guests would like to help out picking fruit in her orchard.

The children duly assembled, and were given a stern warning not to eat while they were picking. There would be time enough for that at the end of the day when the job was done, they were told. To children who had been close to starvation in Gurs, this sounded more like an invitation than an admonition. They fanned out into the orchard and simply sat down under the trees, munching their way through as many ripe apples and plums as they could handle. Madame de Félice had rather less to show for the day's labour than she was expecting. The children, on the other hand, could begin to see that life in this strange new world of the Plateau had its advantages.

• • •

The *garde champêtre* (roughly 'country policeman') is a unique institution in rural French villages, combining the roles of general busybody, town hall enforcer, snoop and town crier. In Le Chambon, the *garde champêtre* was in the habit of taking up station at strategic points around the village, beating on a drum and shouting: '*Avis! Avis!*' ('Hear ye, hear ye!') until enough people had gathered around to hear the latest public pronouncements. In winter, when the streets were covered with snow, he fought a losing battle with the village kids, resident and refugee alike, over sledding. He would whack his drum and proclaim: 'It is forbidden to slide down the village streets on sleds.' Realising that mere words wouldn't do the job, however, he would wait until dusk and then spread ashes on the streets to make them less slippery and therefore less suitable for a mini Cresta Run.

The kids were not to be denied. Minutes after the *garde champêtre*'s ash-spreading spree, an army of them would arrive and get to work with their brooms, which they kept hidden around the village. Then the 'sled trains' could go into action. One of the two most satisfying runs was along the Côte de Molle, which included a fairly steep slope running straight down to the centre of town. The big attraction of this run was that it involved sledding across the railway lines at high speed, which produced a very satisfying shower of sparks. The other run began near the town hall, and involved a road down an even steeper hill and across the town's main intersection, where the roads to Saint-Agrève, Tence, Le Mazet and Les Barandons met. It then led past the school and the Protestant church to a stone bridge over the River Lignon. Fortunately there were no cars about, so the road crossing was less hazardous than it sounds. However, the stone bridge was another matter. One older boy was killed when he lost control of his sled and slammed into the bridge.

• • •

Christmas in Le Chambon was, of course, a major event for the children. Every year the Protestant church featured a massive Christmas tree. It was so big that it had to be dragged into position by a horse, which came snorting through the big double doors and heaved its way down the aisle with the enormous balsam tree in tow. The church elders removed one of the flagstones from the church floor and the tree rested in the hole it left behind.

The French traditionally eat their Christmas dinner on Christmas Eve rather than Christmas Day. But the biggest event for the children began with the ringing of church bells in the afternoon of 25 December. The kids would race down to the church and sit in assigned places, dazzled by the hundred real candles lighting the tree, and tinsel dangling from the branches. André Trocmé and Édouard Theis led the singing of Christmas carols, accompanied on an old reed organ. Then each child would receive a bag of gifts, including an orange or a tangerine. This was no mean feat. Fresh fruit was hard to come by in wartime France, especially exotic fruit not grown locally. There would be some dates to go with the fruit, and some sweets. Each bag contained *bonbons* (candies or sweets) wrapped in paper, with an exploding cap inside, which detonated when the two paper ends were pulled, a forerunner of the modern Christmas cracker, but with sweets inside instead of a feeble joke and a paper hat. (Not to be pulled in church, of course; they had to be saved for later.)

Finally, Pastor Trocmé told a story, which he would have written himself.[21] He would tell it entirely from memory, acting it out as he went. Meanwhile, Roger Darcissac operated a 'magic lantern', which projected the story's illustrations onto a large screen. Trocmé would pace up and down beside the tree, a born showman, laughing at his own funny bits and ad-libbing a few embellishments. For the kids, it was pure magic.

• • •

Catherine Cambessédès, as we have seen, always liked the New Cévenole School. One of its previously unsung attractions was its mixed classrooms.

The classes were co-ed. That might seem like nothing to you, but to us it was a new world. We came from separate girls or boys schools, and suddenly having these different creatures sitting right next to us in the classrooms was amazing. I had four brothers, but they were brothers, not boys! We were, no doubt, quite uptight about boy–girl relationships, with our Huguenot upbringing. Result? We were 'good' girls and boys, except the wilder ones who disobeyed. At Le Chambon there was no hanky-panky, so it was safe to laugh and go out in a gang of girls and boys, even for 'good' girls. And that was sure fun. Egged on by the presence of girls, boys dared to make jokes in class, or even play small pranks. We girls were such a good audience!

Music was permitted in the Trocmé household, but dancing was out. Nelly Trocmé, who was in her early teens during the war years, remembers:

My father had principles: no drinking, no dancing. Music was fine, but dancing was no good, especially locally. The young people went dancing in a bar near the town hall, and then they went to sleep in the hayloft and produced babies.

It's very difficult to be a minister's daughter or son, because you are supposed to live by the standards of your parents and be an example. You can't disobey your parents. But I danced! Not in bars. I had a friend who had an old-fashioned wind-up record player, and we went to her place on Sunday afternoons. There were American jazz records. That's where I first heard Glenn Miller's 'In the Mood'. We were girls only, a bunch of six or eight girls getting together. We turned on the records and we danced! Dad didn't know that. I told him later.

The dancing may have been girls only, but boys were included in swimming parties in the icy River Lignon. There is what is still optimistically called a 'beach' just outside the centre of the village, near the House of Rocks, and a second 'beach' nearer the village, called Tata Zoé (Auntie Zoe). 'It was all very innocent,' explains Nelly. 'We had a special little friend, but we didn't even hold hands. We would try to sit together, maybe. There was nothing happening . . . it was all silent vibes. It was cold, but we swam. And there was no hanky-panky, at least none at our level.'

There were other activities: cycle rides and camping trips in the mountains, Boy Scouts and Girl Scouts, school plays, a basketball team, cross-country runs. In other words, the kids of the Plateau, locals and refugees alike, shared and played and flirted and danced and sang and couldn't wait for Christmas, just like kids everywhere. And that is one of the many miracles of this story.

6

Rebellion

By the summer of 1942, the two streams of refugees were in full flow. As mentioned, there were the 'unofficials'—mostly French and foreign Jews who had been displaced from their jobs, their houses and their businesses, and who had made their own way to the Plateau in the hope of sheltering there—and the 'transfers', mostly children released from the camps. These children were in Le Chambon and other Plateau villages with the full knowledge of the Vichy authorities.

The 'unofficials' could be divided into two groups. The first of these were better-off Jews. Towards the end of 1941, when the anti-Jewish laws of the Vichy government began to bite—particularly those laws leading to the confiscation of businesses—some Jewish people simply sold up while they still had something to sell. A significant number moved into hotels or rented villas away from the large cities, where there was less risk of raids and round-ups. On the Plateau, they favoured hotels on the eastern side, in Ardèche towns like Saint-Agrève, Le Cheylard and Lamastre, although some did settle on the Haute-Loire side, the most significant group in the Hôtel Placide in Tence. A few found their way to Le Chambon.

The second group of unofficials were the 'illegals', the poverty-stricken and desperate who simply came to the Plateau from all over

Europe because they had heard that people there were willing to help. They were generally placed with sympathetic farmers and scattered in remote houses all over the Plateau. They were inevitably well and truly outside the law. If they were Jewish, they naturally did not register themselves as Jews, though the law required it. And they were often using false papers, which was a serious crime.

The poor Jews were generally well received and made welcome. Sometimes the 'illegals' arrived alone. Sometimes they came as whole families. Nobody asked who they were, why they were there or if they could pay. Above all, nobody kept a tally. Some of the refugees needed fresh papers before they could move on. Roger Darcissac could oblige, as could Pastor Édouard Theis, Simone Mairesse, Mireille Philip and others. Mireille Philip in particular took huge risks. She was the wife of André Philip, the deputy who had joined de Gaulle in London, so she was very much a marked woman. Although she was on her own in Le Chambon with five children to look after, she played a hugely active part in the rescue operation and in the Resistance, and was an active forger.

The rich Jews were a different matter. The behaviour of some who settled in the hotels and villas did not exactly endear them to the local population. Apart from resenting their wealth, local people often blamed them for either controlling or creating a black market. The principal source of resentment was their frequent demand that the hoteliers provide them with extra food beyond their rationed allowance.

On 30 April 1942 the mayor of Saint-Agrève wrote to the prefect of the Ardèche complaining that he seemed to be facing an endless succession of 'Jewish summers' and asking the prefect to ban Jews from the commune of Saint-Agrève for the forthcoming holiday season. 'Their presence,' he wrote, 'risks encouraging the hoteliers to feed them illegally, as happened to one hotelier from Lamastre, who was arrested this week on the streets of St. Agrève with 32 kilos of sausages bought without ration coupons.' The mayor continued: 'Their presence also risks the number and scale of direct purchases from farms at uncontrolled prices, which would gravely compromise the already difficult task of feeding the community.' Someone, presumably from the prefect's office, had added a handwritten comment at the bottom of the letter: 'Of course!'

Nor did the Jews in the hotels show much sympathy for their poorer fellow Jews who came to the Plateau looking for shelter. Magda Trocmé went on the rounds of the hotels to ask some of the more prosperous Jews if they would contribute to the support of their co-religionists, particularly those from outside France. She was told: 'These foreigners that you bring to Le Chambon will be the ruin of us. We French Jews are not going to get mixed up with them.'

• • •

The functioning and financing of the various shelters for the transfers seems to have been largely undisturbed by America's entry into the war in December 1941. On 11 December, three days after the Pearl Harbor attack by Japan,[22] Hitler declared war on the United States. Under the terms of the Armistice of June 1940, funds could not be sent directly from an 'enemy' country to France, so they now had to arrive clandestinely via Switzerland. However, the Plateau had a staunch and resourceful friend in Geneva who saw to it that the money continued to flow. As André Trocmé wrote in his memoirs:

> Through the channel of the Ecumenical Council in Geneva, and with the help of Charles Guillon, we had the necessary money to keep our children's and adolescents' homes going, as well as receiving grants for young refugees at the New Cévenole School. Brave couriers crossed the frontier secretly, carrying the funds.

It is highly likely that Guillon himself was one of the couriers. He made several clandestine trips to the Plateau in this period, and he was not the sort of man to arrive empty-handed.

The terms of the Armistice also prevented the Vichy French government from keeping an army. To get around this, on 1 August 1940 the Vichy government created the LFC or Légion Française des Combattants, a quasi-military force largely made up of ex-soldiers who supported Pétain. They were hardly a formidable force, but they brought a good dose of right-wing zeal to the task of rooting out communists. Over the winter of 1940–41 they launched a succession of investigations on the Plateau in search of communist sympathisers. In December 1940 they latched on to Paul Charreyron, a cabinet maker working in Le Chambon. Charles Guillon, still acting as mayor despite his resignation, assured the legionnaires that Charreyon was harmless. On 20 January 1941 the LFC came up with the names of seven suspected Plateau communists, six of them from Le Chambon, including Charreyron again, and Roger Darcissac. Nobody followed up on any of this, and nothing happened as a result.

Nevertheless, the creation of the LFC led to one of the first acts of petty rebellion on the Plateau. The Vichy government decreed that 1 August 1941 should be a public holiday to celebrate the LFC's first anniversary. At noon, all the church bells in every village were to be rung for fifteen minutes at top volume. André Trocmé showed the government notice to his bellringer, but made it very clear that he wouldn't be at all sorry if his bells failed to sound. On the appointed day, the Catholic church's bells rang. The Protestant church's bells stayed silent. As Trocmé wrote afterwards: 'It was the first time the parish openly said "non!"'

The parish said *non* rather more stridently at the end of that month. Pierre Laval was a controversial figure throughout the Vichy era. The former foreign minister had been Pétain's Minister of State in the first Vichy government until Pétain sacked him in December 1940. He hovered on the fringes of right-wing causes, a much-disliked and distrusted figure. Then, on 27 August 1941, a would-be assassin shot and lightly wounded him. He quickly recovered, to the dismay of his critics. However, on the night of 30 August, a Saturday, a group of young men from Le Chambon gathered noisily in the town and marched down to the bridge over the River Lignon, carrying a coffin-sized box with a swastika painted on the side. They proceeded to throw it into the river, chanting: 'Laval is dead.'[23]

Their actions did not go unnoticed. Four days later, on 3 September (the second anniversary of the declaration of war), a group of gendarmes arrived in Le Chambon from Tence. En route they had seen dozens of chalk signs proclaiming 'V'—Churchill's symbol of Allied victory—and the forbidden double-barred Cross of Lorraine, de Gaulle's icon for the Free French Army. Alongside one of the chalk signs someone had written: '*Vive de Gaulle!*' ('Long live de Gaulle!')

All of this was brought to the attention of Robert Bach, the new prefect of the Haute-Loire. Bach was very much one for the peaceful life. He dismissed the defiant chalk marks as 'a ridiculous nonsense'. However, the head of the gendarmerie in the Auvergne region took it all much more seriously. In his view it was clearly the work of Jews and Freemasons, and he blamed it all on outsiders. 'Most of these people have left their homes and moved to the eastern Haute-Loire, where a lot of them have properties,' he wrote in a report. 'You can see it particularly in Le Chambon, Tence and Montfaucon, where these people are congregating. There are a lot of people wearing the Cross of Lorraine, and that's where the propaganda is at its height.' All this disloyalty was spoiling the area for law-abiding holidaymakers, in his opinion.

• • •

Throughout this period, it was still possible to send letters to and from the internment camps. Hanne Hirsch stayed in touch with her mother, still in Gurs, and with Max Liebmann. The first news she received was good. Max had been transferred from Gurs to a farm near Lyon, not too far from Le Chambon. The farm was run by, of all unlikely organisations, the Orthodox Jewish Boy Scouts. Then came the bad news. Hanne's mother was ill. The OSE and the Swiss Red Cross arranged for Hanne to be allowed to travel from Le Chambon to Gurs to see her. She set off unescorted, arriving in Gurs on 5 August 1942.

My mother had been very sick for some time but nobody told me about it. Eventually I was told I had better come and see her. On my way to Gurs, since you have to pass through Lyon, I went to see Max. The mail worked, you see! Then I went on to Gurs but I couldn't get into the camp. It was under lockdown. I found out that after lockdown, the next day was deportation.

I saw my mother in the camp from a long distance. We had a shouted sort of conversation. Then, with the help of the Organisations [the OSE and the Swiss Red Cross], they arranged that I could be in the freight yard. So I went down to Oloron on foot.[24] I slept in the street during the night. About five in the morning I walked over to the freight yards. The trains were standing there. They had already been loaded. Where was my mother? There were 1000 people there. I was sort of standing there when a French gendarme said: 'What are you doing here?' I said: 'I'm looking for my mother.' He said: 'Do you know where she is?' I said: 'No.' How could I know among 1000 people? He said: 'I will find her for you. What's her name?' Then he asked me, like a good Frenchman, would I like a drink out of his hip flask? I said: 'No, thank you,' and he went off. Before he went he said: 'What goes on here tears my heart out.' He had to be there, he was there, but he did as little as possible. But he did find

*my mother, and I had about an hour with her. Then the trains left.
These were freight trains, standing room only, cattle cars. Some had
straw on the floor, some did not. There was a pail in the corner.
People took whatever luggage they still had on the train. The Quakers
had supplied some food. That was it!*

That was the last time Hanne saw her mother. On her way back to
Le Chambon, she went to see Max Liebmann again, near Lyon. When
Max told her about the round-ups then going on in the Lyon area, it
was the first time she had heard the word 'round-up'.[25] She told him:
'If you're not safe here, come to Le Chambon.'

A couple of weeks later, Hanne was walking to school with a group
of other girls. At that time of the morning the boys from New Cévenole
School tended to mill about in the village, ogling the girls. Suddenly
there was the familiar sound of a wolf whistle. Hanne kept her nose
determinedly in the air, but one of the girlfriends couldn't resist taking
a look. What she saw was not the usual grinning Cévenole schoolboy.
She shrieked to Hanne: 'Turn around!' Hanne wasn't having it. Her
friend, who had been in the Gurs camp with Hanne, was insistent.
So was Hanne. The friend grabbed her by the shoulder and spun her
around. The whistler stood a few yards away, smiling. Max and Hanne
were back together again.

• • •

By August of 1942, the mood of the Plateau towards the Vichy government had well and truly soured. The newly arrived refugees came with
tales of persecution and injustice. With rationing and shortages, life
was uncomfortable for everybody. So there were few reasons to be
cheerful, or even grateful. The pinpricks of the likes of the LFC were
a constant irritation. For the very few who could afford it, the need
to top up everyday items like petrol and food on the black market

simply made things worse. The government blamed the Jews for the black market and, as we have seen, there were some Jewish black marketeers who did their fellow Jews no service. But the population wasn't fooled. The problem was not the Jews: it was the war, the defeat and the Occupation. And the government seemed incapable of doing anything about any of it.

The sheer frustration of it all is illustrated by this conversation in Le Chambon, remembered by Catherine Cambessédès. 'I heard the lady in the grocery store say to a customer with coupons that she was out of (one at a time) sugar, also flour or coffee or eggs. The customer then asked: "Well, what *do* you have for sale then?" Answer: "Baking powder."'

Sourness turned into open hostility on 9 and 10 August 1942. The Vichy government's Minister for Youth, Georges Lamirand, decided to pay a visit to Le Chambon to see for himself the admirable ways of France's young Protestants. He had heard good things about the New Cévenole School, about the UCJG's Camp de Joubert, about the Boy Scouts and Girl Scouts, and even about the hostels for young refugees. What better way to show his appreciation of all this cheerful adaptability than with a bit of on-the-spot head-patting, cheek-kissing and palm-pressing, personally congratulating the youth of the Plateau for the fine example they were setting the rest of France? Prefect Bach wrote in advance to André Trocmé: 'I'm sure that in your heart you will want the visit to be a brilliant success.'

It was nothing of the kind. The whole enterprise was pretty much doomed before it began. The Vichy government had tried to merge all French youth movements into one large organisation called the Compagnons de France (Companions of France). But with their fascist salutes, their flag-waving and bugle-blowing, their parades, their work camps, their uniform blue shirts and their wild-eyed zeal for Marshal Pétain, the Companions looked too much like Germany's Hitler Youth for comfort. So the government's attempts to corral the youth of France produced the opposite result: the various youth movements clung tenaciously to their independence, and generally resented government attempts to talk them out of it. The youth of the Plateau were stroppier than most. The various pastors of the Plateau had all been preaching against totalitarianism, with a strong dose of pacifism to accompany it. The young people knew what to do about visits by government ministers. And they were about to show it.

Perhaps sensing trouble, the authorities tried to make sure everything went smoothly. On 8 August, the day before Lamirand's arrival, nine gendarmes from Tence descended on the town and set about sanitising it. It was a Saturday, and therefore market day, so the town was crowded. The gendarmes set themselves up at the bus stops, the railway station, and in the market place, demanding to see papers and identification. They checked out the hotels and bars. Two gendarmes guarded the main road south of the town, while two others blocked the route to Le Mazet. Nobody was going to escape their keen scrutiny. The official records of this particular operation have long since disappeared, but as far as anyone remembers, nobody was arrested, no false papers were found, and the town could safely be declared 'clean'. The gendarmes drove back to Tence, presumably congratulating themselves on a job well done. After that thorough sweep of undesirables, what could possibly go wrong tomorrow?

When Lamirand arrived by car the next day, wearing a splendid military-style uniform with more than a hint of the German Army about it, the streets were deserted. No flags flew. No bunting hung from windows. Nobody waved. Nobody smiled. There was nobody there. Lamirand had been promised a 'banquet' at, of all places, Camp de Joubert. Instead he was served a thin meal of typically rationed food. The minister tried to make the best of it. 'It's better this way,' he said. 'It's what the marshal would want—it's more patriotic.'

Lamirand then moved on to the sports ground, accompanied by the prefect, the sub-prefect and the deputy mayor. The various pastors refused to join them, though they had been around for the 'banquet'. About a hundred curious children had turned up at the sports ground to take a look at the minister. These were small numbers, far from the cheering, enthusiastic crowds of two thousand or more that Lamirand had addressed elsewhere.

'*Bonjour, m'sieur,*' a couple of the bolder children said, trying to take the minister's hand. This is more like it, Lamirand must have thought. '*Bonjour, bonjour,*' he replied jovially. That was about as affable as things got. Pierre Brès, an athletics teacher at the New Cévenole School and the head of the local Boy Scouts, made a brief and grumpy speech taken from Romans 13, saying that Christians had a duty to obey the laws of the state. Lamirand had planned to follow up with a long, rousing speech praising the wonders being performed by the Protestant youth of the Plateau. This clearly wasn't the moment for it, so he contented himself with a few words before heading to the Protestant church for a service, the next scheduled stop on the itinerary.

If what had gone before was bad, things now got worse. Both Theis and Trocmé had refused to preside over the service, so a Swiss pastor, Marcel Jeannet, spoke instead. His message was not what Lamirand wanted to hear. Jeannet echoed Pierre Brès, saying it was the duty of Christians to obey the state. There was, however, a gigantic *but*: it was the duty of the state to make sure it didn't bend the laws of God.

When the service ended, Lamirand walked out of the church to be confronted by a dozen senior students from New Cévenole School. They handed him a document that began:

Minister, we have been informed of the scenes of terror which took place three weeks ago in Paris, when the French police, under orders from the occupying power, arrested at their homes all the Jewish families of Paris and dumped them in the Winter Velodrome.

This was a reference to the notorious round-up and deportation to Auschwitz of some 13,152 Parisian Jews on 16 and 17 July 1942. The students then drove their point home. 'We know from experience,' they told the minister, 'that the decrees of the occupying power are, after a brief delay, imposed in Unoccupied France, where they are presented as the independent decisions of the French head of state. We believe that these deportations of Jews will soon start in the south.'

Then came the sting. 'We want you to know,' the students continued,

that there are a certain number of Jews among us. We can't tell the difference between Jews and non-Jews. If our friends, whose sole fault is to adhere to a different religion, receive deportation orders, we will encourage them to disobey those orders, and we will do our best to hide them.

Lamirand knew when to retreat. He brushed the students aside. 'These questions don't concern me,' he said. 'Ask the prefect.' He then stomped off to his car and drove away.

Prefect Bach was furious, and clearly blamed Trocmé for the disaster. He turned to him and snapped: 'This should have been a day of national harmony. You create division.' Trocmé snapped back: 'It's hardly a question of national harmony when our friends are threatened with deportation.' Bach was adamant: 'The plain fact is I've received my orders, and I'll carry them out. The foreign Jews living in the Haute-Loire aren't your brothers. They're not part of your church, and they're not part of your country. In a few days, we'll have a list of names of every Jew in Le Chambon.' Trocmé was sceptical. 'Even we don't know if someone is a Jew,' he offered. 'We just know they are people.' At this, Bach turned threatening. 'Monsieur Trocmé,' he warned, 'be very sure to take care. Seven of your fellow citizens write to me regularly to keep me up to date on your subversive activities. I haven't kept count of their letters up until now, but I'm well informed. If you aren't careful, it will be you that I'm forced to intern. So, a word to the wise . . . watch it!'

• • •

What Bach knew—and Trocmé did not—was that on 3 August 1942, a week before the calamitous Lamirand visit, the Vichy government had instructed the prefects of all departments in the Unoccupied Zone to come up with a register of all Jews in their area, and to arrest all foreign Jews. The list of names Bach referred to was part of this Vichy operation.

Trocmé may not have known about the specific order, but he sensed looming trouble. On 14 August he went to the prefecture in Le Puy and spoke to the chief of police. He told him (entirely speciously!) that three children's homes in Le Chambon had diplomatic immunity: these were The Flowery Hill, the House of Rocks and The Shelter. The three were under the protection of the neutral Swiss, the neutral Swedes and the United States. They could not be touched.

Whatever the chief of police made of this, it did not stop the authorities from pressing on. At four thirty on the morning of Tuesday, 25 August, Auguste Bohny, who ran The Shelter, was woken by a fearful pounding on his front door. Gendarmes, eight of them, had the house surrounded. With them was a police Inspector of Security from Le Puy. At the time, Bohny was looking after a group of children from The Wasps' Nest, but they were sleeping in the communal dining room and the games room rather than in the bedrooms.

Bohny made his way to the front door by way of the cellar, as he normally did. What did the gendarmes want? They wanted to see a

Monsieur Steckler, to check his papers. Monsieur Steckler was at The Wasps' Nest, not The Shelter. Bohny would take them there, if they would give him a minute to get dressed. He dressed 'at speed' and they duly covered the few hundred metres between the two houses. At The Wasps' Nest, the gendarmes told Steckler to pack his bags (but not his shaving gear).

When they got back to The Shelter, they found that the most senior gendarme had decided not to wait around outside and had marched into the house. He hadn't got far. One of the staff, Joseph Godefryd, had bailed him up and harangued him non-stop until his boss's return. At this point the gendarmes seemed uninterested in the boys, who were sleeping in the games room, but wanted to check the two girls, who were sleeping in the dining room. The girls turned out not to be on their list of names.

Bohny now challenged the gendarmes. These young people were under his protection, this was Swiss government property, and he would not allow any further action without confirmation from the chief of police himself. There's a mug born every minute, and Bohny was lucky enough to be surrounded by nine of them. The gendarmes accepted Bohny's demand and all eight gendarmes plus the Inspector of Security left The Shelter at around 6.30 am.

Bohny now woke the children, fed them a good breakfast and bundled them out the door. They headed straight for the woods. When the gendarmes returned at 9.30 am the place was empty. They were furious, and threatened Bohny with arrest. Meanwhile, they had brought a bus to the village—it would take more than a car to accommodate their expected haul of Jews, they thought—and in it sat the unfortunate Monsieur Steckler, alone. Well, not quite alone: the bus was surrounded by villagers wishing Monsieur Steckler well, offering him food, even a bit of precious chocolate. The sympathetic crowd looked on as the bus set off for Le Puy. That afternoon, Bohny received a letter from the Social Services in Le Puy. Monsieur Steckler was only quarter Jewish. He could go free, as he did the next day.

Despite this setback, the authorities weren't finished with Le Chambon. At five o'clock the next morning the gendarmes were back at The Shelter and The Wasps' Nest. They kept coming back every day for the rest of the week, always leaving empty-handed. The children had all been dispersed. By Saturday the gendarmes were totally exasperated. They summoned André Trocmé to the town hall and demanded that he lead them to the hidden Jews. If he refused, he would be arrested, along with Édouard Theis and the directors of the three children's homes. No deal. And no arrests.

On Sunday, notices were posted all over the village announcing that anyone who sheltered foreigners without declaring them would be sent to a concentration camp or heavily fined. Nobody responded.

On 3 September, private houses were searched for the first time. No result. On 10 September the village was given advance warning: the penalty for hiding a foreign Jew was two to five years in prison. Yet still no one came forward. Nothing happened.

After three weeks the police gave up. They had searched the houses and the surrounding forest without catching so much as a single refugee. The story was the same all over the Plateau. Between 19 August and 13 September, French gendarmes based in Yssingeaux mounted no fewer than 35 raids, looking for Jews. They found one, whom they later released.

The whole thing was a fiasco. In a document understandably marked 'secret', the company commander of the gendarmes, Squadron Leader Silvani, set out the results from the commune of Le Chambon. They had checked the papers of 879 individuals on the roads, in buses and on trains, and a further 496 individuals in hotels and hostels, and had raided 625 private homes. The result: two arrests. The report shyly omits the fact that of the two arrested, one, Monsieur Steckler, had been released the next day. So 2000 searches had produced one arrest. Silvani concluded: 'This proves that the Jews we were looking for have left the Plateau.'

The commander of the group of gendarmes specifically targeting Le Chambon agreed. His report concluded:

> *On the advice of people we can trust, all of them living in Le Chambon or the surrounding area, none of the foreign Jews we were looking for are still in the commune or living nearby. Nobody has seen these Jews. The Chaumargeais sector of the commune of Tence, rumoured to be sheltering Jews, was searched minutely, day and night, without result.*

By the prefecture's own reckoning, three months of diligent raiding throughout the whole department of the Haute-Loire had produced not very much. Draft 6483(2) of the prefecture's report dated 30 October 1942 states:

> *In accordance with the instructions of 3 August (and subsequent):*
> *160 foreign Jews have been located—*
> *85 arrests have been carried out, 73 are still in custody—*
> *75 Jews, of whom 7 were foreign workers and 5 minors, got away—*
> *among these, 8 including the 5 minors have been authorised to move*
>   *to Le Chambon in the care of Swiss Aid.*
> *16 have been recaptured, of which 2 were caught in the Haute-Loire,*
>   *8 at the Swiss border, and 5 are still in Switzerland.*[26]
> *So 46 out of 160 are still on the run.*

This puts the best face on what was essentially a disaster. The 85 Jews arrested included 73 picked up in two raids in the northwest of the department, well away from the Plateau. What's more, these Jews

100

were hardly well hidden: they were already penned up in two labour camps for foreign workers, at Brioude and Saint-Georges-d'Aurac. The 73 were shipped off to the euphemistically named Collection Centre in Montluçon, not far from the town of Vichy, presumably to await 'deportation'. In summary, the prefecture had managed to arrest only 85 out of 160 foreign Jews they had identified and whose names and addresses they had, and 73 of the 85 were not exactly on the loose: they were already locked up in labour camps. The gendarmes had managed to find only two of the 75 who had given them the slip. It was not exactly a triumph. Indeed, if the raids had any effect at all, it was to add eight young Jews to the 'transfer' population of Le Chambon. Otherwise, despite Bach's threats, the Plateau's rescue mission continued undisturbed.

It is worth taking a look at the number of Jews that the likes of Bach were chasing. As we know, there were no records kept, so everything is dependent on anecdotal memory and guesswork. The numbers that follow probably exclude the children released from the camps. But even in the middle of 1942, when both streams of refugees were flowing into the Plateau, the numbers were surprisingly low. In his memoir, André Trocmé writes:

> How many Jews were in Le Chambon in the summer of 1942? Not too many: 100 to 150 at most. We knew them all. A lot of farms sheltered them. Others were scattered around the village or in the seven refugee houses. We had two of them at our place.

• • •

By late 1942, although the atmosphere on the Plateau was clearly getting tetchier, things could have been worse. The Quakers, the Cimade, the OSE and the Red Cross continued to win the release of children from the camps and transfer them to the Plateau.

Then, at the end of 1942, three closely related events changed everything. On 8 November, Allied forces, largely British and American, landed in the French territory of Algeria in North Africa as part of 'Operation Torch'. The Vichy French resisted, but their hearts weren't in it, and the Allied forces, led by General Dwight D. Eisenhower, soon established total control. A large Allied force was now hovering over southern Europe, and an Allied invasion of mainland Europe, probably via France, looked imminent.

Operation Torch also showed the Germans that the Vichy French weren't exactly snarling rottweilers when it came to resisting Allied invasions. What if the Allies mounted an attack on the Unoccupied Zone of France? Would the Vichy French be able to throw them back into the sea? The omens weren't good. So Hitler decided that if southern France was to be defended against Allied attack from North Africa, the only way to do it was with German troops. He ended the sham of the 'Unoccupied Zone' and took over the rest of France. On 11 November, German troops raced south, meeting no resistance. Within days, the whole of France was in German hands, with the exception of a small chunk in the southeast corner, which was occupied by the Italians. There was no longer an Unoccupied Zone. This was naturally unpopular with the French people, and had the effect of turning the whole of France into hostile territory for the Germans, while making de Gaulle and his Free French Army, in the eyes of the French population, seem like a more useful bet than the marshal.

The third development was that the Russians started to push the Germans back on the Eastern Front. Over a year earlier, on 22 June 1941, Hitler had invaded Russia. The German Army initially rolled over Russian opposition, and began to close in on Moscow and Stalingrad. But, like Napoleon before him, Hitler never quite managed to deliver the fatal blow, and the battle dragged on through the bitter winter of 1941–42, then through the spring and into the summer of 1942. The

Russians consolidated, and by the middle of 1942 they were holding their ground. As early as May 1942, Marshal Zhukov, field commander of the Red Army, was beginning to claim the odd victory over German forces. By the end of 1942, the badly mauled Germans were on the back foot. The Russians were pushing them out.

In other words, around the end of 1942, Hitler started losing the war. And that made him desperate.

Part III

...

OCCUPATION

7

Fresh blood

It is impossible to overstate the importance of the changes that took place in France at the end of 1942. Quite simply, the occupation of the whole country,[27] instead of the northern three-fifths, changed everything.

Let's start with Pétain. As we have seen, in the beginning he enjoyed widespread acceptance, at times adoration, as 'the man who saved France'. Although France had been soundly defeated, Pétain had managed to negotiate a deal with Hitler whereby he hung onto some control of two-fifths of the country, and was nominally in charge of all of it: even the occupied Northern Zone was theoretically under the control of the Vichy government, though in practice Germany wrote the rules there and made sure they were obeyed.

But now that the whole country was occupied, Pétain's claim to be the saviour of the nation no longer had any real basis. Meanwhile, de Gaulle's Free French Army took control of a succession of French colonies. With the Allied capture of Algeria in Operation Torch, it was clear to the French population that the Allied side increasingly looked like the winners. Pétain's authority and popularity did not evaporate overnight, but by the end of 1943 they were in terminal decline.

With this decline came some real uncertainty on the part of the Vichy officials, in the gendarmerie and in the various departmental bureaucracies. Very early in the war, the left-wing deputy André Philip—who had voted against Pétain and the Armistice and moved his family to Le Chambon, before joining de Gaulle in London—said in a speech at a wedding that after the eventual liberation of France those who supported Pétain would be shot as traitors. At the time it seemed completely mad. Who in 1940 could imagine that the all-conquering Germans would be kicked out of France in a little over four years, and that with their departure Pétain's Vichy regime would be consigned to the dustbin of history? But now, in late 1942 and early 1943, with the Germans on the back foot, it was a different story. The least that could be said was that this one could go either way. So the French police, the gendarmerie and the bureaucrats quietly concluded, not collectively but individually, that it might be prudent to take things a bit easy.[28]

Last but not least, it was increasingly clear that there was no French government *in France* to be loyal to. Up until the occupation of the Southern Zone, there was a good case to be made that the Vichy administration was the only legal government of France, and that any Frenchman who sought their overthrow was at best misguided and at worst a traitor. But after the Occupation, did that still hold good? De Gaulle had set up a government in exile in London (with André Philip as his Minister for the Interior). Maybe that was the legitimate government? In which case, anyone clinging ostentatiously to the side of the Vichy government had better watch out!

In particular, the occupation of the whole of France gave a different complexion to the idea of armed resistance. Up until the end of 1942, with the World War I hero Pétain leading a French government, taking up arms against the authorities looked positively treasonous, not to mention dangerous. But with the fading power of the French government, and the rising sense that the German enemy *could* be beaten, armed resistance looked like a much more attractive option.

This last eventuality was one of the great fears held by André Trocmé and Édouard Theis, the two leading pacifist pastors of the Plateau. They had preached non-violent resistance. As Trocmé said in his 'weapons of the spirit' sermon: 'To love, to forgive, to show kindness to our enemies, that is our duty.' There was no ambiguity: violence against the Germans was as much to be condemned as violence against the Jews.

Robert Bach, prefect of the Haute-Loire, was one of the first to sense fresh trouble ahead in the wake of the extended Occupation. On 23 November 1942, twelve days after the German push south, he sent a formal note to the head of the gendarmerie of the department of the Haute-Loire.

The events of recent days have provoked population movements that cannot fail to attract more foreigners and Frenchmen into the department, particularly Jews. It is vital that I am given very full and accurate information about these arrivals so that, if this happens, I can take all effective steps to limit their numbers so that they don't exceed our ability to provide accommodation and food. I'm sorry to have to say that among the people leaving their homes for reasons to do with the present circumstances, there will be some suspicious and even dangerous elements, and that their presence in the Haute-Loire could lead to trouble.

He was right about that.

• • •

Pierre Fayol had lived most of his life in Marseille. He was born there in 1905, and he rejoined his wife and son there after his demobilisation from the French Army on 30 July 1940, five weeks after Pétain signed the Armistice. Marseille was in the Unoccupied Zone so, as a French-born Jew rather than a foreigner, Fayol was in less danger than the many Jews who had fled to Marseille from Germany, Austria and other Nazi-ruled countries of Eastern Europe. However, the Fayol family was well known in Marseille, and Pierre Fayol had stepped forward to do what he could to help Jewish and other refugees. If things got tough, he was a marked man.

This was brought home sharply on 9 June 1942 when a provisional administrator, a Monsieur Foulon, came to take stock of the Fayols' possessions, including their flat and its furniture. The writing was on the wall. Fayol already had a plan. He had heard about a Protestant pastor in a remote mountain village of the Haute-Loire who was urging his congregation to defy the Vichy government by sheltering refugees, including Jews. Fayol's cousins, the Coblentz family, confirmed the story. Originally from Strasbourg in eastern France, the Coblentzes had been evacuated south in the early days of the war. They now lived on a farm in Le Crouzet, just outside Le Chambon, and they recommended the Plateau. The clincher came when they mentioned the New Cévenole School: that sounded ideal for the Fayols' thirteen-year-old son. So in August 1942, at about the time Georges Lamirand was making his ill-fated visit to the Plateau, Pierre Fayol decided to take a look for himself. He went to Le Chambon with his family for a visit.

They stayed in a farmhouse called Panelier, which looked a bit like a small fortress. They were not the only guests. A promising young French-Algerian writer named Albert Camus had just moved into Panelier with his wife, Francine. Fayol and Camus struck up a friendship that continued for the rest of the war. Camus had moved to the Plateau for the mountain air, which was reputed to be good for tuberculosis, from which he suffered. He spent his time at Panelier working on a novel, which he called *La Peste* (*The Plague*).[29] Published in 1947, it was a towering allegory set in the small Algerian town of Oran. Bubonic plague strikes, but the people of the town are frozen in disbelief. The disease becomes a metaphor for the plague of Nazism sweeping Europe. It was mostly written on the Plateau, and in his book *We Only Know Men* the philosopher and historian Patrick Henry says he can hear echoes of André Trocmé in the sermons of Camus's fictional priest.

On the Plateau, the Fayols also met up with the Coblentz family, Pierre's cousins, who had already begun to search for somewhere for the Fayols to hide if things got too dangerous down south. All in all, the Plateau looked like the answer. The Fayols returned to Marseille to await developments, their escape plan in place. On 11 November, as the Germans began their sweep south into the Unoccupied Zone (reaching Marseille on 22 November), Fayol knew the time had come to move. Time to get out, and go underground.

As we have seen, there was little or no armed resistance in France before the end of 1942. However, in August 1940, in Lyon, Henri Frenay, a former captain in the French Army, and his remarkable female co-conspirator Berty Albrecht had set up the Mouvement de Libération Nationale (National Liberation Movement), or MLN, which later came to be known as Combat. It operated mostly in the Unoccupied Zone and had six regional networks: Lyon, Marseille, Montpelier, Toulouse, Limoges and Clermont-Ferrand. Pierre Fayol was already in loose touch with the Marseille branch. Now he turned to them for help obtaining false papers. Pierre Chaix-Bryant, who later distinguished himself in the liberation of Marseille, was able to oblige. Fayol became 'Simon Lehay'.

The Fayols had planned to move in January 1943, but Fayol's wife, Marianne, wanted to get out straight away, in November. She was proved right. Gestapo raids began on the platforms of Saint-Charles, the main railway station in Marseille, the day after the Fayols left.

The Strasbourg cousins had found accommodation for them on a farm at La Celle, about three kilometres north of Le Chambon. The

'Lehay' family occupied the first floor of the house, while an old farmer and his nephew lived on the ground floor. It was not exactly five-star comfort. There was no running water, so they had to fetch whatever water they needed from a spring. On the other hand, their accommodation included a sink with a plug, a rare luxury. They chopped their own wood to feed the stove, which also provided the only heat. For Pierre Fayol, one of the big attractions of the house was its layout. The house was built on a forested hillside, with the main door at the back of the building. The raised and doorless front of the house had a clear view of the lane that led from the main road. It would be hard to be taken by surprise, and easy to do something about it.

Fayol had agreed to stay in touch with the Combat organisation. He was highly motivated and a trained soldier, just the sort of man a guerrilla army needs most. The radical pacifist pastors continued to set the mood of the Plateau, preaching love for their enemies. They remained adamantly opposed to armed resistance; among other things, it would put the rescue operation in jeopardy, and their mission was too important for that. Nevertheless, the changed mood in France after Operation Torch and total occupation meant that across the country armed resistance was looking both more inviting and more possible.

The arrival of Pierre Fayol meant that the Plateau had its Secret Army[30] leader-in-waiting.

• • •

Lyon was just south of the Demarcation Line that had separated Occupied and Unoccupied France, so it was one of the first cities occupied by the Germans in November 1942. In the process, it acquired one of the most unpleasant Gestapo chieftains in the whole of Europe, the notorious Klaus Barbie, nicknamed 'the Butcher of Lyon'.

Virginia Hall, still working as an SOE agent under her cover as a journalist for the *New York Post*, realised that it was time to get out. By now there were well-established escape routes to neutral Spain, used mostly by Allied airmen shot down over France. The escape routes were well known to Hall through her SOE work. She had a choice of two 'pipelines' out of France—the Pat Line and the VIC—and she chose the VIC, because she knew it was less busy at the time.

Details of her journey are hard to come by. However, most of these pipelines involved a mixture of train, bicycle and foot journeys, and being handed on from farmer to villager to town dweller along the way. For someone with a wooden leg, it must have been the purest hell. The last part of the journey was on foot across the Pyrenees, involving a climb to 3000 metres in deep snow. At one point she telegrammed London to report progress, adding: 'Cuthbert [her wooden leg] is being tiresome, but I can cope.' Whoever received the telegram was clearly not familiar with her story, but showed a nice line in ruthlessness. 'If Cuthbert tiresome,' he replied, 'have him eliminated.'

Virginia was travelling with two companions, one French and one Belgian. To guide the party to the Spanish border, she appears to have paid a Spanish *passeur* (a French word for ferryman or boatman, but which in this context means 'people smuggler'—I have occasionally translated it simply as 'guide'). At the border, they did not have the necessary entry permits, and were promptly arrested and imprisoned at Figueres in Spain, about 30 kilometres from the border, near the Mediterranean coast. She shared a cell with a Spanish prostitute, who was due to be released very soon. Her cellmate agreed to post a letter to the American consul in Barcelona. The consul pulled the necessary strings, and by the beginning of 1943, Hall was back in England awaiting fresh orders.

• • •

Oscar Rosowsky, the forger we first met in the Prologue, arrived on the Plateau at about the same time as Pierre Fayol, in late November

1942. On 17 November, after her release from Rivesaltes internment camp using forged papers supplied by Oscar, Mira Rosowsky returned to the family apartment in Nice. The two Rosowskys discussed their next move. Mira's husband, Reuben, had been arrested, and neither mother nor son knew where he was. They clearly could not stay in Nice—it was too dangerous. So what next?

Of all the possibilities—try again for Switzerland, try for Spain, try for a safer part of France—the stories of Le Chambon as a shelter for Jews made it sound like the best prospect. The two agreed that Oscar should go there and take a look around. He travelled alone as Jean-Claude Pluntz, using his friend's borrowed papers. He liked what he saw, and went back to Nice to collect his mother. They travelled together by train. When they arrived in Le Chambon, they went straight to the apartment of Marcelle Hanne, the mother of Oscar's friends Charles and Georgette Hanne from Nice.

Madame Hanne wrote popular novels. Her best-known book carried the rather unpromising title *Coeur de vache* (*Heart of a Cow*) and was the story of an Alsatian cattle dealer. It was quite a popular success, and reprinted four times. Her others, *Des princes quand même . . .* (roughly *Princes Despite Everything . . .*), *Bourrasques* (*Squalls*) and *Les cahiers de Simone* (*Simone's Notebooks*), seem to have done rather less well. Oscar describes her as having wild hair that stuck out at the sides. She lived alone in a small apartment on the fourth floor of a new apartment block on the Rue Neuve in Le Chambon village, across the road from the Salvation Army headquarters.

Oscar remembers well the first meal Madame Hanne produced at the apartment.

To feed us, she went off to the butcher and came back with a lot of beef offal. She put it all in an enormous pot, which she cooked for hours. There was the liver, the lungs and the heart. It made an

*incredible soup, delicious. Then she cooked some potatoes in the
coals of the wood stove . . . We spent four stunning days there.*

As described in the Prologue, Oscar and Mira Rosowsky couldn't
stay in Marcelle Hanne's tiny apartment for any length of time.
They needed to find somewhere with a bit more space, and ideally
not together so no one would guess they were mother and son (and
therefore using false identities). There is no record of who found
Mira her new lodgings, but all the descriptions point to Simone
Mairesse. Mira Rosowsky, now the middle-aged Turkish Russian
spinster 'Mademoiselle Grabowska', according to her forged papers,
had a great stroke of luck: Simone (if indeed it was her) placed her
with the very new pastor in Fay-sur-Lignon, Daniel Curtet.

Curtet was only 25 years old, and unmarried. He arrived at his
new parish on 22 October 1942, a month ahead of the Fayols and the
Rosowskys. He was one of six Swiss pastors now established on the
Plateau: Marcel Jeannet (Le Mazet), Henri Estoppey (Intres), Georges
Grüner (Mars), André Bettex (Le Riou) and Daniel Besson (Montbuzat).
The Swiss link became vital to the whole rescue operation from early
1943 onwards. The Plateau had a loyal and well-connected ally already
established in Geneva in the form of Charles Guillon. Each of the
Swiss pastors also had his own network of friends and contacts in
Switzerland. They would need every single one of them before much
time had passed.

The young Curtet seems to have plunged unhesitatingly into the
rescue operation from the moment he arrived on the Plateau. He soon
became a willing accomplice in a process that would have been more
at home in the pages of a spy novel than in the day-to-day workings of
a group of Protestant parishes. At their regular *pastorales*, the pastors
would set the password of the month. In the next four weeks, someone
might ring one of the pastors' doorbells and say: 'I've come to remind

you of the *pastorale* in Le Mazet.' If the pastors' last get-together had indeed been held in Le Mazet, no problem. Otherwise, handle this particular visitor with caution.

Curtet's father was also a pastor. Daniel Curtet wrote regularly to his parents, who kept his letters and postcards, so that they form a record of his time on the Plateau. As everybody concerned was familiar with the Bible, Daniel wrote to his parents in a biblical code that now seems perilously easy to crack. For instance, on 23 January 1943 he wrote:

Continuing my study of first names (Mark 13/14b), I seldom come across the name Hans. On the other hand my collection [of names] has grown to include those of the 12 sons of the patriarch, and I have noted with pleasure that my parishioners and the Darbyists love them all.

In Mark 13:14 is the phrase: 'Let him that readeth, understand.' In other words, I'm writing in code. 'I seldom come across the name Hans' doesn't need much interpretation: there are no Germans about. The next is a bit more obscure. The twelve sons of the patriarch in the Bible are the twelve sons of Abraham: in other words, Jews. So what Curtet was telling his parents, in code, was that there were no Germans in the area, but that there were increasing numbers of Jews, and his parishioners were helping them. His non-biblical code didn't take too much cracking, either: for example, he would refer in his letters to the *chiens au tri*, which might—at a stretch—be translated as 'dogs at a sorting office', but otherwise meant nothing at all. However, the French word for Austrians is *autrichiens*, so it would not have taken a genius code breaker to work out to whom Curtet was referring.

Curtet recalls that 'Madame Grabowska' arrived in Fay-sur-Lignon understandably very distressed by both the disappearance of her husband and by her experience in Rivesaltes internment camp. She stayed for a while in the presbytery, recovering her health, before moving on to the Hôtel Abel, and finally to an apartment nearby. She was, says Curtet, a popular figure in the village. She also did a good job of maintaining her false identity: two years later, the villagers of Fay-sur-Lignon were astonished to find out that the charming spinster who had been living so happily among them was in fact married to a deported Latvian Jewish husband, whereabouts unknown, and was the mother of 'Jean-Claude Plunne', the eminent forger.

Oscar Rosowsky was still only eighteen years old when he arrived in Le Chambon. He was also slightly built, so he could easily pass for a schoolboy. After leaving Marcelle Hanne's apartment, his first 'home' in Le Chambon was the guesthouse Beau-Soleil, which acted as a dormitory for the New Cévenole School. Oscar had returned Jean-Claude Pluntz's borrowed papers to his friend, and had created a new identity for himself as Jean-Claude Plunne, deliberately taking a name that sounded almost identical to the old one in case anyone remembered it.

Beau-Soleil was Oscar's introduction to the clandestine world of Le Chambon.

An extraordinary couple, Monsieur and Madame Barraud, managed Beau-Soleil. Monsieur Barraud was a carpenter and joiner, and a communist, who left to join the maquis in 1943. There were twenty boys from the school in residence, plus a few young kids. There were some amazing people. One of them was Marc Eyraud, who went on to become a French movie star. There were the two Pupier brothers, sons of the famous Pupier chocolate family from Saint-Étienne. There was a young Jew called Roger Klimovitzky, four years older than us, who was high up in the Boy Scouts, and who had been a soldier. Then there was Madame Barraud's daughter Gabrielle, who had applied for a job as a teacher. We quickly became mates.

• • •

In their sweep south to occupy the remainder of France, the Germans had bypassed the Plateau. Given that they covered more than 300 kilometres to Marseille on the Mediterranean coast in eleven days, the three weeks it took them to get around to occupying the Haute-Loire suggests that the area was not a high military priority. They didn't have far to come, either—the Demarcation Line was only about 150 kilometres north of the Haute-Loire. They finally arrived in Le Puy on 5 December 1942. On 15 December the most senior officer of the Haute-Loire occupying force, Major Julius Schmähling, arrived in Le Puy and took command. It was an entirely bloodless operation.

Although the Germans set up a garrison in Le Puy, the Haute-Loire's capital city, they did not occupy the whole department. In particular, the Germans did not occupy the Plateau at all. No German Army units were stationed there at any stage during the entire war. However, German Army uniforms now appeared on the streets of Le Chambon for the first time, in slightly odd circumstances. Mountain air is famously healthy, and the Germans decided Le Chambon would make an ideal convalescent home for soldiers, particularly those returning from the Russian front. In December 1942 they took over the Hôtel du Lignon in the main street of Le Chambon, and installed anything from twelve to twenty soldiers there. The soldiers were all unarmed. In general they were the 'walking wounded', and no doubt they were grateful to put as much distance between themselves and the Russian front as they could. The villagers and the soldiers ignored each other. The Hôtel du Lignon was right next door to the guesthouse Tante-Soly (Aunt Soly), which was packed with young Jewish children. German soldiers occasionally sheltered in Tante-Soly's doorway on rainy days, but otherwise they left the house and its young guests alone. If the German soldiers had been very alert, they might have picked up on the fact that the headquarters of the Resistance was just across the street from their hotel. Nevertheless, the number of watchful eyes in Le Chambon now grew. There is no police station (*gendarmerie*) in Le Chambon to this day. However, at the beginning of November 1942, Prefect Bach considered a plan to set up a seasonal gendarmerie there. It would operate from 1 July to 30 September each year, the main tourist season, when the village was packed with non-locals. Nothing came of the plan, but sometime around the end of 1942 the powers-that-be decided that Le Chambon could not be left entirely to its own devices. Somebody should be keeping an eye on things. So they installed a plainclothes Inspector of Police in the town.

The various police forces in France are still pretty labyrinthine, and it would take a whole chapter to explain them all, now or then. Suffice to say that there is a municipal police force answerable to the local commune, and a national military force called the *gendarmerie*, which does work that in other countries would be left to the regular police force: investigating crime, policing the roads and so forth. In general, the gendarmes operate in rural areas. They report to the local prefect, as the representative of the central government.

There is also a national police force, known until 1949 as the Sûreté Nationale, which does the same work as the gendarmerie but concentrates its attention on the larger cities (those with a population of over 10,000). Prefect Bach decided to make an exception to this division of labour. Although it would have been normal to use the gendarmerie to police the rural Plateau, Bach decided instead to send a city policeman to Le Chambon. Léopold Praly was an inspector of the National Police. His job would be to report goings-on in the town to Prefect Bach, and hence to the Pétain government. Were there any Jews there, for instance? Praly moved into the Hôtel des Acacias, sharpened his pencils, filled his pen with ink and got ready to write some reports.

• • •

Things were now changing throughout France. The introduction of the STO forced labour law in February 1943 turned all young Frenchmen into potential fugitives. The Germans were insistent: young German men were being diverted away from factories to put on military uniforms and fight, particularly on the Russian front. These factory workers had to be replaced by young men from the occupied countries, including France. The Führer had ordered it. This led those same young men to go into hiding. They formed their own maquis.[31]

The fact that the whole country was now occupied meant that there was no longer any need to be squeamish about armed resistance. The Germans (and, to a lesser extent, the Italians) were unambiguously the enemy. They were there to be attacked. So while the pacifist pastors of the Plateau continued to preach pacifism and non-violence, their voices found a less ready audience in a population beginning to get a whiff of victory and liberation.

On the Plateau, the raids that had started on 25 August and continued for three weeks afterwards sent a clear signal: the Plateau was no longer safe. The residents could not trust the Plateau's isolation to keep the enemy away; and sure enough, within a few months the enemy was right there among them, in the form of Inspector Praly and his reports, and in the visible presence of uniformed German soldiers now walking freely on the streets of Le Chambon.

Finally, it was clear that the Jews on the Plateau were no longer safe. It also meant that it was not enough just to keep the Jewish refugees out of sight. They needed to be moved out of harm's way, and that meant getting them from the Plateau to Switzerland. The great rescue operation was no longer simply about running legal shelters for children released from the camps and hiding 'illegal' Jews in scattered farmhouses. From now on the Plateau would have to be one end of a dangerous and treacherous pipeline, with its other end in Switzerland. The operation would need forgers to supply false papers, guides to lead parties safely across the mountains, and money to keep the rescue mission running smoothly. Happily, it was able to meet all three needs.

8

Forgers

Despite the absence of accurate figures, there seems to be near-universal agreement that the number of 'illegals' in the Le Chambon area was comparatively small up until the end of 1942. André Trocmé estimated the number at 'between 100 and 150' in the summer of 1942, and this probably didn't increase by much until after 11 November and the German push south.

There were other non-locals on the Plateau, of course. There were the mostly Protestant holidaymakers and second-home owners who opted to stay on when war broke out, some of whom stayed for the duration of the war. There were the city children who regularly stayed in guesthouses on the Plateau during summer holidays and whose parents agreed should stay on after the outbreak of war; some of them may still have been there three years later. And from May 1941, when The Wasps' Nest children's home opened its doors, there were the various Jewish 'transfer' children released from the camps, perhaps as many as 200 by the end of 1942. So anybody looking at the village of Le Chambon's core population of 900, and then at the number of people living in and around the village at the end of 1942, might have come to the conclusion that there were thousands of refugees. Not so.

However, after 11 November, refugees began to arrive more quickly. The Rosowskys and the Fayols were typical of these arrivals. Once they had found accommodation, they needed ration cards to buy food and other essentials, and they needed 'clean' identity cards and supporting documents in order to survive round-ups. There was only one way to get them: forgery.

• • •

Until Oscar Rosowsky's arrival on the Plateau, the principal forgers were Roger Darcissac, Édouard Theis, Mireille Philip and Jacqueline Decourdemanche, the secretary at the New Cévenole School. All of them remained active in the forgery business after November 1942, and some (notably Decourdemanche) worked with Rosowsky. But there can be no doubt that the genius of the Plateau's forgery industry was Rosowsky, and he combined this remarkable talent with a manic energy. He was quick, clever, thorough . . . and tireless.

The creation of Rosowsky's forgery bureau was almost an accident, part of a conversation in November or December 1942 between four of the Beau-Soleil's young guests. Rosowsky started the ball rolling. 'I was telling them how I had used an art pen to trace the missing quarter of the official seal on the photograph on my first identity card, for Jean-Claude Pluntz.' Gabrielle Barraud (known as Gaby), daughter of the Beau-Soleil's managers, immediately saw a new possibility. Tracing was too slow, and too difficult. Primary school teachers regularly used a primitive hand-printing press to produce multiple copies of material for their pupils. It consisted of not much more than a large felt roller with a layer of gel wrapped around it. Gaby explained how it worked. 'They write a text on the gel with special coloured ink, and then they print it off for their students. They can roll off 50 copies at a time, and they hand them out to their students.'

Rosowsky picked up the idea. If he could get hold of some tracing paper, he could place it over the official seal or stamp on a genuine document, then trace it very accurately with the special ink. The trace could then be transferred to the roller, and bingo, 50 official stamps or seals were ready for their new home on somebody's fake identity card or other document. 'I was pretty skilful at the time,' says Rosowsky. 'I told them: leave me alone and you'll see. In half an hour I can copy even a complicated French official seal.'

Best of all, as Gaby told them, the printing kit used by the primary school teachers was in almost universal use and therefore readily available. A stationery shop in Tence stocked the necessary rollers, gels, and a range of inks in blue, red, violet and black—the colours used by the official stampers, sealers and pen pushers in the various town halls, prefectures and police stations. Previously on the Plateau, creating forged official stamps had involved painstaking work with engraving tools, cutting copies of the stamps out of copper, rubber or linoleum. But with Gaby's ink and roller, they could reproduce any official stamp they needed, all in a matter of minutes.

The other two members of the group now chimed in. Louis de Juge was a free-spirited young Protestant who was already in touch with the Resistance. He was the son of a senior French officer in Toulon, and came from a wealthy Protestant family from the Camargue. His mother had left him in Le Chambon in 1940. She wanted to rejoin her husband in Brest, with Louis's brother and sister. But Louis was in the middle of a love affair, and he wanted to stay in Le Chambon. His family left him behind but refused to support him, so he earned a living as a supervisor at the school while he worked on his baccalauréat. Roger Klimovitzky, the fourth member, was an ex-soldier; he, too, was in contact with the Resistance. Now all four could see the possibilities of setting up a full-time forgery factory. They agreed to take the idea to Léon Eyraud, the local Resistance leader.

Rosowsky made the case to Eyraud.

I explained that soon everybody was going to need false papers. The STO had just been announced. People would soon need false papers. A Resistance was now being organised, and they would need them, too. The children and the Jews who were going to head off into the mountains, they would need them. Everybody needed them.

Eyraud jumped at the idea. So did other members of the Resistance. This in itself was something of a miracle. As Rosowsky said later: 'They were all a bit paranoid, a bit mistrustful, every man for himself.' But they quickly accepted the young forgers, and this acceptance was a major step forward for the entire enterprise. The Resistance had access to a network of sympathetic officials in town halls and prefectures all over France, and it had other forgery teams who could exchange information. The Plateau's forgery bureau would not be operating alone.

The bureau began with a staff of three, all residents of Beau-Soleil: Rosowsky, de Juge and Klimovitzky. Gaby Barraud continued to support the forgers, but she ceased to be a key member of the team. They worked from the guesthouse. This meant working in the open, where everybody could see what was going on. It also meant storing their highly incriminating forgery tools in a cupboard where they were likely to be found in even the most perfunctory search. The situation couldn't continue, and in March 1943 the forgers agreed that they had to move from Beau-Soleil. Rosowsky succeeded in finding a new home at his first try.

I borrowed a bicycle and set off into the countryside. I took the road leading to Le Mazet. About four kilometres from Le Chambon, there was a girl sitting knitting in a window. I said to her: 'You wouldn't happen to know of a room to rent?' She said: 'Yes, four hundred metres up the hill, go to my father's place. He might be able to arrange something.' I told the farmer I was a student at the New Cévenole School. And that's how I moved to the Héritiers' house. They had this minuscule room that had the advantage of having their cows behind it, giving plenty of heat, and lots of straw on the floor. There was a bed, a stove, and a sink for water, but no water. No problem. There was an excellent source of water ten metres away, in the courtyard. So we rented it for a ridiculously small amount. The forgery workshop started up straight away.

Klimovitsky and de Juge stayed on at Beau-Soleil, dropping out of the day-to-day forgery business, although they remained in regular contact with the forgers and were active in the Resistance. Another young Protestant, Sammy Charles, the son of a local blacksmith and his primary-school-teacher wife, replaced them. He and Rosowsky became a team of two. They both lived with the Héritiers at La Fayolle. Says Rosowsky:

For two years we ate at their table, and Madame Héritier washed our clothes, all for a token price (when we could pay them). There were seven of them, and two of us. I was given a bicycle belonging to one of the small daughters, so I extended the saddle rod, while Monsieur Héritier registered me as his farm worker at the Bureau of Agriculture. This was one of my protections in my travels outside the department, since farmers were still exempt from the STO.

Rosowsky may have been naturally skilful, but he came to the forgery business with very little practical experience. For just two months, in Nice, in September and October 1942, he had done a little forgery work with Charles and Georgette Hanne, and a young Jew named Anatole Dauman. Then he had altered Jean-Claude Pluntz's papers on his own behalf to allow him to travel, and he had successfully forged his mother's residency permit to get her out of Rivesaltes camp. Finally, he had created a set of papers for his mother that had cleared the way for her to move from Nice to Fay-sur-Lignon. That was about it: he was not an absolute beginner, but close to. However, he was knowledgeable about the inner workings of typewriters and duplicating machines, in particular the machines used in prefectures. He also turned out to have a singular skill at what might be termed artwork: copying signatures, tracing official stamps and seals, and matching papers and materials.

Whenever we could, we filed away a sample form of genuine papers that served as models for the signatures, stamps and seals. After we made our copies, the originals were destroyed so that the beneficiaries could not possibly be tempted to have two sets of papers on them, one genuine and one false. That mistake led to more than one victim during the occupation.

Most of all, Rosowsky had a keen brain and street know-how well beyond his years. Some of his forgery techniques were almost comically simple. Men who had been prisoners of war and who were released on medical grounds naturally arrived back in France with no papers other than a single, scrappy and hastily prepared discharge document. It was usually a single sheet of paper with an indecipherable signature, which had been sealed and approved by a blurry rubber stamp. Creating a false version was all too easy. As Rosowsky explains: 'These papers gave ex-prisoners of war the right, on simple presentation at the town hall or police station, to a complete set of papers necessary for their return to civilian life: identity card, food ration coupons, clothing rations, tobacco rations, everything.' For men of military age who needed new papers, this approach was perfect; in particular, Rosowsky often used it to create new identities for Resistance fighters. Just run up a scruffy POW discharge and let the bureaucrats do the rest. Who was going to challenge a hero soldier, someone who had already suffered enough as a prisoner of war, and who was now so ill that he had to be sent home? Here are your papers, *monsieur*. And may I take this opportunity of wishing you a speedy return to health?

Some papers didn't need to be forged at all. Blank versions of the ubiquitous *carte d'identité* could be bought at any bookshop or tobacconist. The idea was that, having bought a blank card, the owner took it along to the local town hall or prefecture together with a passport photograph and supporting documents such as a birth certificate. The officials mounted the photograph, and signed and stamped the card: job done. Rosowsky simply spared the officials the trouble. All he needed was a suitable photograph, and he could do the rest. He and Charles even had that rarest of luxuries, a thoroughly convincing typewriter. 'Our typewriter came from a Protestant missionary friend of Sammy Charles' parents, who brought it back from Lambaréné in Gabon, an old German colony [in central Africa].'

Some of the forgers' work needed the cooperation of sympathetic local officialdom, and this was where the links with the Resistance came into their own.

There was the son of a town clerk who had been with us in Beau-Soleil. His father took care of public works, a man named Paya from Saint-Agrève. I went there by bicycle with the son. The guy was in the Resistance, and he said: 'No problem.' He had ration cards by the carton. He even had the necessary rubber stamp for the identity cards. We bought tax stamps at the tobacconist. We bought identity cards at the booksellers for five francs each.[32] We could make ordinary identity cards by the hundred. We could make them wholesale!

Rosowsky graded his customers by degrees of difficulty. French Jews were the simplest. In general, all they needed was a new set of papers not stamped 'Jew'. This would be enough for them to move to a new part of France. So it was important to steer well clear of Jewish-sounding names. Foreign Jews from countries allied to Germany were just as easy: Hungarian and Romanian Jews, for instance, simply needed a clean set of papers that did not brand them as Jewish.

Not all of his customers were Jews. Some were young Frenchmen anxious to avoid being packed off to Germany to work in factories under the STO. In the early days, the STO laws applied to those born in a particular year, although young men in certain professions—farming was one—were exempt. Thus avoiding the STO generally involved altering the man's date of birth or changing his profession to an exempt category. 'Some youths changed their age and profession several times in this way,' says Rosowsky. 'For myself, J.C. Plunne was born successively in 1925, then 1927, and was sometimes a farm labourer, sometimes a schoolboy, and sometimes a medical student.'

Among the non-Jewish customers, members of the Resistance needed the most attention to detail. Their false papers needed to be particularly well crafted, and their identities needed to be verifiable against official records.

It was a matter of coming up with a host of supporting papers that we thought could occasionally tip the balance our way in the event of a sudden identity check. Indeed, the opposition knew well that France was awash with false identity papers . . . Their technique consisted of closely watching the behaviour of the suspect while searching his wallet and so on. So it was a matter of looking the policeman right in the eye while remaining calm and not being aggressive, but also having in your wallet all sorts of supporting papers, the more varied the better: student cards, Boy Scout cards, social security cards, driver's licences, fines, certificates of employment, diplomas and other documents. It was sometimes these additional 'plausibility papers' that made the police let someone go.

Misfortune could even be turned to advantage. Rosowsky made delivery runs at night on his bicycle. That meant travelling without a light. One night he got caught. 'I picked up a very lucky infringement notice for not having proper lights. It was issued under my false name of J.C. Plunne, and I kept it reverently among my other "plausibility papers", which I always had with me.'

According to Rosowsky, the forgery workshop was soon producing identity and other papers at the rate of seven sets a day, 50 sets a week. Given the incredible detail involved, including the creation of library cards, trade union cards and the like, it was a remarkable achievement.

The forgers' techniques were simple. Ration cards? Get a genuine set of coupons, wipe them clean with correcting fluid, re-stamp them, then scuff them up a bit to make them look older. Military service records? Same technique: clean a genuine record, and reuse it. No genuine originals available? Go to a friendly town hall and see if they can come up with some blanks. Demobilisation papers? No problem. 'Demobilisation cards were fairly easy to forge, as many of the originals had been made on Roneotype machines at the various demobilisation centres in 1940.' The 'Roneo' machines produced papers that were blurry and messy. The problem was not so much making papers good enough to pass inspection, but rather making them look bad enough to pass for the genuine article.

Exotically, some of the material was literally parachuted in to the forgery team. Parachute drops of weapons for the Resistance are well known. What is less well known is that the boxes drifting down on parachutes from Allied aircraft occasionally included some rather less aggressive loads—fake ration cards, for instance. Explains Rosowsky:

One time . . . we had a batch of food ration cards and papers of all kinds, entirely made in free Algeria, which had been parachuted in to us. The reproduction pages copied from genuine originals didn't cover the whole surface of the parachuted pages and we had to improvise the cutting-up ourselves.

Some high-risk strategies depended heavily on sympathetic officials.

For the women, it was essential to work with a cooperative town hall or police station where it was possible to lodge a declaration of loss of papers together with a false birth certificate to obtain a complete set of regular papers. When this was possible, we would choose an unverifiable place of birth where the archives had been destroyed.

The most perilous tactic of all in this regard involved appropriating a real identity: someone made a declaration on their own behalf that they had lost their papers and needed them replaced; at the same time, somebody else used the supposedly 'lost' papers. This put two people at risk: the borrower and the lender. Both were committing a serious crime.

A final trick wasn't too different from the classic technique of appropriating an identity by searching through graveyards for people who had died young. In the case of the Plateau forgers, the resource was the *Journal officiel* of France, a unique French institution that contains a record of just about every official act that takes place in France. As well as recording new laws and the proceedings of Parliament, it records company results, wills, marriages, births, deaths and a mountain of other information, including civil events like naturalisations.

There was a final resort to the Naturalisation Decrees that appeared in old issues of the Journal officiel, *by which we 'naturalised' those*

who spoke French with a foreign accent. Thus my mother became
Madame Grabowska, born in Turkey of White Russian parents and
naturalised as a French woman on 30 December 1926 under the
Presidency of Gaston Doumergue (Journal officiel, 11 January 1927).

• • •

As always, there are no reliable numbers for the forgers' output, but
Rosowsky's figure of 50 sets of false papers a week is a good place
to start. He estimates that roughly two-thirds of the papers were for
Jews, with the rest mostly for young Frenchmen dodging the STO.
This suggests that Jews were arriving on the Plateau at the rate of
about five a day, with another two or three Frenchmen joining them.

Simone Mairesse continued to scour the countryside for spare rooms
or barns that could take in refugees. Madeleine Dreyfus, a psychologist
from Lyon who worked with the 'Circuit Garel', an organisation which
placed Jewish children in isolated farmhouses all over the Plateau,
now joined her.

There is a wonderful sequence in *Weapons of the Spirit*, Pierre
Sauvage's 1989 documentary about these events (which, of course,
takes its title from the 1940 joint declaration by Trocmé and Theis),
where Dreyfus explains how she worked. Against all security rules, she
kept a small notebook with a list of farmers' names and the number of
children they might take in. It looks for all the world like a suburban
housewife's shopping list, with names crossed off as spare rooms are
filled. She tells a particularly revealing story of the problem she had
placing two fourteen-year-old boys. Young children were easy: they
didn't eat much, and they didn't answer back. But teenage boys were
a problem—they ate like wolves, and they gave cheek. Nobody wanted
her two boys. Finally, in desperation, she blurted out to a farmer's wife:
'The truth is that these children are Jewish. They are being hunted.
Their parents were arrested.' The woman was dumbfounded. 'Why

didn't you say that in the first place?' she demanded. Straight away, she took in the two boys.

When he could spare a minute from his forgery activities, even Oscar Rosowsky did a bit of placement work.

I had the great privilege of being able to consult constantly with the baker of Fay-sur-Lignon, Monsieur Robert, whose son was a prisoner in Germany. He was vice-president of our parish council and completely in touch with everything there was to know, someone with absolute discretion (his wife knew nothing of our discussions, for instance). He knew all the parishioners and always advised me well on how to find somewhere for families to stay.

By early 1943, the forgery team had become a key element in the rescue operation. Looking back on it now, it seems incredible that this onerous and crucial burden rested on the skinny shoulders of an eighteen-year-old Latvian Jew with no experience of or contact with the dark underworld of criminal forgery, and whose frustrated ambition was to become a doctor.

9

Arrest

André Trocmé was in a meeting with youth leaders of the parish when two gendarmes knocked politely on the front door of the presbytery at around suppertime on 13 February 1943. Magda Trocmé answered the door, and the two men asked to speak to her husband. This didn't surprise her much. 'The entire world always wanted to talk to my husband,' she wrote in her memoir. 'I told them that he wasn't there, but that I was completely up to date with his work and what he was doing. If they had any questions, they could ask me.' This didn't suit the gendarmes at all. 'No,' they said, 'it's something entirely personal.' Well, he wasn't there, she told them, so they would have to wait. They could sit in André's study.

Both Trocmés had talked to numerous inmates of internment camps over the years and they knew one thing with absolute certainty: it's best to have your bags packed in advance, because if you have to leave, it will be in a hurry. So back in August 1942, after the first big raid on Le Chambon, and after the threats to André from Prefect Bach, they had packed a suitcase of clothes in case he was arrested. However, in the intervening six months the weather had grown colder and the clothes were pulled from the bag one at a time whenever they were needed. The bag was now empty. Magda continues:

My husband arrived home very late. I was in the kitchen, knitting. When he came in, he went straight to the study and found himself face to face with the two gendarmes. You won't believe me but I'd forgotten all about them! A few minutes later, he came in to me and said: 'It's happened. I've been arrested.' I said: 'Oh, no! The suitcase is empty.' One of the policemen said: 'Which suitcase?' I told him: 'You see, we've been ready for this arrest. I prepared a suitcase for my husband with everything he'll need if he's going away. But it's been so cold I've used up all the clothes in it.' The policeman said: 'We're in no hurry. You can do whatever you want.' By the time we'd repacked the suitcase, it was suppertime. That evening we were going to eat vesces.[33] I'd been cooking them myself for three hours, and they were still pretty hard. They bounced on the plate like marbles. Anyway, I said to the gendarmes: 'It's dinnertime, would you like to eat with us?' They were very surprised. As gendarmes, they weren't used to being invited to dinner when they went to arrest somebody. I didn't do this out of generosity. It was dinnertime, that's all. They were very embarrassed. One of them had tears in his eyes.[34]

Magda then asked the gendarmes if it would be all right to tell a few senior people in the parish that André had been arrested. There would be problems if he left without saying goodbye. Emphatically not, said the gendarmes. No one should know that they had arrested Monsieur Trocmé. Magda did not find out until later that there were five police cars lurking outside, and that someone had cut off the presbytery's telephone.

As it happened, that night Suzanne Gibert, André's goddaughter, had something she needed to tell the Trocmés. She arrived at the presbytery and saw the gendarmes, then ran straight into the village to alert everybody. Soon people began arriving at the presbytery with gifts for the pastor. 'It was really very moving,' Magda writes. 'At one point, someone arrived with a roll of toilet paper, which was hard to come by at the time, and very valuable. Much later, when my husband opened the package in the camp, he found on it handwritten Bible verses full of encouragement and counselling patience.'

Among the last gifts to arrive was a candle, another rare and precious item. The Trocmés didn't have any matches to light it. One of the gendarmes fished a box of matches out of his pocket and placed it on the table with the other gifts. 'That's a gift from me,' he said. 'And I will be making a report explaining how all this happened.'

By this time, villagers and students from the New Cévenole School had arrived and were standing in two lines outside the presbytery, forming a guard of honour. André Trocmé marched out of the presbytery between the two lines, while the students sang Martin Luther's towering sixteenth-century hymn 'A Mighty Fortress is Our God'. The pastor climbed into the waiting police car.

The gendarmes hadn't finished with Le Chambon. They now proceeded to arrest Édouard Theis and Roger Darcissac. All three men spent their first night in captivity in the gendarmerie in Tence, only a short distance away. They had been arrested on a Saturday night, and they were moved on Sunday to the regular prison in Le Puy. There they slept on beds without sheets, and had to endure the demoralising sound of a heavy key turning the heavy lock of their cell doors. On Monday they were moved to the Camp de Saint-Paul d'Eyjeaux near Limoges. This involved a lengthy train journey, with a change of trains at Lyon. They were spared the indignity of handcuffs, but the three men walked between two guards; passers-by could only take them for common criminals, a strange experience for two pastors and a headmaster, and one that left them feeling humiliated.

They were not charged with any offence. Neither André nor Magda Trocmé makes any reference in their respective memoirs to an interrogation, and I have not been able to find any record of the questioning of the three men. This in itself is pretty odd. It is hard to see why the authorities would pass up this golden opportunity to put a few pertinent questions to all three of them, but they seem to have decided that locking them up was enough. Without charges and without a line of questions, it is impossible to know just what lay behind the timing of the arrest, or what triggered the arrest itself. However, the intention was very likely to get them locked away where they could do no more damage, and to intimidate them. If that was the plan, it didn't work.

• • •

The Camp de Saint-Paul d'Eyjeaux was a strange place. It was comparatively small, usually holding about 600 people. Some accounts describe it as a 'concentration camp', but that goes too far. Its official title was a Centre de Séjour Surveillé (Supervised Accommodation Centre), and it was really an internment camp, rather like Gurs, Rivesaltes and the rest, but with far better conditions. It was not designed principally to hold Jews; instead it was filled with 'undesirables', a handy euphemism for political prisoners. About 75 per cent of them were communists. The rest were made up of a mixture of Jews, Freemasons and anarchists. There were inmates of all ages and from all walks of life: factory workers, farmers, public servants, tradesmen, shopkeepers, even mayors and other elected officials.

The arrival in this company of two Protestant pastors and a primary school headmaster might have been expected to create a bit of a stir, but it made next to no impression. A good number of the communists could quote Karl Marx verbatim, particularly his oft-repeated maxim 'Religion . . . is the opium of the people', and they weren't about to raise their non-existent hats to a trio of pacifist God-botherers. Anyway, if they had any religion at all they were Catholics, and there were already several Catholic priests on hand. Furthermore, non-violence was not part of their agenda: as far as the communists and anarchists were concerned, nothing important could happen without a violent revolution. After that . . . well, after the revolution there might be time for peace and brotherhood. But until the streets ran red with blood, things would never get better.

From Trocmé and Theis's point of view, this was rather like an old-fashioned Christian missionary suddenly coming upon a whole fresh tribe of heathens ripe for conversion. There was work to be done. The two pastors asked the camp superintendent if they could conduct Protestant church services in the camp. The superintendent agreed. After all, he had said yes to the same question from the Catholics, and he was a fair-minded man.

The first service attracted only three people, but the numbers gradually swelled to twenty and then to 40. Trocmé preached peace, non-violence, equality and brotherly love. The listening communists might have had a problem with the non-violence, but the rest sounded fine. They formed discussion groups, and even found coded ways to discuss touchy subjects. There were teaching classes. Roger Darcissac organised a singing group. If the idea of internment had been to silence the two pastors and the schoolteacher, so far so very ineffectual.

And if the idea had been to give the authorities a quieter life, that didn't work either. The arrest of the three men was followed by something akin to uproar. One of the most significant protests came from Marc Boegner. As we have seen, the head of the Reformed Church in France had not exactly rushed to Trocmé's support in the past. Indeed, in the early months of the Vichy government, he was inclined to give Marshal Pétain the benefit of the doubt. Boegner served on the National Council of Vichy, a strange, unelected body of 300 representatives appointed to advise the government. But after the round-ups of Jews in 1942, he had seen the light. He wrote repeatedly to Pétain protesting strongly over the Vichy regime's treatment of Jews.

On 22 September 1942 he had issued a statement read in almost every Protestant church in France. It said:

The Reformed Church of France cannot remain silent in the face of the suffering of thousands of human beings who have found asylum on our soil. Divine law cannot accept that families willed by God can be broken, children be separated from their mothers, the right of exile and compassion be unrecognised, respect for the human person be violated, and helpless individuals be surrendered to a tragic fate.

Boegner kept a logbook of his daily activities. On 14 February 1943, the day after Trocmé's arrest, he wrote: 'Received two telegrams last night from Le Chambon telling me of the arrest of Trocmé and Theis. By which police? Where are they? I still don't know anything, and what can I do? I'm ashamed.' On 19 February: 'Went to see Bousquet this morning [René Bousquet, secretary general of the French Police]. He knew nothing about any of this. He promised he would write to me this evening, responding to my questions.' So we can be fairly sure that Boegner used his contacts within the Vichy regime to demand that Trocmé and Theis either be charged with a crime and tried, or released.

Most histories credit Robert Bach, the prefect of the Haute-Loire, with high-level intervention on behalf of the three men. Some go so far as to say that he too approached Bousquet. But none of the histories quotes from a specific document, and my extensive trawls through the departmental archives in Le Puy produced nothing, so these stories may be apocryphal. What we do know is that on 4 March 1943, Bach sent a report to the central government that included a section headed 'Public reaction to the internal policies of the government'. After dealing with the STO—which, Bach said, was causing 'deep emotion'—he concluded his report by dealing with the arrest and internment of Trocmé, Theis and Darcissac. This had been 'very unpopular', he wrote. It was particularly unfortunate because things had been going swimmingly on the Plateau after the visit of Lamirand in August 1942. 'Since [the visit], the population has been won over to the policies of the government,' Bach wrote. This was complete hogwash, and well Bach knew it. So at least it can be said that he was prepared to lie to his masters to assist the release of the three men. He concluded his report with the words: 'I am afraid these measures will send this improvement in public opinion into reverse if they carry on too long.'

At the local level, the uproar was even noisier. One of the more popular figures in Le Chambon was the doctor, Roger Le Forestier. He was a remarkable man. Having worked with Albert Schweitzer in Africa, he had arrived in Le Chambon in 1936 and become a key member of the community. Now he was up in arms. He related his actions with characteristic glee and self-mockery in a letter to André Trocmé dated 21 February 1943, and received by Trocmé at Camp de Saint-Paul d'Eyjeaux.

We are thinking of you.

The church in Le Chambon is not really like the dove of the Holy Spirit, it's more like a duck . . . after its head has been cut off, it still runs about automatically. I found out from elsewhere that the whole of Protestant France knows your story. Some are furious that the Church and Christians are being persecuted anew, others pin their hopes on God. Stay courageous and strong, God is at work.

When I left you, I went with Daniel Trocmé to Vichy. The following Tuesday I was received by the chief of staff of Monsieur Cadot, who is from the general secretariat of the police and Minister of the Interior. I handed over the letter of introduction right at the beginning, which went something like this: 'I request an audience on the subject of the internment of three friends. They are respectively the pastor of a parish with 1200 members, the headmaster of a school with 400 students, and the father of 8, 4 and 3 children.[35]

I had some beautiful phrases at the ready: 'You have struck at the heart of French Protestantism,' or 'You will be handing the martyr's palm to my friends, and they don't want it,' or 'Their freedom cannot be subject to conditions, because these men of God are all from a single block, they preach the Gospel and Divine law overrules human law,' etc . . ., and this one: 'You have been misinformed by agents who are strangers to Protestantism and the Chambon community.' Finally I demanded 'that a serious inquiry be set up, not using sneaky informers' but involving prominent citizens.

I have learned that the Prefect Bach asked for a similar inquiry, and that it was set up in the last few days.

Finally, I advise you to stay in the camp where you are. There you have men who are sturdy and of mature age to bring to Faith and Salvation. Here there is nothing but a few women who have already been saved. The friends from Le Chambon, whose names are too many to list here, join with me in telling you of their faith and total affectionate friendship.

R. LE FORESTIER

So the outcry functioned at three levels. On the ground, if Le Forestier is to be believed, the whole of Protestant France was up in arms. It all smacked of a return to the bad old days, when Protestants were hunted down and relentlessly persecuted. The authorities had to be stopped before the new persecution got out of hand. At the departmental level, the prefect Robert Bach was unhappy with the spreading row on his patch, and no doubt dreading the thought of receiving endless delegations from Protestants from all over his department demanding the release of the men. And at the highest level, Marc Boegner and others were tugging at any string they could find.

It is impossible to know exactly what triggered off the next step, but it is a fair guess that high-level string-pulling did the job. Boegner's protests in particular may even have travelled as far as the desk of Pierre Laval, the Vichy prime minister, perhaps passed on to Laval by Bousquet. Boegner had had repeated meetings with Laval over the years, so the two men knew each other. There is no record of a direct approach by Boegner to Laval on this occasion, but Laval was nevertheless implicated on 15 March, when the camp commandant summoned the three prisoners and told them they were to be released that morning and put on the train home at 10 am. The release order had come from the office of the prime minister himself, the commandant said. The three men should gather up their belongings then come back to sign a few papers and they would be on their way.

This proved to be easier said than done. When the three men read the paper to be signed, they found it contained a clause requiring them to swear allegiance to the government of Marshal Pétain and to undertake to obey its orders. As school headmaster, Roger Darcissac had no choice. He was a public servant paid by the government; if he didn't sign, he would lose his job and be unable to support his family. So he signed, and left on the five o'clock train.

However, the two pastors refused. It would be a breach of the Ninth Commandment, they explained, which forbade bearing false witness. The camp commandant urged a bit of cynicism on them. Just sign, he said, nobody will pay any attention afterwards, it's just a formality. The two pastors stuck to their position. To the commandant's astonishment, they returned to their prison hut, where their fellow inmates couldn't believe what they were hearing. You'd let a worthless promise on a piece of paper stop you from getting out of here? You must be mad.

Given the power politics now apparently involved, we can only assume that the camp commandant went back to whoever had issued

142

the original release order—Laval's office, perhaps—for further advice. The next morning, he summoned the two men again. He had new orders. They could leave without signing the paper. They were free.

We can only guess at whether the following fact was known to the camp commandant at the time of the men's departure, but it was almost certainly known to whoever ordered their release. A few days later, all the prisoners in the camp—about five hundred men—were packed onto trains and deported to Poland and Silesia. There is no record of any of them being heard from again.

• • •

On 18 March 1943, two days after the release of the two pastors, Boegner wrote to Trocmé: 'I have heard this instant that you and Édouard Theis are to be released. I want you to know straight away how glad I am. Your parish, the school, and the Church all need you.'

Boegner may have been delighted, but the release of the three men sowed a seed of doubt elsewhere. Until November 1942, it is fair to say that Trocmé's views, shared by Theis and other pacifist pastors, dominated the thinking on the Plateau. Resist, yes, but without violence and hatred. In fact, love your enemies. So how could evil be overcome? Answer: with the power of reason. Talk to your enemies, make them see sense, that was the way forward. The fact that the pastors had been released peacefully by this very process meant that it had been given fresh credibility. But that, in the eyes of some, presented a problem.

The change that was about to take place in the dynamics of the Plateau is brilliantly echoed in a classic film. All Westerns are morality plays, and *High Noon* has a pretty good claim to being the greatest Western of all time. Grace Kelly plays the brand-new Quaker bride of the former town marshal, played by Gary Cooper. The newly married couple leave town at a brisk trot in a splendid horse-drawn carriage.

But Cooper knows that a man he sent to prison is returning to town that day with a couple of henchmen, sworn to kill him. He decides he can't run away and, over Grace Kelly's protests and threats, turns the carriage around and goes back to town to face the killers, alone.

Grace Kelly watches the ensuing gunfight fearfully through a window. She is a Quaker and abhors all violence. She naturally fears for her new husband's life, and she looks on powerlessly. Now two of the killers have Gary Cooper trapped inside a saddlery shop. Cooper is outnumbered and caught in their crossfire. He's never going to make it. Then, to our shock, an unseen gun fires and one of the killers falls, shot in the back from close range. Gary Cooper has a chance. We switch to Grace Kelly, holding a smoking Colt .45 behind the window. It is one of the bleakest moments in all film history because it seems to say, eloquently and powerfully, that fine principles are one thing, but in the end violence is the only answer.

At first there had been something approaching a deal between André Trocmé and the Resistance that violence was to be avoided, particularly any violence aimed at the unarmed and convalescing German soldiers in the village. In his book *Le Chambon-sur-Lignon sous l'occupation* (*Le Chambon-sur-Lignon under the Occupation*), Pierre Fayol writes: 'Pastor Trocmé, Léon Eyraud and myself were all agreed that not only should no action be taken against the unarmed men but also that the young people should not do anything reckless that would have grave consequences for the village.' Oscar Rosowsky gives a slightly different slant to this in a contribution he made in 1990 to a symposium, *Le Plateau Vivarais-Lignon: Accueil et Résistance 1939–1944* (The Plateau Vivarais-Lignon: Welcome and Resistance 1939–1944). He told his audience:

> *There was agreement at the beginning between the Resistance and*
> *André Trocmé that it was acceptable to give the impression that*

this region was peaceful, one where the opposition remained strictly
spiritual. This view of Le Chambon was also the one adopted by
the national leadership of the Reformed Church and, we now know,
by Mark Boegner.

In other words, it suited the newly forming Resistance to lull the
Vichy and the Germans into believing that the Plateau was a peaceful
haven of high-principled pacifism and not a bubbling source of violent
trouble. That cover story would give the Resistance time to recruit,
arm, organise and train. It would also mean that the rescue operation
could continue. In Rosowsky's view, Trocmé's arrest, and the probability
that he would be arrested again, threatened that timing:

If the pastor had been deported, there was a risk that reprisal
actions against the convalescing German soldiers stationed in Le
Chambon would get out of control, because the general tactic at
the time consisted of hitting back every time someone was hit. The
whole action strategy up until then of clandestine refuge and silent
preparation for the battles to come, which was the policy of the
Secret Army, was placed in danger.

Presumably, though, this is far from the whole story. Surely
André Trocmé presented a bigger problem than that for the
Resistance? All guerrilla armies depend on the support of the
local population, particularly the rural population: the Viet Cong
needed the peasants, the IRA needed the Catholics, the jihadists
today need the villagers. The Secret Army would need the support
of the local rural population. Yet André Trocmé opposed all
violence. His often-stated fear was that the civil disobedience he
preached would transform itself into armed insurrection. If that
happened, there was a chance he might feel obliged to denounce the

violence of the Resistance from the pulpit. He had a long history of consistency, after all. And if he denounced the Resistance, then his unique authority might threaten the absolutely vital support of the local population for the maquis.

Fayol was clearly aware of this. He wrote: 'The pastor Trocmé was a conscientious objector, not just in matters military but in the true sense of the word, objecting to anything which offended his conscience. He knew that his words would be listened to.' Rosowsky also hinted at this same problem:

> *Trocmé clung to the idea of a liberation that could be achieved without any military participation. From this point of view, there was a conflict not only with the tradition of military resistance by French-speaking Huguenots but also with all those who were rejoining the various sections of the Resistance.*

Trocmé's arrest and release in early 1943 planted the first tiny seed of a previously unthinkable thought. After his return, Trocmé continued to preach anti-government resistance and civil disobedience. In the past, his tactics with the authorities had included marching into the lion's den and demanding to be heard. There was a genuine risk that he would do this once too often, and that the authorities would simply arrest him, intern him, then deport him, as they did to so many others. That would unleash forces that the Secret Army would rather have kept in their box. Timing was everything, and Trocmé's activities put that timing at risk.

It is important to make clear that throughout the conflict the Resistance wished Trocmé and his family no harm; indeed, quite the opposite. His arrest, deportation and subsequent death would be a disaster for them all. For that reason alone, members of the Resistance were anxious that he should remain safe. But always in the background was the thought that his arrest might wreck the timing of Resistance plans. So, with Trocmé's arrest, began the first tiny glimmer of the unthinkable thought: for his own sake, for his family's sake, and for the sake of the Resistance, Trocmé must go.

10

Switzerland

Praly, the policeman, struck for the first time on 25 February 1943. The villagers of Le Chambon had noted with something approaching amusement that Praly regularly walked from the Hôtel des Acacias to the post office and sent off large envelopes, presumably containing reports on their activities. Something had to come of all this, and on 25 February (while Trocmé, Theis and Darcissac were still in Camp de Saint-Paul d'Eyjeaux) trouble finally arrived. It was a repeat of August 1942. The usual collection of buses and gendarmes assembled in the middle of the village. All school classes stopped, and the children and teachers were ordered to assemble at the town hall.

Jacob ('Jack') Lewin had been transferred from Gurs internment camp to Le Chambon in September 1941. He had moved around the various houses, including The Wasps' Nest and The Shelter, but after the August 1942 raid he had been moved to a farmhouse. He was apprenticed to a master carpenter, a Monsieur Astier, and had been working there four weeks when the knock came on the door.

On 25 February Monsieur Praly of the National Police arrived at the workshop with some other policemen to arrest my brother and me. 'At last,' Praly said to us, 'I've got you.' We were taken to the

148

town hall and guarded there by the police. We had to wait there for a long time. I don't know how many people were arrested. Eventually they put us all on a bus and we set off in the direction of Le Puy. Dr Le Forestier followed us in his car. However, they let us go because we were too young. Dr Le Forestier drove us back to Le Chambon.[36]

In fact, eight people were arrested in the raid, including the unfortunate Monsieur Steckler, who had already been arrested and released in August 1942. As with the earlier occasion, he turned out to be only one quarter Jewish and that was enough for him to be released. Jack Lewin's older brother Martin remained in custody and was sent back to Gurs to await deportation. However, he managed to keep himself well hidden inside the camp from 28 February to 4 August. Then he was sent back to Le Chambon.

The raid was not exactly a triumph for Inspector Praly, but in combination with the arrest of the pastors and Roger Darcissac, it produced two results. In the growing mood of disillusionment with the Vichy government, sympathisers began to appear in unexpected places, not least among the gendarmes themselves. Madeleine Barot, one of the founders of the Cimade, tells the following story:

When the gendarmes from Tence received an order to arrest somebody, they were in the habit of dawdling along the road and making themselves highly visible. Then they would stop at a café just before they reached the steep path up to The Flowery Hill and say loudly to each other that they were going to 'arrest a few of these dirty Jews'. A lookout post set up inside a woodheap in front of the house would give the alarm. When the gendarmes arrived, the people they were looking for would have disappeared. Often the runaways hid in an underground passage in the forest nearby, after we showed them where it was. It was the sort of hiding place that had been used by persecuted Huguenots.[37]

Other warning systems sprang up. Magda Trocmé recalls in her memoirs that the phone would ring at the presbytery and an anonymous female voice would say: *'Attention! Demain!'* ('Watch out! Tomorrow!') Then the phone would click, and the line would go dead. Magda never knew who made these calls. It was probably some comparatively junior official in a town hall somewhere, or in the prefecture in Le Puy. In any case, Magda knew what it meant. There would be a raid tomorrow, so she was to get the children out into the woods first thing in the morning and wait for the buses to go away empty.

The second effect was more far-reaching, and it was reinforced by subsequent events. In the August 1942 raid, the gendarmes had searched the children's homes as well as private houses. After raiding the Flowery Hill home, for instance, they produced a list of 26 names of foreign Jewish children who were alleged to have left the area illegally. At least, the two searching gendarmes said, they had looked in every room and couldn't find them, although all their belongings were still there. Now, in the February 1943 raid, the schools had been emptied and the children had been told to assemble at the town hall. If schools were no longer a sanctuary, clearly there was nowhere safe on the Plateau.

Ironically the various children's homes were easier to target than the schools. The prefecture knew the names of the children transferred to homes from the camps; indeed, they were there with the prefecture's permission. Once a month the various homes were required to submit a list of their residents' names to the authorities. In return, they received a token sum from the prefecture. So while they might have had more children in residence than they were admitting—and this they almost certainly did—they nevertheless had to come up with a credible list of residents' names every month. So the authorities had a pretty good idea of the identities of those staying in the homes, including who was staying where.

The schools represented quite a different problem. While almost all the children sheltering on the Plateau went to school, somehow the two headmasters, Roger Darcissac and Édouard Theis, never managed to get their school registers up to date. No doubt it was a combination of pressure of work plus the sheer difficulty of keeping up with the many comings and goings among the children. That must surely have been the reason why so many children who attended the primary school or the New Cévenole School never found their way onto the register. Nobody would be so untrusting as to suggest that the two headmasters deliberately left names off to keep them away from the prying eyes of the authorities, now would they?

Sometimes their forgetfulness went beyond the register. For example, on one occasion, schoolchildren all over France were required to write a letter of appreciation to Marshal Pétain, praising the wonders and benevolence of the Vichy regime. The pupils in Le Chambon did as they were told. But—and this is surely one of those lapses that happens in even the best-run institutions—the refugee children's letters were never sent with the others. Inadvertently, I'm sure, Darcissac and Theis spared the authorities all the trouble of collecting refugee children's names from the signatures on the bottom of the letters.

• • •

Of course, all these children's homes, guesthouses and hostels constantly needed money. Food was not free, nor was rent, bedding, furniture, electricity, heating, clothing or schoolbooks, while adult staff were needed to cook, clean and manage. Add to this the fact that nowhere was safe anymore, and two questions demanded an answer. Where would the money come from, and where could the refugees go that was safe? Both questions turned out to have the same answer: Switzerland.

Officially, Switzerland didn't want the refugees. On 13 August 1942, at about the time that raids and round-ups started in earnest all over occupied Europe, the Swiss closed their borders. The arguments sound familiar: Sorry, we're full. The refugees are bogus—they're all spies. Or communists. Or (whisper it) they're Jews and we're a bit anti-Semitic here. In particular, the Swiss government would not accept that Jews were political refugees entitled to political asylum. So the refugees were unwelcome and would not be allowed in if the Swiss could help it. That was the official policy.

However, under pressure of international public opinion, the Swiss softened their stance. In August and September 1942, thousands of refugees, mostly Jews, crossed from what was then the Unoccupied Zone into Switzerland. Then, on 26 September, the Swiss announced that they were again tightening the rules, restricting entry to the elderly, unaccompanied children, pregnant women, the ill, and families with children younger than sixteen years. They tightened this further in December, saying they would accept families only if they had children under six years.

Then a convention sprang up. The Swiss police, customs officers and military at the regular border crossing points could be tough, applying the rules and turning people back when they could, even handing them over to the Vichy police for internment in Rivesaltes, followed by deportation. But the Swiss authorities away from the border were much less zealous. If you could make it across the border and into Switzerland, most of the time things would be fine.

Geneva became the key. The geography all pointed that way. The city of Geneva is at the far southwestern tip of the huge Lake Léman (also known as Lake Geneva), which drains into France and becomes the River Rhône. The border between France and Switzerland runs down the middle of the lake, which jabs its way deep into territory that might otherwise be French. The result is a long neck of Swiss land poking into France, with Geneva at the extreme tip. The French city of Annecy is a mere 40 kilometres from Geneva, and the major French city of Lyon is only 110 kilometres away. The two sides of the long neck of land form a very long border around a very small patch of ground. Best of all, the Geneva 'neck' was at the far northern end of the part of France occupied by the Italians, not the Germans. The Italians were a great deal less zealous than the Germans both in policing the borders and rounding up Jews, which made life simpler for smugglers.

As is true to this day, in 1942 Geneva played host to a huge number of international organisations. The city was particularly important to the Protestant churches. The various ecumenical movements that eventually became the World Council of Churches were based there. Charles Guillon, now secretary of the World Federation of the YMCA, lived and worked there. Numerous other organisations, including the FESE, the European Fund for Student Support (which funded the House of Rocks in Le Chambon, for example), and the International Red Cross, were based in Geneva. As we've seen, the Quakers could send money from America to Switzerland without too much difficulty, and in general it went to Geneva. From there, men like Guillon—'Uncle Charles' in all correspondence—arranged to get the money to its proper destination, usually in occupied countries. So Geneva was a hub.

The first party of Jews left the Plateau for Switzerland sometime in early September 1942, just after the first big raid in August but before the German occupation of the Southern Zone. We have no reliable record of who led it, but it was probably Pierre Galland, one of the first regular guides. The group probably left on 2 September, and there were probably six Jews in the group. A second and similar group left a week later, on 9 September. They all appear to have made it safely into Switzerland. So the 'pipeline' got off to a good start.

In 1943 the operation settled into a pattern. There were two established *filières* or paths: the western route, through Saint-Étienne and

Lyon, and the eastern route, through Valence and Grenoble. Who guided the escaping Jews? Be ready for yet another revelation from the Plateau . . . they were mostly led by volunteers from no less a group than those pointy-hatted, clean-living, well-prepared, knot-tying devotees of the healthy outdoors, the Boy Scouts. Pierre Galland was a Boy Scout, for instance.[38]

• • •

Pierre Piton was seventeen years old in September 1942 when he came clandestinely to the Plateau. He had been working as an apprentice boilermaker in a factory in the Occupied Zone, but had decided he wanted to go back to school. He was French and Protestant, and he had an introduction to Édouard Theis. So he crossed over to the Unoccupied Zone and headed for Le Chambon. Theis organised some accommodation for him, and then introduced Piton to Mireille Philip. As mentioned, André Philip's wife had turned out to be a dab hand as a forger, and had become one of the key figures in the Resistance on the Plateau. When she met Pierre Piton, she liked what she saw.

Mireille Philip clearly knew real talent when she came across it. From her point of view, Piton had a perfect CV. He had resumed his studies at New Cévenole School, with the intention of becoming a missionary, so nothing to excite the authorities there. He was clearly a self-starter, with plenty of initiative. He had a job as a school supervisor, and that would be a good cover story. His tender years meant he could move about without attracting too much attention. Best of all, he had been a Boy Scout leader, so he had all the necessary Boy Scout skills.

Pierrot Galland, who had run numerous missions from Le Chambon to Switzerland, had recently come to the end of the road. He was *grillé* (a French expression that translates as 'grilled', and means that his cover was blown), so the chain was currently broken and no parties of Jews were being taken to Switzerland. Would Pierre Piton care to take his place, and get things moving again?

Mireille started him off with a simple task: find places to hide Jews in the surrounding villages. Once he'd proven himself, he moved on to escorting the Jews to their new homes. Every third night he would wait until everybody in the Golden Broom home fell asleep, then he would creep out. The winter of 1942–43 was particularly severe, and the Plateau was deep in snow. Pierre would grab his sled and drag it behind him while he set off to an established rendezvous point in someone's house to meet that night's party of Jews, usually a small group of two or three people. First he would make a careful check to be sure they weren't spies sent by the Gestapo, or by Inspector Praly. Having satisfied himself and swallowed a hot cup of what passed, during the war, for coffee, he would pile the group's belongings on a sled and lead them off on foot through the snow to their new home.

Pierre describes his role:

I hid Jews in a lot of villages around Tence, Fay-sur-Lignon, Le Volamont, Le Mazet-Saint-Voy, Villelonge and so on . . . I will give you an example from this last village, where I succeeded in hiding one or two Jews in every farm without a single one of the farmers knowing what their neighbours were doing. I would usually arrive around one in the morning with my two or three Jews and my sled. I had personally warned the farmer in advance and I would wait for him to light a kerosene lamp in his living room . . . that was the signal. I would open and close the door as fast as I could so that the neighbours wouldn't notice. Around three in the morning I would head back to Le Chambon at high speed, this time on my sled. When I got close to Le Chambon I needed to keep my eyes open for Gestapo from Saint-Étienne or

Lyon. Then I would park my sled and, making as little noise as I could, go back to bed for about two hours, as though nothing had happened.

I want to single out the village of Villelonge. Everyone in the village hid at least one Jew and one maquisard, *all for free, all at risk of their lives or of reprisals. The road sign at the edge of the village should read: 'Here every farmer hid at least one Jew, one STO dodger or one Resistance fighter.'*

• • •

Catherine Cambessédès is hugely likeable. She is clever, funny and modest. When I interviewed her, she was inclined to wonder why I was talking to *her*. She was just one of many, she told me, and others had done much more dangerous jobs.

In this narrative, we first met Catherine in September 1939, when her parents had rented a large house just outside the village of Le Chambon (and, by coincidence, just across the road from the Héritier farmhouse and what would become the Rosowsky forgery bureau). When war broke out, she and three siblings stayed on with their mother in Le Chambon rather than return to Paris. They would be safer there. Or so they thought. Catherine explains:

Le Chambon was a hot, hot centre for the underground. There was a little group that was organised by the International YMCA in Geneva. There were four members. We would do errands for the maquis, bringing them clothes (always khaki), bringing them bandages, whatever they needed. And money. They would send me to get money—a suitcase full of money. If [anyone had] opened my suitcase, [they would have known] it was for the maquis. I was asked to join because I was a girl. It was a big advantage. The other three were men. I wasn't too good because I was scared. The people who did this kind of thing could not afford to be scared. When you're scared, you don't react very well.

Catherine's first mission took a week.

The first trip was to deliver a message to another maquis. It was written on a tiny piece of tissue paper. I was told that if soldiers made a check on the train, I was to swallow the message.

On the way to Nîmes there was an alert, so the train stopped. Everyone got off and hid in the bushes. In the distance we could see the plane dipping to bomb the area. When the bombing was finished we all got back on the train and continued down the valley.

Eventually I did get to Nîmes and stayed with my uncle, who lived there. He kept pumping me with questions. 'Does your mother know about this? Who are you going to see? Where exactly are you going?' I couldn't tell him anything. For a while I thought he wouldn't let me go.

From Nîmes I took a train to Ganges, on the other side of the Cévennes, and there I contacted a Monsieur Monnier and told him I had to go to the maquis of so-and-so. He wasn't exactly eager to take me there as it was 40 kilometres away and he had gone there two days earlier. The only means of transport was his tandem bicycle. But okay, he would take me there at night. 'Come to my house at 11 pm.'

It turned out to be an incredible, magical ride. When on earth would anybody ever expect to spend a night cycling through the mountains? The air was balmy and there was a strong scent— lavender, thyme—of flowers as we pedalled until about 3 am. There was a bit of moonlight, fortunately, as we didn't dare to use a bike light. But Monsieur Monnier knew the way and he was in front, doing the hardest pedalling!

All of a sudden, we heard: 'Halt!' Monsieur Monnier stopped right away and gave a password to the sentry in the shadows. They knew him and let us pass. We were now in the 'other' maquis.

I was told to go to sleep in a barn with the soldiers. I wasn't much to look at[39] but I was a girl and they hadn't seen one in a long time. They took care of me like you would a doll, bringing me blanket after blanket, two mattresses, and a pillow, and I spent what was left of the night with 40 soldiers!

At about 6 am the head of the camp came and I gave him the message that told him, in code, that there would be a parachute drop. I can still remember the message: Jean sera à la fête de Pierrou et il apportera trois cadeaux *('Jean will be at the Pierrou party and he will bring three gifts'). It meant: There will be a parachute drop at Pierrou and it will bring armaments, food and sundries.*

What was interesting was that Trocmé, on the basis of being a Christian, was a pacifist. Olivier, the head of this maquis, was also a minister but felt that the Christian thing to do was to get rid of evil—in this case the Nazis—by any means necessary, including force.

Olivier's maquisards filled my suitcase with items they had received by parachute: bandages, soap, khaki shirts, medicine and cigarettes.

Then I did the same trip the other way round, back to Le Chambon. But I did a very foolish thing. I was too young and too scared. At one point I needed to tie up my shoelace, so I laid my suitcase on one of those flat railway cars. As I was tying my shoe I saw the train start to leave. My God! So I ran after it with one shoe off. Miraculously it stopped and I was able to recover my suitcase. Phew!

Catherine inevitably carried a lot of information in her head—names and addresses, for instance. If she had been caught by the Gestapo and forced to talk, the damage could have been substantial. However, the Resistance was crafty enough to keep the problem to a minimum.

> *You never knew very much, only the next step. That way you didn't know any of the other people involved . . . I was never stopped and searched on the train. I got away with it. They didn't stop everybody. But that's what I was scared about. What the hell would I say? How could I explain this?*

Catherine's first trip may have brought back to the Plateau nothing more dangerous than soap dropped in by parachute. But soon she became the last leg in a relay team bringing in something far more incriminating. Money. From Switzerland.

11

Smugglers

The money that was smuggled to the Plateau from Switzerland appears to have been delivered by a relay team rather than a single courier. As already mentioned, one of the most important rules in any clandestine operation is to keep all the parts separate and make sure each member of the team knows as little as possible about the rest. So Catherine Cambessédès has no idea to this day how money travelled between Geneva and Lyon. She would simply receive a message consisting of not much more than an address to go to, and a password. That was all she needed. The people at the first address would brief her on the next step, and so on. That kept to a minimum the amount of information that could be dragged out of her by the Gestapo if she was caught.

This trip was less dangerous than the trip to the maquis, because there were no guns involved. I was given an address in Lyon and I went there. You got to wherever you were sent and said a password so they would know you were genuine . . . They gave me a suitcase that had money in it. I have no idea how much. It could have been ten francs or a million. I sat on it all the way home. The train was full so there were no seats. I saw a friend of mine on the train, and he sat on the other end of the suitcase. I'm pretty sure the money came from Charles Guillon in Geneva. I delivered it to Camp de Joubert in Le Chambon, and Joubert was Charles Guillon's baby. I handed the money over to somebody there, probably Charly Durand. He belonged to one of the families living at Joubert. Getting back to Le Chambon always meant safety. In Lyon, or Saint-Étienne, I didn't know anybody. But in Le Chambon, if anything happened, I knew plenty of places to hide. I was always anxious to get back there. I remember being scared. If a German walked by I'd think: Oh, dear!

Catherine never kept a record of any of these missions, so it is impossible to know how many courier trips she made, but she thinks it was as many as ten, a hefty burden for a schoolgirl—to Lyon, to Valence, to Nîmes, wherever the Resistance asked her to go. Everything she brought back was incriminating, and could be easily linked to the Resistance. If she had been caught she would certainly have been arrested, and the penalties for aiding the Resistance were dire, including death or deportation.

Things didn't always go smoothly.

I was in the Lyon train station one night and it was hot as hell. Fresh from Le Chambon where there was no hanky-panky, I said: 'I'm going outside to get some fresh air.' A man followed me out, not a lot of people as I expected. I got into a train because I thought I could sleep on a seat. He followed me in there. It was obvious what he was going to do. I was so stunned, because . . . well, you never thought that way in Le Chambon. And I said: 'No! No!' as he made a move. Just then, the [Allies] started bombing the station. Believe me, at that point you don't think of anything but to save your life. I got off that train. He did too. And everybody from the station started to run, trying to get to the tunnel close to the station. It was very awkward and slow, running over the rails, but we all scrambled

madly in the dark. As we were running, one woman dropped a
suitcase and I . . . said: 'Madame, you dropped your suitcase.' She
didn't even turn around to look. She just kept running. Then, from
the sky, came parachutes with lights attached so the pilots could tell
what they were going to bomb. Suddenly we were in broad daylight.
That made running a little easier. We all made it into the tunnel,
and soon it started to shake and tremble: the Allies were bombing the
other end of the tunnel. That was my scariest experience, for sure.

• • •

The other side of the smuggling operation—getting the refugees across
the border into Switzerland—was no walk in the park either. For a
start, the refugees themselves presented all sorts of problems. They
were mostly foreign Jews, many of whom spoke no French. They would
give themselves away if they so much as opened their mouths. Also,
they had to be briefed beforehand in their own language. German was
most frequently needed, and that presented few problems, but Polish
was more difficult.

They travelled in small groups, perhaps two or three people at
a time, plus their *passeur*. They would spend the night before the
journey in a safe house in Le Chambon where, Pierre Piton recalls,
a briefing similar to the following would take place on the evening
before departure, usually in German or Polish:

A man ([i.e. Piton, or another passeur*] will come looking for you at*
this house. Follow him at a distance. Just before you depart he will
give you your train tickets. If someone asks for your ticket or your
proof of identity, act as though nothing important has happened and
you aren't bothered. Don't speak. For as long as you can, pretend to
be asleep during the whole day and night of the train journey. In the
railway station waiting rooms, you should doze off. Don't let anybody

start a conversation with you. If you lose sight of your guide, don't worry; he'll be back as soon as he can. If you are arrested but your guide isn't, you must leave without giving any sign that you know him. Don't chat with your two or three companions in your own language. Try to relax, and avoid eye contact. If somebody seems to keep staring at you, pretend to fall asleep. You will have a chance to relax and talk among yourselves during the various stops you will make at the homes of friends of your guide.

Leave behind your little suitcase and your bundle of belongings; your guide can't take you and your bags. It will be necessary for you to go under the barbed wire one at a time, and you mustn't worry about your companions, not even your wife or husband. Once you are in Switzerland, don't talk about your guide. You are hereby warned that the trip involves risks and that there is no guarantee for everybody. If you agree, good luck!

They tended to agree. As Pierre Piton points out, they already trusted him; after all, he was often the one who had earlier led them to their original farmhouse shelter.

In general, the people being smuggled out under the protection of Mireille Philip used the western 'pipeline', through Saint-Étienne and Lyon. It was quite a journey. Before they set off, the party of refugees and their guide would all be equipped with false papers, courtesy of Madame Philip. Then, according to Piton, this was how it worked:

We would leave Le Chambon by train in the morning, and arrive at Dunières around midday. There our brave travellers would do as they'd been told and park themselves on a bench seat at the station and sometimes sleep, a bit embarrassed, with their hats tipped down. I would then go and get a ticket for Saint-Étienne and hand it over to them. Then they would follow me and we would catch the next train for Saint-Étienne. I got into the habit of not sitting down with them. I would be in my Boy Scout uniform, wearing shorts, seventeen years old, and I would travel in the corridor. If the conductor came along, I would take a quick glance in their direction to see how calmly and naturally they showed their tickets. At Saint-Étienne my three friends would follow me and we would go to the home of Henri Rivière, who owned a large transport business. Monsieur Rivière lived in this huge house. He was very much the patriarch, with a large grey beard. We would all eat, me in the house with Henri Rivière, and my friends in a barn above the stables. After the meal I would go to the station and buy third-class tickets from Saint-Étienne to Lyon and on to Annecy. At around five o'clock in the afternoon we would leave for the railway station, and arrive in Lyon around six thirty.

There everything would be different, because although there was sometimes an identity check between Saint-Étienne and Lyon, it would be carried out by the French gendarmes. From Lyon onwards we were stepping on hot coals! Lyon had already become something of a hub, and was crawling with the men in leather jackets and felt hats.[40] We would arrive at the railway station at between six thirty and seven o'clock in the evening, but our train for Annecy didn't leave until around midnight. It eventually arrived at Annecy at six thirty in the morning, travelling all night, so my little world of responsibility could sleep, safe from the wrong kind of attention. In general, the German military police checked identity cards once during the night, but happily they did it inside the railway cars, where the light was terrible!

At Annecy my three friends would follow me, and I would go the short distance from the station exit to the Protestant church and the home of Pastor Chapal. He offered free food for everybody, which for me meant the chance to move about freely. I would go in my

Scout uniform to see the Abbé Folliet,[41] who would tell me that the driver of the nine o'clock bus from Annecy to Collonges-sous-Salève [a village north of Annecy on the French side of the border, but so close to Switzerland that it was almost a suburb of Geneva] was already 'in the know' and that in principle the day was looking good. I would go back and look for my friends, who would follow me as far as the bus. I would pay as nonchalantly as I could for four people, give them each a ticket, and then sit well away from them so that I could look at the view. At Collonges the bus driver would see to it that we were let out at the top of the road that led to the home of Abbé Jolivet, the parish priest of Collonges. And there, once I had given the password, the abbé would open the door and immediately take my friends to his attic.

It would then be around eleven o'clock [in the morning]. I would stay there all day to get the latest briefing on the patrol routines of the Italian border guards and, the first few times, to take a discreet look for myself at what the problems might be on the route from Collonges to Annemasse, and to use the daylight to find a good place where I could pass my Jews under the barbed wire. From the attic, I could point out to my friends the green fields of Switzerland, the line of barbed wire and, behind the poplar trees, the Swiss Army sentries.

As the refugees could see from the priest's window, Switzerland was only 500 metres away. But there were patrols to dodge, barbed wire to climb over and all sorts of dangers still to be faced. Understandably, the refugees would become more and more agitated as the hour of the crossing approached. It was generally set for around nine o'clock at night. At about that time, Abbé Jolivet would go down to the road to look out, and race back as soon as the Italian patrol had passed. Pierre Piton had established that the patrols came by about every twenty minutes. He would give 'his Jews' the thumbs-up, and tell them to follow him out of the presbytery. Once he was walking ahead of them he couldn't see them, so he simply had to trust that they were still behind him.

When he arrived at the asphalt road he stopped to listen, and tried to see the lights of Switzerland far off in the night. Once they had joined him, he told his group to lie down in the ditch on the presbytery side of the road and wait while the second patrol passed. He would wait on the other side. About five minutes later they would hear the boots approaching. Thud, thud, thud. The soldiers tramped by within feet of them, talking. By this time the group's eyes would have become accustomed to the dark. Once the patrol had passed, Piton would cross the road, back to his three charges, and tell them that the moment had arrived. They should follow him.

Across the asphalt. Softly, softly. Up to the barbed wire. Gently, gently. Lift the wire. One by one, crawl under the wire. Even the old men and women. That's Switzerland on the other side of the wire. You're through. Run, run, run, towards the first Swiss soldier you see. When they challenge you, answer. But watch it: sometimes the Italians patrol on the Swiss side, not on their own side. If that happens, don't hang about. Keep running. Find a Swiss soldier.

Once his Jews had crawled under the wire and taken off, Piton would go straight back to the presbytery. He would spend the night there and catch the next morning's bus to Annemasse, then catch the train to Lyon. Arriving at Lyon in the afternoon, he would have to hang around in the station until the next morning to catch the train to Saint-Étienne. All night the Gestapo patrolled the station, together with French gendarmes and German military police.

Nobody has any way of counting how many successful missions Pierre Piton ran from Le Chambon to the Swiss border, but it is generally thought to have been at least twenty. He is rightly regarded as one of the best and brightest of the *passeurs*. And he was seventeen years old.

Le Chambon village covered in snow. There is no accurate date for this picture, but it was probably taken in the winter of 1941–42. *Roger Darcissac collection, courtesy Lieu de Mémoire, Le Chambon-sur-Lignon*

A tourist poster from 1926 reads: 'Protestants, take your holidays in Le Chambon-sur-Lignon.' *Courtesy Lieu de Mémoire, Le Chambon-sur-Lignon*

A young André Trocmé displaying film star good looks.
Courtesy Nelly Trocmé Hewett

Magda Trocmé around the time of her marriage.
Courtesy Nelly Trocmé Hewett

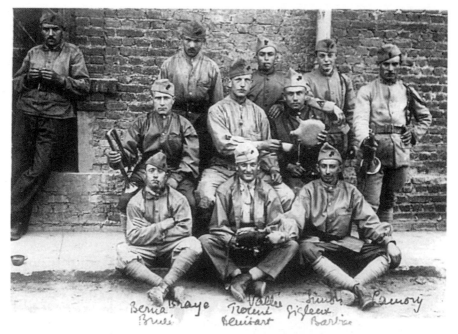

André Trocmé in his French Army uniform, probably in 1922. The young pacifist is in the centre of the middle row, holding a cup. *Courtesy Nelly Trocmé Hewett*

Hanne Hirsch
Courtesy Hanne Liebmann

Left to right: Nelly Trocmé, Marco Darcissac and Catherine Cambessédès photographed in Le Chambon in wartime.
Courtesy Catherine Cambessédès

Charles Guillon
Courtesy Lieu de Mémoire,
Le Chambon-sur-Lignon

André and Mireille Philip. Mireille Philip moved to Le Chambon shortly after the German occupation of France in June 1942. She was an active forger and Resistance worker. André Philip, an elected deputy in the French National Assembly, joined General de Gaulle's government-in-exile in London. *Courtesy Lieu de Mémoire, Le Chambon-sur-Lignon*

One of Oscar Rosowsky's forged identity cards, this time for himself as Jean-Claude Plunne. For puzzled readers of French, Oscar's hair colour ('Cheveux') is not 'cat' ('chat') but 'chestnut' ('châtaigne', abbreviated). Note the detailed interest in the size of his nose ('Nez'), supposedly a giveaway of Jewishness. Oscar modestly put his size as 'moy', short for 'moyenne' (medium). *Courtesy Oscar Rosowsky*

The Héritier barn, where Oscar Rosowsky had his forgery bureau. Oscar and Sammy Charles lived and worked behind the low white door on the left. Dr and Madame Cambessédès rented the large house across the street, beyond the white gate, and Catherine stayed there for the early part of the war. *Contemporary photograph by the author*

Refugees arriving by train at Le Chambon railway station. *Roger Darcissac collection, courtesy Lieu de Mémoire, Le Chambon-sur-Lignon*

Gurs internment camp. Those who survived it remember terrible food, disease, rats, and above all, mud. Each of these small huts was supposed to accommodate 60 people. *Photographer unknown*

La Guespy (The Wasps Nest) was the first shelter for children 'transferred' from Vichy French internment camps to Le Chambon. This photograph appears to have been taken around the time La Guespy opened, in May 1941. *Courtesy Mémorial de la Shoah, Paris*

L'Abric (The Shelter), another of the guesthouses in Le Chambon. *Archives of Contemporary History, ETH Zurich, NL August Bohny-Reiter*

The children's guest house Tante Soly sheltered 15 to 20 children at a time, mostly Jewish. German soldiers were in the habit of taking cover from the rain under the little balcony near the gate.
Contemporary photograph by the author

La Maison des Roches (House of Rocks) *Contemporary photograph by the author*

Beau-Soleil (Lovely Sunshine) *Contemporary photograph by the author*

Winter on the Plateau, 1942–43. *Roger Darcissac collection, courtesy Lieu de Mémoire, Le Chambon-sur-Lignon*

Teachers at the New Cévenole School. *Third from right, standing*, Magda Trocmé, who taught Italian; *fourth from right, standing*, Jacqueline Decourdemanche, school secretary and active forger; *fourth from right, seated*, Hilde Hoefert, who taught German and has some claim to being the first Jewish refugee in the village. She arrived from Vienna in 1938 after Hitler annexed Austria.
Roger Darcissac collection, courtesy Lieu de Mémoire, Le Chambon-sur-Lignon

School play at the New Cévenole School during wartime, precise date unknown.
Courtesy Catherine Cambessédès

Kid's sack race on school Sports Day. *Roger Darcissac collection, courtesy Lieu de Mémoire, Le Chambon-sur-Lignon*

Jewish children dancing the *Hora* in the woods near Le Chambon. *Courtesy Chambon Foundation, Los Angeles*

A wartime Christmas in the Protestant Temple, Le Chambon.
Roger Darcissac, courtesy Lieu de Mémoire, Le Chambon-sur-Lignon

George Lamirand addresses the youth of Le Chambon. Note the quasi-military dress, unnecessary for a civilian minister. The uniformed figure to the right of Lamirand is Robert Bach, Prefect of the Haute-Loire. *Collection Roger Darcissac, courtesy Lieu de Mémoire, Le Chambon-sur-Lignon*

Inside the internment camp at Saint-Paul d'Eyieaux. *Left to right*: Édouard Theis, Roger Darcissac, André Trocmé. *Collection Roger Darcissac, courtesy Lieu de Mémoire, Le Chambon-sur-Lignon*

Boy Scout camp at Domino on the Île d'Oléron, 1919. André Trocmé (far right) was embarrassed to find himself 'wearing only a bathing suit and exposing my body to the burning sun'. *Courtesy Nelly Trocmé Hewitt*

Pierre Fayol *Courtesy Lieu de Memoire, Le Chambon-sur-Lignon*

Pierre Piton *Haute-Loire departmental archive, Pierre Piton collection*

Virginia Hall *Courtesy Lieu de Memoire, Le Chambon-sur-Lignon*

Julius Schmähling as a prisoner-of-war *Courtesy Lieu de Memoire, Le Chambon-sur-Lignon*

YP company of the FFI (French Forces of the Interior): 'Y' for Yssingeaux, 'P' for *parachutage*, a reference to the parachute drops which took place at Villelonge, near Yssingeaux. The female figure in the centre is Virginia Hall. *Collection Roger Darcissac, courtesy Lieu de Mémoire, Le Chambon-sur-Lignon*

Parachute drop of arms. Each canister also contained a packet of tea marked 'Diane', intended for Virginia Hall. *Collection Roger Darcissac, courtesy Lieu de Mémoire, Le Chambon-sur-Lignon*

The wrecked train and bridge at Chamalières. As this was a single line railway, the attack effectively blocked the rail route to Saint-Étienne and Lyon.
Courtesy Éditions L'Harmattan, Paris

Surrender of German troops at Estivareilles on 22 August 1944. *Private collection, courtesy Musée d'histoire du 20e siècle, Estivareilles*

Liberation of Le Chambon, 3 September 1944. Troops from the Free French Army of General Jean de Lattre de Tassigny receive a warm welcome as they pass through the village.
Collection Roger Darcissac, courtesy Lieu de Mémoire, Le Chambon-sur-Lignon

• • •

Even the most serious stories have their moments of comedy. Above, Pierre Piton describes an escape along the western route, which involved travelling by train and bus. The alternative, eastern route, via Valence and Grenoble, involved an early commitment to the healthy outdoors. Valence and Le Chambon are about 67 kilometres apart, and the refugees and their escort would make the first part of the journey on foot.

'They would dress these Jews as Boy Scouts, as though they were going on an outing,' says Catherine Cambessédès. 'They looked really ridiculous, because some of these guys were hardly young.' So unlikely parties of middle-aged Jews, bare knees on display below their Boy Scout khaki shorts, pointy hats on their heads and whistles in their pockets, set off across the Plateau at as jaunty a pace as they could manage, hoping to be mistaken for a group of fourteen-year-olds. Incredibly, it worked.

• • •

The pastors themselves were not above doing a bit of people smuggling work. Édouard Theis made several trips, escorting parties of refugees, as did André Morel, the pastor of Devesset. Max Liebmann, whom we last saw being reunited with Hanne Hirsch in Le Chambon in August 1942, was one of the first to make it to Switzerland. He managed to cross the border in September 1942, escorted by André Morel. He was promptly interned in a Swiss work camp at Sierre, in the central-south Swiss canton of Valais. It wasn't a bad life: there were no guards, and no barbed wire, and you were actually paid for work done. However, there was no Hanne, and he missed her.

Hanne, for her part, grew increasingly restless. She was lonely, she missed her family and she missed Max. By early 1943 she'd had enough.

She spoke to Auguste Bohny, the manager of The Wasps' Nest, saying she wanted to leave the country. She was lucky: she had an aunt who lived in Switzerland, and the aunt arranged an entry visa for her. But that was only half the battle. She would also need an exit visa to leave France. She was given a set of false papers for the journey from Le Chambon to the Swiss border.

I went by myself. Most of them went two or three together. I was alone. Between Annecy and Thonon, which is a tiny little place, I walked along the highway. There was a French customs office, and I passed it [without going in]. A customs office? Wartime? What traffic could there be? Naïve reasoning. Before I knew it, I was called back.

'Where are you going?'

'To Thonon, to the priest.' That was the plan, the arranged thing.

'Papers?' So I showed him my phoney papers, all the papers, and everything that goes with it. He was a young man, the customs officer, and he looked at me and said: 'Are you Jewish?'

Oops! A question I didn't think of, okay. And within a second I caught my breath and said: 'I've got nothing to do with that dirty race.'

'Okay, you can go.' And he gave me a little smile, and gave me my papers back. Had I said yes, if I hadn't been so quick with my answer—well! Also I wasn't carrying any luggage, anything. All I carried was a briefcase, which I still have.

Hanne made it to Switzerland, where she was again united with Max.

• • •

By the time he had completed about twenty missions, young Pierre Piton was full of confidence, and that probably contributed to his undoing. He had got his party, consisting of a husband and wife and a German nurse, as far as the barbed wire. The husband and wife both got through. The German nurse was next. The top 50 centimetres of her made it into Switzerland but the rest was still in France when the Italian soldiers sprang out from behind the poplars, blinded Piton with torchlights, yelled at them and fired a warning shot.

The nurse prudently went into reverse, and she and Piton were both standing on the French side of the barbed wire when the Italians arrested them. Two soldiers with fixed bayonets guarded them on either side, and marched them to the guard post in Collonges-sous-Salève. There, two specialist interrogators bombarded them with questions, while a stenographer took notes. The German nurse's fake papers said she was French, from northern France, but she spoke French very badly and with a heavy German accent, so that story didn't convince anyone.

The Italians then ordered them into a military transport. With the pair still guarded by two armed soldiers, the vehicle set off without anyone telling the two captives where they were going. As they drove, Piton tried to work out where they were heading. He recognised Annecy, and that was ominous. Could they be headed for Lyon, where the Italians would hand them over to the Gestapo? But they were lucky. Just outside Annecy the military transport turned left. They stopped briefly at Chambéry, then continued on. Finally they drove into the courtyard of a military barracks and were marched into an old armoury, where they found themselves locked up with about fifteen others, men and women.

I warned the nurse not to talk to any of the others, in case there were spies planted among the prisoners. One of the prisoners told me he was a primary school teacher from Annemasse imprisoned for no reason. He started to ask me questions, and I restricted myself to telling him: me too—I've no idea why I'm here. Then I asked him where we were, and he told me Grenoble. The next day he was released!!??

I still don't know why, but neither the nurse nor I were interrogated. My one fear was that we would be handed over to the Germans. We were kept there for about three weeks, then released. A soldier with fixed bayonet marched us out to the guard post where, to my great surprise, two French gendarmes took charge of us. They asked us plenty of questions, all done very properly and politely. Then, I think on account of my age, they let us go. There we were, on the street, free.

The question was: where to next? Piton decided that he couldn't simply dump the nurse and leave her to fend for herself. He would have to try again to get her under the wire. He knocked on the first door he came to, and asked where he could find the local Protestant church. At the church they were taken in, given a bed for the night, fed well and given enough money to buy two rail tickets from Grenoble to Annecy. The Grenoble pastor telephoned Pastor Chapal in Annecy and, in heavily coded language, told him to expect two arrivals around noon the next day.

The next morning they boarded the train to Annecy. As they approached Chambéry there was the usual inspection of papers. The gendarmes looked at the nurse's papers then demanded to know if she knew Piton. Yes, said the nurse, breaking all the rules she was given before leaving Le Chambon, before adding: 'I'm not Jewish, I'm Protestant, the young man will confirm it for you.' The gendarmes clearly weren't persuaded, and hung around in the corridor between Chambéry and Annecy, keeping an eye on them. Just before Annecy, they handcuffed them both, one to each gendarme. Piton knew that Pastor Chapal would be waiting for them at the station exit, so he stood as tall as he could, in order to be easily spotted. Chapal was quick-witted enough to size up the situation, and made no move towards Piton. Instead he called Abbé Folliet and told him what he had seen.

Meanwhile, the gendarmes escorted their two prisoners to the gendarmerie, where the pair waited on a bench for about an hour. Finally they were led into the room of a senior officer, a captain or commander, who ordered the two escorting gendarmes to release the prisoners from their handcuffs. He then said he wanted to talk to the prisoners alone. 'He was brief. "I don't know what you've done that's brought you in front of me. I congratulate you. I'm going to release you, but I'm also telling you never to come back here, and you must stop doing this kind of work."'

Once they had left the gendarmerie, Piton and the nurse went straight to Pastor Chapal. They agreed that Piton would remain just long enough to have something to eat, then he would catch the next train back to Le Chambon. The nurse would be handed over to Abbé Folliet, who would arrange her crossing using a different route and with a new guide.

Back in Le Chambon, Piton went to Mireille Philip for the usual debriefing. They agreed that Pierre was now well and truly *grillé* and that he had better make that his last mission to the Swiss border. He could concentrate instead on setting up a network of safe houses for the young Frenchmen now arriving on the Plateau to dodge the STO forced labour laws. In this role, he would report to Pierre Brès, the scoutmaster.

Piton appears to have accepted this new role with good grace. However, in one of his accounts, he adds a postscript. 'It so happens,' he wrote, 'that later on I managed to do one or two trips with Jews for the Cimade and Madeleine Barot.' You can't keep a good smuggler down.

• • •

The young *passeurs* were sometimes pressed into service at the last minute. Catherine Cambessédès remembers the story of a friend from the New Cévenole School, Didier Moulin. 'Theis arrived one night and said to him that Mireille Philip had been arrested. Could he take some people across to the border? A teenager! The school principal is asking him to do that! That's how desperate things sometimes got.' Didier agreed. And returned safely.

12

Germans

The number of German soldiers arriving on the Plateau increased a little from the beginning of 1943 onwards. The convalescing veterans from the Eastern Front who took over the Hôtel du Lignon in December 1942 must have flourished, because the German Army now commandeered a further three of Le Chambon's seven hotels: the Hôtel Central, the Hôtel du Commerce and the Hôtel du Midi. They didn't use them much, or for long, but all were available to them. More importantly, they arranged to billet some soldiers in Tence. The highest-ranking officers reserved a chateau that boasted six bedrooms, two reception rooms and some storage space. They booked 80 beds in hotels for lower-ranking officers, and 90 beds in dormitories for ordinary soldiers.

As before, there was little or no contact between the German soldiers and the local population. They simply ignored each other. It was better that way. However, the presence of the Germans could not be dismissed entirely. The managers of the various children's homes smelled trouble. At The Flowery Hill, the staff dusted off an old plan to find alternative shelter for their guests on farms in the immediate area, and asked André Trocmé and Édouard Theis to be on the lookout for suitable farms and willing farmers. It was not going to be easy: with the arrival of the German soldiers, the farmers were more cautious.

After all, they were the ones being asked to run the greatest risk. In December 1942, Pastor Lhermet, from The Flowery Hill, wrote to Madeleine Barot of the Cimade: 'In September [1942] the danger for the Jews was insignificant, but in the light of what the Germans have been doing lately, the storm could hit us any day.'

Meanwhile, the German high command grew more and more restless. It was clear that young Frenchmen in significant numbers were going into hiding rather than agreeing to be packed off to German factories under the STO order. Many of them hid in the forests, maquis in the more literal sense of the word. They tended to link up with the maquis of the armed Resistance, who were now beginning to make their presence felt all over France (though not yet on the Plateau).

To add to the German high command's problems, their soldiers were deserting in worrying numbers. Among the Le Puy garrison, desertions were in part attributable to the bizarre method of recruitment of the troops themselves. Basically, the Germans had told large numbers of Russian prisoners of war that they faced a simple choice: either they joined the German Army and fought alongside the Wehrmacht, or the Germans would shoot them. Unsurprisingly, the Russians opted overwhelmingly to join the Wehrmacht. However, they were hardly dedicated Axis soldiers.

The German garrison in Le Puy included large numbers of these Russian conscripts. Joseph Bass, leader of the resistance 'Network André', set about exploiting this weakness. Bass was a Jew from Marseilles, who worked closely with a Catholic priest, Père Marie-Benoît, to move Jews in safety in less risky regions of France, including the Plateau. He later moved himself and his network to the Plateau. At great risk to everybody involved, Network André produced leaflets in Russian, which they posted in cafés and bars around Le Puy. A typical leaflet read:

COMRADES

Those who address themselves to you are your comrades who have been forced to wear the shameful German uniform. We have concluded that it is our duty to switch to supporting the French Partisans in order to continue the struggle for our country, for our families, for our children.

So far, so straightforward, you might think. However, Bass's men now issued a none-too-subtle threat.

Don't think that your country has forgotten you. The high command of the Red Army knows what has happened to every combatant. Our information service has been told of each prisoner who has been forced to join the ranks of the Fascist army, and what everybody has done.

The time has come for you to recognise the great shame you have brought on yourself and on your family. Switch to the French Partisans, who are struggling against Hitler's Germany and thereby supporting the Red Army.

THE FRENCH PARTISANS DO NOT SHOOT THOSE FORMER SOVIET SOLDIERS WHO JOIN THEIR RANKS VOLUNTARILY.

You can go to any French farmer for more information.

WE ARE WAITING FOR YOU.
YOUR COMRADES.

No record of precise numbers exists, but there is general agreement that the Russian-language leaflets met with some success, particularly in 1944 when deserting Russian soldiers thoughtfully brought their German weapons with them.

The first uncertain moves towards forming an armed resistance on the Plateau were taken at about the same time as the Germans began arriving in increasing numbers. There is little doubt that the village of Yssingeaux and Jean Bonnissol were the first to take active steps in this regard. Although comparatively young for a Resistance leader, the 30-year-old Bonnissol was a stalwart opponent of the Vichy government, and had consistently argued against defeatism. On 1 March 1943, he joined the departmental committee of the MUR (Mouvements Unis de la Résistance, or United Resistance Movements), which brought together the groups Combat, Franc-Tireur (roughly 'French Gunman') and Libération. He was quickly appointed head of the armed resistance for the whole of the Plateau. He took the name 'Borel', then 'Dunbois' and finally 'Soumy'.

Pierre Fayol, who had been in contact with Combat back in Marseille, now entered the fray. As we have seen, he had set up home with his wife and son in the tiny village of La Celle, not far from Le Chambon. A local farmer, Alexis Grand, put him in touch with Resistance leaders in Tence. He was not exactly snapped up. The Resistance had investigated him in advance, and found that he had been in the French armed forces. Could he be a spy from the Vichy government? They were not going to rush things. Eventually they accepted him, and sent him to Jean Bonnissol. Fayol, now variously known as 'Simon' (the name on his false papers), 'Rivière', 'Vallin' or 'Roux', became head of the armed resistance in Le Chambon. Léon Eyraud ('Noël'[42]) remained in charge of civil resistance.

The Secret Army leaders set themselves a recruiting target. By the end of 1943, they wanted 400 armed, trained and willing men on the Plateau, all ready to take on the Germans. Fayol began recruiting Secret Army cells, known as *sizaines*. These were groups of six soldiers, consisting of a leader and five men. It was vital that the groups were kept separate, and that men in one group knew nothing about any of the other groups.

At first they had limited supplies. They had a few Sten submachine guns smuggled in from Britain, some maps and some compasses. The Sten gun was much beloved by commandos, and by partisans, throughout World War II. It was a simple, close-combat weapon firing 9-mm rounds from a 32-round magazine. The maquisards learned how to strip it and clean it, how to maintain it and how to fire it. Because the gun was simply made, it presented few opportunities to go wrong. Best of all, the Germans also used 9-mm ammunition, so it fired captured rounds beautifully.

It may have been a handy weapon, but there were too few of them to go around. Proper training was a further problem. The early Sten guns made a dangerous racket when fired, loud enough to alert the gendarmes, the Germans and the neighbours. Ammunition was also scarce, so there was little opportunity to practise firing live rounds.

Training took place at night, and consisted of finding the way in total silence around a triangular course with sides three kilometres long, in the dark, without a light, using only a compass. It was hardly adequate preparation for guerrilla warfare against a tough and ruthless enemy. Still, it was a start.

• • •

When researching this book, I put the same questions to everybody I talked to: Were there any informers on the Plateau? Were there denunciations? Did anybody from the Plateau spy for the Germans or the Vichy? The response was universal. No, no and no again. There was no fifth column. Nobody snitched. Nobody broke ranks. The Plateau stayed solid.

The only mildly dissenting voice is that of the excellent Protestant historian François Boulet. In his book *Histoire de la Montagne-refuge*

(*History of the Mountain Refuge*), he says that the chain of events that led to the most horrific episode in the whole story of the Plateau began with a French informer. Boulet is a painstaking and thorough researcher. He doesn't name the informer or give any details, but I would happily bet that he knows what he is talking about.

In his version, 'somebody French from Le Chambon' wrote to the German military police in Saint-Étienne to let them know that an Austrian named Kaller, who had deserted from the German Army, was hiding in a guesthouse in the village. On the morning of 23 April 1943, by coincidence Good Friday, two German military police from Saint-Étienne arrived in Le Chambon on their motorcycles and made a beeline for Inspector Praly's office. They were looking for an Austrian deserter called Kaller, they told the policeman. Could the inspector lead them to him? The three men scoured Praly's files, looking for a foreigner named Kaller aged between 30 and 35 years. No luck. Clearly Kaller was living under an assumed name, probably with false identity papers.

The House of Rocks was unlike other shelters on the Plateau. As it had the status of a mini-university, it was generally for older students rather than the schoolchildren transferred from the camps. In fact, the ages ranged from seventeen to 35. The manager, Daniel Trocmé, was an earnest young man who saw the role as a test of his ability to do something worthwhile with his life. The House of Rocks could accommodate as many as 50 students in 32 rooms, and the students came from all over Europe. For the two military policemen, it sounded like a good place to start looking for their deserter with false papers.

So the policemen hopped on their motorcycles and set off for the House of Rocks, which was on the edge of the village of Le Chambon. There they questioned all the students. Name? Place of birth? Date of birth? Okay, now let's see your papers. There was no sign of the elusive Monsieur Kaller, but the policemen were visibly disturbed by what they had seen and heard. They were particularly suspicious of Daniel Trocmé. 'You speak German too well to be French,'[43] they told him. 'You're certainly using forged papers, and you're definitely Jewish.' They returned to the village on their motorcycles and had lunch at the Hôtel du Lignon. Then they headed out of Le Chambon towards Saint-Agrève, clearly very unhappy.

Four days later, on 27 April, four German non-commissioned officers were taking an evening stroll outside the village of Le Chambon. It was about nine thirty at night. Around 500 metres from the village, on the Tence road, they came on two students from the New Cévenole School, Roger Debiève and Jacques Marchand, painting something on the road. It turned out to be a huge 'V'—Churchill's famous victory sign—and the forbidden double-barred Cross of Lorraine. They topped this off with a giant '1918', the year of Germany's defeat in World War I. The four German soldiers grabbed the two teenagers and marched them off to Inspector Praly's office. The little party arrived there at about ten o'clock at night.

A German officer, a lieutenant, now joined them and demanded to know the captives' names. Praly questioned them and, having established who they were, passed their names on to the German officer. The whole questioning process took about an hour. The officer left, after telling Praly without any explanation that he could let the two teenagers go. The next day, the lieutenant sought out Praly and told him: 'Do nothing about this affair, because I'm going to let the German police know about it and they'll arrange with me to come here.'

Around the end of May 1943, two German military police went to the House of Rocks and arrested a young German called Ferber. The military police were usually on the lookout for deserters.

The significance of all this is not so much the raids and arrests themselves as who carried them out. Up until now, French gendarmes had done all the raiding. But the gendarmes were deliberately sabotaging their own efforts (as testified by Madeleine Barot in Chapter 10), while others were ready to sabotage the raids for them (for example, there is good evidence that someone in Prefect Bach's private office was tipping off those about to be raided by the Vichy forces). Faced with this, the Germans now brushed the gendarmes aside and took over the job of raiding and rounding up for themselves.

Things were clearly getting a whole lot more dangerous. Oscar Rosowsky and his host Henri Héritier discussed the problem. Rosowsky's forgery equipment was seriously incriminating: it needed a more secure hiding place than the little room in the barn. Héritier had an idea. He had fourteen beehives, but the bees had set up house in only twelve of them. What about using the two spare hives to store the forgery kit? It would take a Gestapo man of more than ordinary courage to stick his hand in there.

On 8 June, three French con men dressed as policemen arrived in Fay-sur-Lignon. They were there with the connivance of the German authorities. The 'policemen' managed to swindle 110,000 francs from a rich Jewish father and son from Marseille, Armand and André Nizard. They then 'arrested' them both and handed them over to the Germans. The gendarmes in Fay-sur-Lignon refused to intervene. The normally sharp Daniel Curtet, pastor in the village, hesitated for several days before reporting the matter to Emile Romeuf, the head of Franco–German relations for the area. Curtet's hesitation was probably recognition of a simple dilemma: if he explained the circumstances of the swindle, he might have to answer a whole lot of awkward questions about other Jewish refugees in the village.

Prefect Bach got to hear about the affair and tried to intervene. It was all to no avail. The two Nizards were shipped to Drancy holding camp outside Paris then put on the train to Auschwitz. They never returned.

• • •

The refugees sheltering on the Plateau were now faced with that classic dilemma so beloved of animal behaviourists: fight or flight. For many, flight seemed the better choice. The arrest of Ferber from the House of Rocks meant that the German police of the RSHA (ReichsSicherheitsHauptAmt or Reich Security Main Office, which included the Gestapo) now had their hands on someone who had plenty of beans to spill. If the Gestapo went about questioning him with their usual brutality and thoroughness, he would be very likely to tell them all. So from the end of May 1943, the House of Rocks was totally compromised.

Some of its residents could see the writing on the wall. Pastor Curtet recalled:

I often hid two Austrian Jews, Lipschutz and Schmidt, who left the House of Rocks when they realised that Daniel Trocmé was being naively over-confident. After the grilling of the House's management around Easter 1943, the two Austrians were sent to me and I understand that they did not return but kept constantly on the move, changing their address all the time, and turning up at my house in the middle of the night. In June 1943 they were established at the parish hall, which was always open, and from which I heard them move out around five in the morning.

However, most of the residents at the House of Rocks remained in place. Daniel Trocmé was given plenty of warning that there was trouble ahead. 'Oscar Rosowsky and Jacqueline Decourdemanche saw Daniel Trocmé in person and told him that the residents of the House of Rocks should be dispersed,' Pierre Fayol wrote later. 'Grouping them all in the one place put them all in danger, a danger which Daniel Trocmé didn't want to accept.'

Even after the arrest of Ferber, Daniel Trocmé continued to resist the idea of dispersing his residents. 'Straight after this first alert, Daniel Trocmé was warned again,' Fayol wrote. 'Unhappily, he believed it was his duty to refuse. On the other hand, five of the residents of the House of Rocks pulled out despite the fact that they had no idea at the time whether they would be able to find another refuge.'

In fairness to Daniel Trocmé, it should be said that he was doing no more than continuing an existing policy on the Plateau. The line taken by his prominent cousin, André Trocmé, together with Pastor Theis and the other champions of passive resistance, was simply to stand your ground. Do the right thing, whatever the law says. But do it openly. Our enemies are human beings, too. Reason with them. Show them a better way.

Then, at about six thirty on the morning of 29 June, fourteen plainclothes German police burst into the House of Rocks. They were heavily armed, with submachine guns as well as the usual side arms beloved of police forces everywhere. They came in two front-wheel-drive Citroëns painted dark grey, together with a canvas-sided truck with bench seats. They clearly meant business: they arrived with guns drawn, and four policemen armed with submachine guns were posted around the house to make sure nobody got away.

There is some doubt to this day as to which police force the raiders came from. All early accounts say they were Gestapo, but they may have been Kripo (Kriminalpolizei) or even German military police (Feldgendarmerie). Without uniforms, who could tell? They had come all the way from Clermont-Ferrand, the capital of the large French region of the Auvergne, which includes the Haute-Loire. No matter who they were or where they came from, they were an unpleasant bunch of thugs.

First they stormed all over the house, throwing open the bedroom doors and barking in German: *'Raus! Raus!'* ('Out! Out!') Then they assembled the students in the large dining room and began the interrogations. At about seven thirty, they realised Daniel Trocmé was not there. Where was he? He's at The Crickets, they were told. A party of policemen went off to arrest him. Daniel had enough warning and enough time to escape into the woods behind the house, but he chose to stay at The Crickets. He was the director of the House of Rocks, and he felt he had to be there with his students. He was promptly arrested and taken back to join the others. Magda remembers that Suzanne Heim, one of the staff at The Crickets, burst into the presbytery, shouting: 'Madame Trocmé, run, they've arrested Daniel Trocmé.'

I grabbed my bicycle and with Suzanne raced to the House of Rocks, where I went in while Suzanne rode back to The Crickets. Why did they let me in? I don't know . . . the doors were open, but the doctor had tried to go in to see a child who was sick, and they blocked the way. As for me, I left the presbytery in such a rush that I hadn't taken my apron off. Maybe the Germans thought I was one of the staff. I went in through the kitchen and what did I see in the big dining room? On one side of the room was a table with three or four men from the Gestapo[44] plus the management of the House of Rocks, including the accountant. Each man from the Gestapo had a submachine gun. On the other side of the room, all the students were lined up against the wall. At the very back was Daniel Trocmé. Did they know that Daniel was someone important?

I tried to approach him, but a Gestapo man shouted at me . . . I stopped in my tracks then headed back to the kitchen. Nobody moved. They must have thought I was a cook or a chambermaid. I sat down. Time slipped away, then the students started to walk past me, one at a time, into a little storeroom at the back of the kitchen. There the Gestapo, who had a large directory list of names, demanded that they identify themselves. When they came back, some of them had black eyes and all of them looked badly frightened. Some of them gabbled: 'I've got a bit of money in my room, go quickly and look . . .' or 'I have the address of my mother, or my fiancée . . .' or 'I have a gold watch, go and take it . . .' The poor kids didn't realise that the Gestapo had already searched everywhere and taken everything.

By ten o'clock the Germans were hungry. Magda managed to rustle up a bit of food—two scarce eggs each, and a bit of bread. In the process, she was able to have a quick word with Daniel. He reminded her that a few weeks ago a Spanish student from the House of Rocks had saved a German soldier from drowning in the River Lignon. 'Go to the Hôtel du Lignon,' Daniel urged her, 'and tell them that the Gestapo are arresting everybody here, and remind them of the rescue . . . Who knows, we might be able to save a life.' Magda jumped back on her bicycle and pedalled for dear life into the centre of the village.

The sentry at the Hôtel du Lignon didn't want to let her in, but Magda spoke reasonable German and was a well-known figure in the village. Finally, the sentry relented.

There were two or three officers sitting at a table by a window on the first floor. I approached them, and they asked me what I wanted. I told them I wanted to know which of them had been in Le Chambon for a long time. One of them said to me: 'I've been here for weeks.' I said: 'Remember the German soldier who was about to drown in the Lignon?' 'Yes, yes,' he said, 'I remember it very well.' I said: 'It was one of the students from the House of Rocks who saved him.' 'Yes, I remember it perfectly.' 'Well, this morning the Gestapo arrived . . .'

Before Magda could finish, the Germans butted in. They had nothing to do with the Gestapo, they said. Magda was unfazed. 'It's a matter of honour,' she told the officer. 'I am a woman. You are an officer. We are both people of honour. I'm simply asking you to tell the truth, to testify that the rescue took place during your time in Le Chambon.' Two German officers reluctantly agreed to accompany Magda back to the House of Rocks. They walked, one on each side of her, while she pushed her bicycle. They had not gone far when Magda met two girls from her Christian Union, both on bicycles. Could the German officers borrow their bicycles? If it was important, yes. So this rather odd trio of cyclists, Magda and two German officers on girls' bikes, pedalled back to the House of Rocks.

This time it was not so easy for Magda to get inside. When she first arrived she had been dismissed as unimportant. But now it was apparent that she spoke German, and that she was talking to two German officers, whom she had brought back with her. She certainly couldn't just slip past. She made the two German officers repeat their promise to tell the story of the rescue in the river. Meanwhile, she asked one of the police officers if she could talk to Daniel Trocmé. No, she was told. But come back at midday and you can talk to him then.

She came back as ordered, with her son Jean-Pierre. This time an entirely different scene greeted her. The students were lined up in single file on the outside staircase, with Daniel Trocmé at the head of the queue. She went over to him. As she did so, she could see on the balcony at the head of the stairs two or three of the raiding policemen beating up a young Dutch Jew, shouting at him: 'Pig Jew! Pig Jew!'

Daniel tried to reassure Magda. 'Don't worry about me,' he said. 'I'll go with my students. I'll do my best to explain these things to them, and I'll defend them for as long as it's possible. Please write to my parents and tell them what happened.' He then offered a little wry humour. 'You know I love travel,' he told Magda. 'I'm not afraid, and

185

it's my duty.' Then, in dribs and drabs, the students climbed into the lorries, and were driven away.

In all the horror of the situation, there was one happy moment. When Magda walked into the dining room after the lorries had gone, she saw Luis ('Pepito') Gausachs, the Spanish student who had saved the German soldier from drowning. The two German officers from the hotel had kept their word.

As well as taking Daniel Trocmé, the German police took away eighteen students: five Spanish, three French, two Dutch, two German, two Belgian, two Luxembourgeois, one Austrian and one Romanian. For inexplicable reasons, the Germans left five students behind, including Gausachs. Another eight students had either prudently made themselves scarce or were simply away for one reason or another. So thirteen avoided arrest.

There was predictable uproar. Prefect Bach wrote to the staff officer of the German occupying force in Le Puy—presumably Major Schmähling—demanding the release of those arrested. He received a reply from a Captain Lange:

> In response to your letter on the subject of the imprisonments carried out by the security forces, the Staff Officer informs you that after communicating by telephone with the Head Liaison Staff Officer, he was informed that he could not be given any information, as the Security Service in Clermont-Ferrand knows nothing about it, and that this affair arose with Vichy. The Liaison Officer recommends that you get in touch directly with Vichy.

On 30 July, Maurice Leroy, Inspector General from the French Ministry of Education, wrote to the head of the French military demanding that Daniel Trocmé be released, adding that Trocmé 'does not have a single drop of Jewish blood in his veins but he has German blood—his maternal grandmother was German'. Others wrote along similar lines. It did no good.

Under pressure from the French government, the Paris headquarters of the RSHA looked into the whole episode, and reported on it no fewer than three times: on 27 August, then on 1 September, and again on 18 November. Each time they came to the same conclusion: the House of Rocks was a nest of 'loathsome undesirables', a bunch of 'German haters' who hid German deserters, STO dodgers and Jews. These reports are quite revealing. Given that of the nineteen people arrested only seven were Jewish, it is clear that the Germans saw the raid as part of their struggle against the burgeoning Resistance movement, rather than as a simple round-up of Jews.

The raid on the House of Rocks also marked the end of the Plateau's reputation as a sanctuary. All sorts of things finished with it. When André Trocmé, Édouard Theis and Roger Darcissac had been arrested in February 1943, the uproar that followed was enough to convince the Vichy authorities that they would be better off letting the three men go. The raid on the House of Rocks demonstrated that the Germans were deaf to this kind of protest. In the past, passive resistance had worked. Not anymore.

Clearly, the 'safe' houses were no longer safe. If machine-gun-toting German police could march into the House of Rocks unchallenged and arrest anybody they chose, then where did that leave The Wasps' Nest, The Crickets, The Flowery Hill and all the other shelters? While courageous farmers scattered across the countryside might still offer their barns, outhouses and spare rooms to hapless refugees, concentrations of refugees in guesthouses and hostels looked increasingly dangerous. It made raids like the 29 June affair look all too easy, and all too tempting for the Germans.

• • •

Of the eighteen students arrested in the 29 June raid, four—all of them Spanish—were not deported. Pédro Moral-Lopez and Sérafin Marin-Cavre were released, from Fresnes prison on the eastern fringes of Paris;[45] Félix Martin-Lopez and Jules Villasante-Dura were released from Royallieu-Compiègne internment camp, 80 kilometres northeast of Paris. All four survived the war.

Less than two weeks after his arrest, Daniel Trocmé wrote to his family from the camp at Moulins, near the town of Vichy. He wrote fourteen letters and postcards in all, from various camps and prisons. Some were written on toilet paper. At Moulins, the Jews were separated from the rest of those arrested and sent separately to the camps in the east. None returned. Five of the arrested students are known to have been part of convoy 57, which pulled out of Paris-Bobigny station at nine thirty on the morning of 18 July, bound for Auschwitz.

Two French Protestant students arrested in the raid on the House of Rocks miraculously survived the war. Jean-Marie Schoen lived through Buchenwald and Mittelbau-Dora. Pastor André Guyonnaud emerged alive from Dachau.

Daniel Trocmé was not so lucky. From Moulins, he was moved to Frontstalag 122 at Royallieu-Compiègne. He was then deported to Buchenwald concentration camp in Germany, and moved internally to Mittelbau-Dora. Dora was a division of Buchenwald camp, whose inmates worked as slave labourers in underground factories building secret weapons. Conditions were appalling. Around 60,000 prisoners passed through Dora, of whom 20,000 died there—9000 from exhaustion, 350 hanged, and the rest from disease and starvation. In January and February 1944, 2000 of the most sick and disabled Dora prisoners were moved to Maidanek camp in Poland, and Daniel Trocmé appears to have been one of them. On 2 April 1944 he was murdered at Maidanek. The Germans never stopped believing he was Jewish.

Part IV

...

RESISTANCE

13

Violence

There are two hotly disputed versions of a (relatively minor) event in the chain that led to André Trocmé's departure from Le Chambon in mid-1943. Here is Oscar Rosowsky's account, set out in his contribution to the 1990 symposium *Le Plateau Vivarais-Lignon: Accueil et Résistance 1939–1944*.

It was vital that Trocmé should leave and go into hiding. The idea came to me to invent the very real threat of a young Resistance fighter taken prisoner and 'turned', who could have undergone a change of heart and warned Léon Eyraud of the dangers of arrest by the Gestapo, of which the pastor would be the object. I headed back to the farm at La Fayolle to draft the main points of this letter, in which we decided also to name Dr Le Forestier. He was going to be asked to confess to his role in a minor anti-German provocation when he gave a fat German orchestra conductor a morning serenade with his car horn in the middle of Le Chambon after this bloke plonked himself in the road and prevented the doctor from passing.

Léon Eyraud liked my idea. I don't know by which route or how in the end he informed André Trocmé and Dr Le Forestier. But the latter never again indulged in troublemaking in public, and André

Trocmé, who was under strong pressure at the time and in the same direction from the Reformed Church, accepted that he should go into hiding until the Liberation.

So in this version it is a forged letter from Oscar Rosowsky that does the trick.

André Trocmé's version of events is the same in spirit but different in method. In his unpublished memoirs, he writes that a young Resistance fighter who had been 'turned' came to see him in person. No letter, no Léon Eyraud.

'I am a double agent,' the young maquisard began. 'I pretend to work for the Gestapo, but I feed them a lot of false information. However, that lets me listen in to the plans of their agents. So, the other day in Valence, they decided to put a price on your life. You are going to be assassinated.'

'Assassinated?'

'Yes. The system works like this. The Gestapo tell French criminals that they can free them from French prison and have their sentence suspended. All they have to do is make some troublesome people disappear. It's a villainous business. If the French police arrest the criminal, the Gestapo insist that he is handed over to them. The Gestapo then change his identity, and he moves somewhere else.'

'That would explain the recent assassinations of perfectly honest people,' I exclaimed.

'You've got it!' the young man replied. 'By doing this, the Germans don't stir up anti-German feeling: nothing seen, nothing known! People just don't see the pattern in these strange assassinations.'

'Are you telling me now that I'm going to be killed?'

'If you don't go into hiding, yes.'

Of course, there is no logical reason why both stories should not be true. However, neither narrative is likely to have made a jot of difference to Trocmé's decision. What surely turned the tide was the argument put to him by the Reformed Church.

The logic of the situation was clear. The arrest of Daniel Trocmé made the arrest of his much more prominent cousin André something close to a certainty. And that would lead to unimaginable trouble on the Plateau. This was clear to Resistance figures like Fayol and Eyraud, as well as to some of Trocmé's fellow pastors. In his memoirs, Trocmé set out his belief that Marcel Jeannet, the pastor at Le Mazet, had discussed Trocmé's exile with Pierre Rozier, president of the Regional Council of the Reformed Church, who contacted Marc Boegner, asking him to intervene.

Boegner did not come to see Trocmé in person, but he sent his number two, Pastor Maurice Rohr, a distant cousin of Trocmé's. In Trocmé's account of the meeting, Rohr got straight to the point.

'With the arrest of Daniel and his students,' he said to me, 'we've already had enough trouble. How would it help, adding another name to a list of martyrs that's already too long?'

'I can serve as an example,' I told him. 'I have preached non-violent resistance. I should stick to my post until the end.'

'The parish is already troubled enough,' Rohr said to me. 'You have a price on your head. You know how these executions are carried out. You go for a ride in a car, and your body is found in a corner of a wood. Or they burst into the house at dinnertime, and the death squad from the Gestapo sprays the whole family with machine-gun fire. How can you live with the thought that not only will you be killed, but you could be responsible for the death or injury of your wife, your children and your guests?' And Rohr listed some recent cases.

'No,' I said.

'Do you think that the parish will stay non-violent if you are assassinated?' he asked.

'I don't believe so,' I replied.

'So, be reasonable. Disappear for a little while. The BBC is saying that the invasion is coming this summer. It will only be for a few weeks. It would be mindless to expose yourself to the worst. We want you alive, not dead.'

Trocmé didn't agree straight away. But in the end he came round to it. Probably he thought that if his arrest led only to his own death, so be it, but if his arrest would lead to armed insurrection and major bloodshed on the Plateau, then it was his Christian duty to do all he could to prevent it. The conclusion was inescapable: time to go. There is no exact date for his departure, but it was sometime in July 1943. He shaved off his moustache, put on a Basque beret and swapped his owlish spectacles for a much larger pair. He carried false papers prepared by Roger Darcissac. André Trocmé had ceased to exist: step forward André Béguet.

His first protector was a Protestant hardware merchant from the village of Lamastre, who drove him in his truck to the parsonage in Lamastre, just beyond Saint-Agrève. Next Trocmé moved to a farm just outside Lamastre, and stayed there three weeks. After that he moved to a large 'half-farm, half-villa' between Lamastre and Vemous, still in the area of Le Chambon. He was unhappy there, and wanted to move on. Finally, Magda found him a safer haven much further south and across the River Rhône, at the Château de Perdyer, in the Drôme valley not far from the town of Châtillon. There he waited for Liberation, in every sense of the word.

André Trocmé suffered from a bad back, so he was not fit for active service. The same did not apply to Édouard Theis, who remained active in the Resistance. He went into hiding at the same time as Trocmé, in his case somewhere near the Swiss border. He has never given precise details of where he went or how he got there, but it is generally thought that he used one of the Cimade routes, and that he headed for the area around Annemasse on the French side of the border, not far from Geneva. He did not settle anywhere, but stayed constantly on the move. Despite his nomadic existence, he remained active with the Cimade, smuggling Jews to safety in Switzerland. After all, changing profession from *pasteur* to *passeur* didn't sound like too big a jump.

So in one move the Plateau lost the two strongest voices supporting pacifism and passive resistance. If the Resistance now chose to take up arms against the Germans and the Vichy Government, there would be no attacks from the pulpit by Trocmé and Theis to give them pause. For the rest of his life, André Trocmé agonised over whether he had done the right thing.

• • •

On 6 August 1943, the Resistance shot Inspector Praly, Le Chambon's resident police spy. Three men came to the Hôtel des Acacias at about nine in the evening. One of them, Jacques Bellin, shot the policeman twice with a 7.65-mm automatic pistol. The three men then fled, Bellin on a bicycle that lost its chain about 60 metres from the hotel. Bellin abandoned the cycle and the three men disappeared on foot into the nearby woods.

This was not a Le Chambon operation, nor was it approved by the Resistance in Le Chambon. The plan in Le Chambon had always been to do nothing that would put the rescue operation at risk. The three assassins—the other two known only as '13.206' and '13.216'—came from the tiny village of La Bataille, about thirteen kilometres west of Le Chambon, at the foot of a mountain called Pic du Lizieux. Many accounts say the shooting of Praly was revenge by the Resistance for the raid on the House of Rocks, but that is not Bellin's version: according to Bellin's report to Jean Bonnissol, the head of the maquis in Yssingeaux, Praly was shot for 'treason'. It was the first assassination carried out by the Resistance in the Haute-Loire.

Understandably, there was uproar. Four brigades of gendarmes fanned out into the countryside around Le Chambon. They came up with nothing. The three men were back home in La Bataille within 23 hours of the shooting, well beyond the range of the searching gendarmes. At one point the police circulated a description of a Jean Brugière, a nineteen-year-old apprentice butcher from Montpelier, but he proved to be equally elusive and probably was not involved anyway. The crime remained 'unsolved'.

Praly was a Protestant, so his funeral service, on 9 August, took place in the Le Chambon temple. Prefect Bach attended, and spoke witheringly about the scourge of terrorism. He made the same point a few days later, on 18 August, in his regular report on affairs in the Haute-Loire.

The population of the Haute-Loire has learned with astonishment of the assassination of Inspector Praly at Le Chambon-sur-Lignon. Many different explanations have been put forward as motive for this crime, but there has been unanimous condemnation of this act, which can justifiably be described as 'terrorist'. The public strongly supports the investigation now taking place, and hopes it will lead to the arrest of the assassins.

Bach may or may not have been right about universal condemnation of the assassination, but that was not the main preoccupation of the Plateau. The biggest fear was some sort of reprisal against the whole village. The fact that the victim was French rather than German *might* save them. If a German had been killed, then his compatriots were perfectly capable of lining the men of the village up against a wall and shooting the lot of them. Still, the assassination was the equivalent of sticking a burning stick into a hornets' nest: a lot of angry hornets come bursting out, spoiling for a fight. The Plateau held its breath.

A few days later, the Resistance received their second parachute drop. The first drop, back in December 1942, had been more of a test run. The BBC French service had broadcast the message *La soupe est chaude* (The soup is hot), which told the Resistance to go to a place called Le Pin (The Pine), near Freycenet. That brought ten containers of guns, eagerly snapped up by Resistance forces from the distant Loire region.

The second drop was originally due on the night of 10 July. The message was the same—*La soupe est chaude*—pointing to the same field near Freycenet. However, the Gestapo had intercepted the first message and lay in wait, slightly in the wrong place. Happily, the RAF plane didn't make it—a frequent problem—and both Resistance and Gestapo went home empty-handed. Nevertheless, that marked the end of the hot soup.

On the night of 22 August, the Resistance finally received their drop, this time a heavy shipment of arms destined for the Plateau itself. It followed the even more puzzling BBC message, *Qui veut noyer son chien l'accuse de la rage* (roughly 'He who drowns his dog accuses it of having rabies').[46] That pointed to a field near Mézères, about ten kilometres west of Yssingeaux, where eighteen containers bringing no less than three tons of guns and ammunition floated gently down into the field. Some 22 men rapidly dispersed the treasure trove. They buried some of it, but the precious guns, including around a hundred submachine guns, were hidden in a shed at the Château de Lavée near Yssingeaux. The Secret Army on the Plateau was now well armed.

They paid a price. The local mayor and the local president of the Legion informed the gendarmes that a farm worker had heard a plane fly low over Mézères, and around five thirty in the morning had seen men handling heavy metallic objects. Two gendarmes set off to investigate, and found the breech of a submachine gun. That led to the arrest of René Garnier, one of Pierre Fayol's team. He was shot on 13 November 1943.

• • •

As well as their regular work solving crimes and policing the roads, by mid-1943 the Plateau's gendarmes faced trouble upholding the law on three further fronts. First, there were the Jews: unregistered, usually with false papers, not living at their assigned address. Then there were the *réfractaires*, the young Frenchmen dodging the STO forced-labour laws. They tended to disappear into the forests, where they linked up with the armed resistance. Finally there was the Resistance itself. Praly's fate demonstrated that the Resistance was now up and running on the Plateau, and dangerous. The gendarmes would have taken note that it was a French policeman, not a German soldier, who had been assassinated.

As we have seen, the gendarmes dealt with the problem of Jews by doing as little as they thought they could get away with. But STO dodgers were another matter. The law was not discriminatory: it applied to all young Frenchmen unlucky enough to be born in the wrong year. The gendarmes were paid to enforce the law, so they set about doing just that. On 23 June 1943 the gendarmes raided the village of Araules, between Tence and Le Chambon, looking for *réfractaires*. They made two arrests. They came back to Araules on 8 and 9 July. Four arrests. Between 17 and 20 July, the government declared an amnesty and offered the *réfractaires* the opportunity to give themselves up without facing penalties. Abject failure. So the raids resumed.

Then there was the issue of the Resistance for the gendarmes to cope with. Some of them appear to have approached this problem with a combination of pragmatism and self-interest. They knew the war was going badly for the Germans. The Russians were pushing them back in the east, and in July 1943 the Allies invaded Sicily, capturing the capital, Palermo, on 23 July. The Italians responded by deposing Mussolini and installing King Victor Emmanuel III as head of Italy's armed forces. On 8 September, Italy surrendered to the Allies, and on 13 October they switched sides, declaring war on Germany. The message was clear: it could only be a matter of time before the Allies set about taking the rest of mainland Europe, including France.

The gendarmes had no particular wish to find themselves on the losing side. They also had to face the fact that they were increasingly outgunned by the maquisards. By the end of November 1943, the Resistance fighters on the Plateau around Yssingeaux had grenades, automatic rifles and submachine guns, as well as the usual collection of rifles and pistols. In general, the gendarmes were not particularly pro-German or even pro-Vichy. Put simply, some of them seem to have come to the view that, to paraphrase Churchill's famous phrase, 'jaw-jaw' might be better for their health than 'war-war'.

Given the gendarmes' ambiguous attitudes, Jean Bonnissol thought it might be worth sounding them out. He asked Lieutenant Alfred Morel, the most senior gendarme in Yssingeaux, if he felt like joining Bonnisol's Resistance network, 'Zinnia'. Morel's reply, according to Bonnissol, was: 'I can't join any network. But I could pass on any information that might interest you.' He meant information about Gestapo agents operating in the area and, again according to Bonnissol, he was as good as his word.

• • •

In the departmental archives in Le Puy there is a dossier of telegrams and other orders issued from Vichy to the Haute-Loire. It includes a list of those to be arrested, or somehow got out of the way. The names of André Trocmé, Édouard Theis and Roger Darcissac are there, of course. However, there is a fourth name from Le Chambon: Charles Guillon. The Vichy government's Commission for Jewish Affairs had issued a report on the Plateau in general, which saw Le Chambon not so much as a place of refuge for Jews but as 'the starting point of a channel for Jews into Switzerland'. They were in no doubt as to who was behind it all: Charles Guillon was organising 'the emigration of foreign Jews'.

At the time, Guillon was something of a Scarlet Pimpernel. He was still based in Geneva but continued to make highly dangerous trips into Occupied France, including to the Plateau. He turned up in Le Chambon on 5 June 1943, not long before the raid on the House of Rocks, and attended the meeting of the town council. He prudently didn't sign the minutes, leaving that to his successor as mayor, Benjamin Grand. There is unfortunately no record of exactly what he was doing in Occupied France—people moving large sums of money clandestinely in suitcases from country to country tend to keep their mouths shut and their notebooks closed—but there is universal agreement that without Guillon's efforts, the vital flow of funds to the Plateau might have dried up. He was the Cimade's most important contact in Switzerland, their *correspondant*. The historian Pierre Bolle has estimated that a Guillon suitcase might contain 'five or six million francs'.

And of course, through all that was going on—the departure of Trocmé and Theis, the new assertiveness of the Resistance—the rescue mission on the Plateau continued unchecked. Jews continued to arrive by train and bus, and all were taken in and sheltered. No one was turned away, no one was asked why they were there, and no one was asked if they were Jewish. They were unquestioningly supplied with false papers, including ration cards. The children's homes continued to operate, though the managers there were inclined to send the children off into the forest rather than keep them concentrated in the houses.

The story of Léo and Barbara Sauvage might have been told by any of the Jews who arrived unannounced on the Plateau. Léo was born in Mannheim, Germany, on 23 February 1913, as Léopold Smotriez. His family moved to Forbach in northern France, and somewhere along the line Léo changed his surname to the more French-sounding Sauvage. He met his wife, Barbara, in Paris, where they both moved in left-wing circles. She was a Polish Jew whose two brothers had already moved to Paris in the 1930s to escape Polish anti-Semitism. Léo and Barbara married in 1939.

Léo worked as a journalist and theatre critic in Paris. Both professions were banned to Jews, but he wasn't going to let this bother him. In 1940, the year of the German invasion of France, he and Barbara decided to move south to Marseille in the Unoccupied Zone, where they hoped for better times. Léo taught German in a local school, and tried to save enough money to escape to America through the Varian Fry organisation. He even started a little theatre troupe, which toured the Riviera but never quite managed to make the Sauvages' fortune. When the Germans swept south at the end of 1942, Léo and Barbara moved to Nice, which was occupied by the much more tolerant Italians.

In the summer of 1943, Barbara became pregnant. Then she developed complications. Peritonitis set in. The doctors advised that if she wanted to save her own life, let alone the life of her baby, she would need to rest, eat proper food and avoid stress. Where could that be done? Léo Sauvage talked to one of his left-wing contacts, Victor Fay, who suggested that the Sauvages take a look at Le Chambon. 'They're Huguenots up there,' Fay said. 'You never know.' The Sauvages moved to Le Chambon, renting a room in a farmhouse in La Fayolle.

The rest, better food and lowered stress had the desired effect, and the peritonitis cleared up by the time Barbara went into labour in March 1944. She was taken to the hospital in Saint-Agrève, where Dr Roger Le Forestier presided over the birth. Le Forestier was not merely a qualified surgeon; his work in Africa meant he was experienced as well as skilful. On 25 March 1944, Barbara gave birth to a healthy boy whom the Sauvages named Pierre. They could not have known it at the time, but they had just produced one of the Plateau's most energetic (and grateful) champions, the documentary maker Pierre Sauvage, writer, director and narrator of the Plateau documentary *Weapons of the Spirit*.

The tolerance and hospitality of the Plateau at times went to incredible lengths. For example, Jewish religious ceremonies survived, with the active support of the Protestant establishment. Rudi Appel, a young refugee, remembers a Hanukkah party in December 1943. Rudi had taught Juliette Usach, the director of The Wasps' Nest, to play the Hanukkah song 'Rock of Ages' on the piano, and the kids all sang along. They also lit Hanukkah candles. There was no synagogue in the village, so the Protestant church handed over a room for use by the Jews on Friday nights. André Hano, the classics teacher at the New Cévenole School and a Jewish refugee, conducted the services.

Parties of children and adults continued to flow down the two 'pipelines' to Switzerland (and were sometimes led to their border crossing by Pastor Theis). Despite the absence of the two pastors from Le Chambon, it was rescue business as usual right across the Plateau.

• • •

By the autumn of 1943, the Secret Army on the Plateau was beginning to look like a serious force. Bonnissol's 'Zinnia' network had no fewer than fifteen active sections, each of them made up of between nine and seventeen armed and trained men, a total of 193 men around Yssingeaux alone. There were also auxiliary services. Pierre Fayol set up a medical service of six doctors willing to help, including Roger Le Forestier, the only one trained as a surgeon. A chemist volunteered to provide medicines. So in the battles to come, the wounded knew they would get help. Fayol's wife, Marianne, headed a social services unit. She had begun by collecting clothing to pass on to the men of the maquis. That expanded into a rudimentary service offering financial and moral support to families in trouble. And, of course, Oscar Rosowsky, Sammy Charles and Jacqueline Decourdemanche continued to produce false papers.

The men of the maquis lived in the countryside, either camped out in the forests or else in abandoned farmhouses. They now trained hard. A typical day began at 7.30 am with physical exercise, followed by breakfast at eight. At eight forty-five there would be a lecture, perhaps on military theory and tactics, then at nine forty-five a practice military exercise. At eleven there would be a course, perhaps in morse code, followed by lunch. At two thirty there would be another course, perhaps in armaments and explosives. At four, more physical exercise. At six, a course in English, followed by an evening meal. At 9 pm, a patrol, a march or, rarely, an actual attack.

All this Resistance activity could hardly pass unnoticed by the neighbours. The Secret Army depended heavily on the discretion of the farmers, and overwhelmingly the farmers protected them. Not all, however.

In October 1943 the authorities came to the conclusion that Prefect Robert Bach was not policing his area with the kind of zeal the Vichy government and the Germans wanted. He was replaced on 16 October by a senior policeman from Clermont-Ferrand, André Bousquet. Bousquet's brief was to clean up the area and get things back under control. Within two days he received some rare help. On 18 October a group of nine farmers wrote to his office in Le Puy.

For some time, a gang of communists pretending to be réfractaires *dodging the STO has arrived in dribs and drabs and set themselves up in the area of Lizieux and Meygal. Since then, numerous thefts of vegetables and chickens have been committed by these undesirables. We see them lurking about at night in the villages, pretending to be guarding them. People living in isolated houses mostly give in to them, and sell them or give them food. We are certain that there are dangerous fugitives from justice among them.*

The letter went on to name those in charge of this group of miscreants. There was a Monsieur Valdener, a barber from Yssingeaux, and his brother-in-law, Monsieur Bonnissol, who went under the name of Dumas. One group occupied an empty house at Robert in the commune of Araules. There was another at Faurie, while the most important had taken over an abandoned house at Meygal near Troussaire. The last lot were armed and dangerous. They were being provided with supplies by a family of foreigners living at Sagnes in a house called Le Sergent. The letter concluded with a plea: 'In the name of the peace-loving people of this region we ask you, Monsieur Prefect, to give the necessary orders very soon to rid the region of these undesirables.'

The letter was a rare piece of treachery and, as we shall see, it was probably a factor in the fate of Jean Bonnissol. The letter underlined the problem of feeding the maquis. Stealing food from farmers was unlikely to win friends, but buying it was in effect black marketeering. The farmers had to declare the whole of their harvest to the authorities, and account for it. However, a friend in the right place could work wonders. In Tence, Pierre Bernard combined the functions of primary school teacher and inspector of harvests. He simply arranged for the farmers to sell to the maquis, while he signed off the necessary declaration of (reduced) harvest. Everyone was a winner.

• • •

By the autumn of 1943, Gestapo raids were taking place all over Occupied France, particularly in the larger cities. The Gestapo's main target was now the Resistance, but if the raids managed to catch a Jew or two, so much the better. Oscar Rosowsky had never given up his ambition to train as a doctor, and on 15 November he enrolled with the Faculty of Medicine at the University of Strasbourg. The university had conveniently moved from Strasbourg to Clermont-Ferrand, about 125 kilometres northwest of the Plateau. At this stage Rosowsky was posing as an Algerian Frenchman from the Alsace.

On 25 November a German soldier brandishing a submachine gun burst into Rosowsky's lecture theatre and shouted: 'Raus! Raus!' (Out! Out!) to the assembled students. The performance was repeated all over the campus, until hundreds of students and lecturers were packed into the university courtyard. They could hear shots, and yells. Some of the students started ripping up their papers.

Rosowsky spotted a narrow staircase and managed to slip away. However, his troubles were far from over. The French had set up a checkpoint outside the university, manned by two civilian police and a *milicien*.[47] The milicien's job was to inspect the identity papers and do any searching. Rosowsky recalls:

I was a bit worried. I handed over my identity card, and then the milicien started his search. He was very professional. He started low down with my legs, listening for the sound of ammunition cartridges rattling when he passed his hands over my pockets. Then he came to my right pocket, and he heard a sound exactly like revolver cartridges in a metal box. He beamed, like a successful hunter. He shoved his hand in triumphantly, and pulled out a box of lozenges for a sore throat. His friends started laughing at him. Having made a fool of himself, he shoved me away, giving me a kick in the arse for good measure. If he had continued his search, it would have led to my sleeves and the fur collar of my jacket stuffed with samples of false papers. I decided then and there that Clermont wasn't the place to

be. I caught the train back to Le Chambon that night. I still treasure
this box of Gonacrine, to which I owe my life.[48]

• • •

The Secret Army now began to plan. They drew two lines on the
map. One line ran in a right-handed arc around the peaks of three
mountains, Meygal, Lizieux and Mézenc, and along the ridge of the
valley of Les Boutières. If that line could be held, then the vital route
from the Plateau through to the Rhône Valley could be kept open or
closed, as required. The other line ran roughly east to west following
the ridges above the Loire valley, and commanded the two key lines
of transport: the main road RN 88, which linked Lyon with Le Puy
via Saint-Étienne, and the railway line, which linked the same three
towns. Ultimately these transport routes led to the Mediterranean coast
and important ports like Marseille. If they could be cut or blocked,
the Germans would have two fewer routes to use for moving supplies
and reinforcements when the Allied landing came. So controlling both
the road and the railway line would be essential once the invasion
became reality.

On 5 October 1943 the Resistance mounted its first serious attack.
Led by Bonnissol, they sabotaged the railway line at the Vaure bridge
between Beauzac and the River Lignon, using explosives supplied from
Britain. The attack targeted a particular train, which was carrying a
contingent of German SS. Having halted the train the Resistance now
set about machine-gunning the trapped troops. Result: no Resistance
casualties, and 'many' Germans wounded or killed.

Less impressively, on 30 October they launched a punitive attack on
a tobacconist near Désaignes. This may not have caused the Germans
too much grief, but it left the maquis well stocked with tobacco. They
'requisitioned' the tobacco 'in the name of the French Resistance'. This
was followed by pinprick raids on a collaborationist petrol station and

a shop. The shop raid ensured that the maquis were well stocked with blankets, cooking utensils and shoes.

On 21 November, the maquisards mounted a very well-planned raid on a dairy in Saint-Agrève. The dairy had been supplying the Germans. The fourteen Resistance fighters came armed with six Sten guns with two loaded magazines each, four pistols, four quarter-kilo packs of plastic explosives, twenty packs of '808',[49] a box of detonators, a dozen explosive caps, five 30-minute fuses and five two-hour fuses. At midnight, two men cut off the telephone lines. They then tried to break in, but failed. So they woke the nightwatchman and demanded to be let in. When he refused, they stood in front of the door and fired three bursts from one of the Sten guns. The nightwatchman then opened the door. The maquisards now had to hurry, but by 12.45 am they had laid their explosive charges, four on half-hour fuses and three on two-hour fuses. The dairy was entirely put out of action, and the maquisards escaped with '60 kilos of butter of excellent quality'.

The run of luck could not continue forever. It ended on 15 December, when the Gestapo arrested Bonnissol. It is a measure of the resilience and good organisation of the Secret Army that they carried on undisturbed. For the record, Bonnissol escaped the fate of many Resistance leaders arrested by the Gestapo. He was first sent to Fresnes prison, then moved to Compiègne, before being put on a train to Auschwitz on 25 August 1944. He escaped from the train, and managed to make his way back to Saint-Étienne in France. After the Liberation, he was appointed president of the Épuration Légale in the Haute-Loire, the French legal body which investigated 'collaboration' during the war.

14

Invasion

By the beginning of 1944, the war was starting to go seriously badly for Germany. On 24 December 1943, President Roosevelt felt confident enough to announce publicly that General Dwight D. Eisenhower would be supreme commander-in-chief for the forthcoming Allied invasion of Western Europe. The British general Bernard Montgomery, hero of El Alamein and conqueror of Germany's legendary Irwin Rommel, would be his field commander. Clearly there was major trouble ahead for the Germans.

On 4 January 1944, the Russians pushed the Germans back across the pre-war Polish border. On 19 January, the Russians broke through at Leningrad, ending the two-year siege of that city. On 20 January, Allied aircraft dropped 2300 tons of bombs on Berlin, the biggest ever raid on the German capital. On 22 January, the Allies landed at Anzio in Italy, around 50 kilometres south of Rome. They achieved total surprise, and met little resistance from the Germans.[50] Men and matériel poured ashore. The Allies were now established on the mainland of Western Europe. To make matters worse for the Germans, the winter of 1943–44 was particularly severe. In appalling conditions, they began the long, bitter retreat from their eastern conquests.

The same harsh conditions applied to the Plateau. The snow was deep, making the roads and the railways slow and unreliable. After a particularly heavy snowstorm on 10 February, the whole Plateau literally ground to a halt. Just about every road was blocked, and they stayed that way, because blocked roads meant no fuel for the snowploughs. Throughout the winter, farmers struggled to feed and shelter their cattle. Food was scarce for human residents of the Plateau, too.

There was also a hint of panic at high level. The Vichy government's STO law turned out to be the most effective recruiting agent ever invented—for the maquis. Nevertheless, the government now extended the law to all Frenchmen aged between sixteen and 60. The chances of the Vichy authorities enforcing this were pretty slim, but it meant that the derelict farmhouses of the Secret Army began to look increasingly inviting to young and even middle-aged Frenchmen, particularly compared with the heavily bombed factories of a collapsing Germany. The recruitment pool for the Resistance swelled accordingly.

For their part, the Germans continued to pin their faith on some kind of super-powerful secret weapon, which Hitler would triumphantly brandish and use to turn the tide. And, indeed, the Germans were about to produce the deadly V-1 flying bomb and V-2 rocket, but those were never going to be enough to win a war already lost.

The nature of the rescue operation on the Plateau had changed subtly but comprehensively by the beginning of 1944. The camps remained open, and the various rescuers continued to do their best to win the release of children there. But now, more and more often, they attempted to gather up children either before or at the time of their parents' arrest, operating clandestine networks across France to save the children before they ever landed behind barbed wire. Sabine Zeitoun worked with Madeleine Dreyfus in the Jewish children's rescue service, the OSE. She describes what happened when children were taken to the Plateau:

Most of the time, the children had already been given forged ration coupons, decked out with an 'Aryan' identity and—whenever we could—prepared psychologically for their move into their new family. Madeleine would explain to the children the strict rules which they had to stick to scrupulously throughout the journey: no talking in German or Yiddish, and no speaking to each other using their real first names or surnames. Accompanied by a small group of children, she would set off from Lyon to Saint-Étienne, usually in the train. Then she would change to the wheezing little train that would take them to Le Chambon.

Madame Déléage and her daughter Eva [both residents of Les Tavas, a tiny hamlet in the commune of Le Chambon-sur-Lignon] played an enormous role in smoothing the contacts with the other communities of the Plateau. Sometimes she checked out several villages in advance to find people ready to accept the children. Once she knew there was a place willing to take them in, Madeleine Dreyfus would take the children there.

It was not uncommon for Dreyfus to bring two or three parties like this every week.

So where previously the children had been transferred legally from the camps, now they were brought clandestinely to the Plateau, already carrying false identity papers. As a result, the focus was on finding shelter with farmers or in remote and tiny villages, rather than housing the refugee children centrally in the large hostels and shelters in and around Le Chambon. And, of course, refugees continued to arrive on their own initiative, and in growing numbers, as Gestapo raids across France grew worse. The rescue operation required the willing participation of farmers and villagers throughout the Plateau, not just in Le Chambon, Le Mazet and Fay-sur-Lignon.

After the debacle of the raid on the House of Rocks, the managers of the various hostels and refuge centres vowed never to be caught napping again. All sorts of warning systems were put in place. Oscar Rosowsky set up one.

The geography of the Plateau played a part, in the sense that the movements of the German troops there could be spotted and the Resistance around Le Chambon could be tipped off about any threats coming from Saint-Étienne or from the Ardèche. This was then relayed via the departmental railway's telephone system, and via a PTT [Post, Telegraph and Telephone] network that I myself organised linking the ticket inspectors on the trains with the lady in the Le Chambon post office. They warned of any threats that might come from Le Puy-en-Velay.

With tip-offs from town halls and from inside the prefecture, with warning systems like the one set up by Rosowsky, and with the gendarmes none too keen, the Plateau was never again taken by surprise.

Nevertheless, the raids on children's homes and guesthouses continued. A typical sequence might go something like this. An establishment would receive a message: the gendarmes are coming, searching for Jews. The management would then brief all the residents, children and adults alike. Most of the residents would elect to hide in the woods, but a few—some literally paralysed with fear—stayed in the house, where they could be hidden in the attic.

In the middle of the night there would be the sound of cars arriving, usually accompanied by a bus, followed by loud knocking on the door. Someone inside would open an upstairs window and ask innocently: 'Who's there?' The door knocker, usually a junior officer, would step into the light to identify himself. Once the door was opened, the gendarme would announce that he had come for any 'non-Aryans' and that he intended to 'transfer' them 'elsewhere'. Whoever had answered the door now set about delaying the search as long as possible. Surely, he or she might ask, this very important task should involve a more senior officer? At this point a commandant would step forward and explain that the Jews were being 'resettled' in Poland, where they could live in peace.

The gendarmes would now come in, list of names in hand, and begin the search. First bedroom, empty. Second bedroom, empty. Third bedroom, empty. 'So where are they all?' the commandant would demand. It was now the job of whoever had answered the door to assume an air of puzzled innocence. 'They were all here last night,' they might say. 'But this isn't a concentration camp. They're free to come and go.'

In one celebrated raid on The Flowery Hill, the commandant brandished the list of names in front of Pastor Marc Donadille, the Cimade representative who had answered the door. One of the names struck Donadille as a little odd. Madame Bormann was indeed a guest, but she was not Jewish and she even claimed to be a distant cousin of Martin Bormann, Hitler's private secretary. Surely there had been some mistake? The gendarmes demanded to see her anyway. Having found her, still in bed, they ordered her to get dressed and come with them. Everybody waited in the corridor outside her room while she dressed. There followed the most horrible screams and cries of distress from behind the closed door. When they opened the door again, the gendarmes saw Madame Bormann wrapped up in her bedclothes, rolling around on the floor, eyes wild, arms and legs flailing, in the middle of some sort of fit. They called a doctor. Before the doctor's arrival, Donadille was alone with Madame Bormann for a brief moment, and winked at her, which magically brought the fit to a temporary halt. However, she resumed for the doctor's benefit, and was duly pronounced unfit for travel. The gendarmes had no choice but to leave her; they searched the rest of the house, found nothing and left with an empty bus. Afterwards, Madame Bormann explained to Donadille that it was not the first time she had used *that* particular trick.

• • •

The Resistance continued to be active, despite the arrest of Jean Bonnissol. Some of their actions were more farcical than heroic. In the very early hours of Sunday 9 January, they raided the main grocery store in Le Mazet. Between fifteen and twenty men armed with submachine guns arrived in two vans. They took sugar, coffee, cocoa, flour, jam, cooking oil, pasta, barley, potatoes, chocolate, baby soap and 780 litres of red wine, then capped it all by towing away the grocer's car, a dark blue Renault. They left behind 8000 francs in cash, and a note promising to return the car by next Tuesday at the latest.

As a result of this sort of operation, a *faux maquis* or 'fake Resistance' sprang up. Any local burglar who fancied his chances did his best to be taken for a member of the Resistance 'requisitioning' his loot. The historian François Boulet analysed 84 raids in the Plateau area in the first half of 1944, and came to the conclusion that 35 were carried out by freelance bandits, while 40 were carried out by the genuine maquis, and the remaining nine could not be classified either way. The situation presented the gendarmes with a huge dilemma. By now many of them believed that their patriotic duty required them to let the Resistance get on with its work, but that did not stretch to allowing the local burglars to do the same. In the end, Lieutenant Morel, the most senior gendarme in Yssingeaux, laid down a slightly satirical set of orders to his men: don't worry too much about catching thieves, he wrote, but see if you can get them to drop the loot while they are escaping. That way, nothing gets stolen and no harm done.

Then, in one monstrous weekend, the German occupiers and their Vichy collaborators turned the Plateau from stubborn civil disobedience to seething anger. The Germans were convinced (not without cause) that farmers were hiding members of the Resistance. On Saturday, 22 April, a force of German Feldgendarmerie together with French members of the GMR (Groupes Mobiles de Réserve or 'Mobile Reserve Groups', a paramilitary force set up by the Vichy government to combat the Resistance) swooped on the area around Yssingeaux and Araules on the Plateau. They stormed onto farms and demanded to be led to the concealed members of the Resistance. What happened next is unclear, but the outcome is well established. After the raids, the bodies of nine unarmed French farmers were found where they had been gunned down. The attackers then burned down three farms.

Not content with this, the Germans and their Vichy allies struck again the next day. Mobile units, reservists and military police mounted raids in the Tence and Yssingeaux area. Eleven men were arrested and taken away. The Plateau was now in uproar as never before. If ever the mood changed from resistance to revenge, it was now.

• • •

An important character was about to return to the Plateau. After her release from the Spanish prison in early 1943, Virginia Hall had initially cooled her heels—or heel—in London, working at a desk job in the American embassy. Despite the fact that she was on a Gestapo wanted list, her one ambition was to get back to France. To her own disappointment, and that of Maurice Buckmaster, the head of Britain's Special Operations Executive, the Americans chose to send her back to neutral Spain. She had arrived in Madrid in May 1943, working under cover as a correspondent for *Time/Life*.

Madrid was an odd and probably unwise appointment. It was awash with spies from both sides, so it could only have the effect of making her face and name better known to the enemy. She was able to do a bit of good, helping a group of old contacts from the French Resistance to escape to England via Portugal, but otherwise the Madrid posting was a waste of talent. The Resistance was clearly going to play a key role in the imminent battle for Europe. She wanted to be part of it when it happened, and that meant getting back to London and then France. Ideally she wanted to be somewhere not too far from Lyon, the territory she knew best and the place where she had already been active setting up Resistance cells.

In January 1944 she demanded to return to London to join the American Office of Strategic Services, the OSS, the forerunner of the CIA. The OSS worked in partnership with the British SOE, arming and coordinating the various resistance movements in occupied Europe. Through old contacts, Hall managed to get an interview with the OSS. It was agreed that she should work for them and not for the SOE: as an American, she should be part of her own country's clandestine service. Nevertheless, she would have to work closely with the SOE. At first the British were not sure they wanted her. The Germans knew her by her true identity, and that left her compromised. And, let it be said, her wooden leg made her easy to spot in a crowd. However, both the SOE and the OSS agreed to take her in.

Her first move once she was accepted was to train as a radio operator. She did not want to bring the extra baggage of a specialist radio operator with her into France; she preferred to travel alone and do the job herself. She also trained with the SOE in sabotage work. She was a quick pupil and already had most of the skills she would need to survive in Occupied France. By March 1944 she was ready to be inserted into France. Her orders were simple. 'In an area limited to Central France, examine the capabilities of the Resistance, in particular their manpower, and establish their requirements. Locate suitable landing fields and parachute drop sites. Assist the Resistance, and plan acts of sabotage.' That left a big question unanswered: where should she go in France? Her bosses thought about Cher and Indre in the Centre region, La Creuse in the Haute-Saône, and Nièvre in Burgundy, before coming up with a brand-new suggestion: the department of the Haute-Loire in the Auvergne. It was ideal. There was even reasonable access to Paris if she needed to go there.

So Virginia Hall ceased to exist. She would now be 'Diane', 'Marie Monin', 'Germaine', 'Marie of Lyon', 'Camille' or, to some, 'la Madone' or even '*la sorcière rousse*' (the redheaded sorceress). To the Germans she was 'Artemis'[51] or *Die Frau die hinkt*, the limping woman. In their estimation she was 'the most dangerous of all Allied spies'.

On Tuesday, 21 March, Hall arrived off the Brittany coast in a British motor torpedo boat. Most agents parachuted in, or were inserted by the extraordinary 161 Squadron of the Royal Air Force, using single-engine Lysander aircraft. However, 'Diane's' wooden leg made her poor parachuting material, so she chose the sea route. She was rowed ashore in a rubber dinghy, with her wireless set. At this point she was junior partner to a Frenchman named Laussucq, who had taken the name Henri Lassot, otherwise 'Saint' or 'Aramis'. Hall was simply his wireless operator. The two agents took the train to Paris. Hall moved into the flat of an old friend, Madame Long. Her new address was 59 Rue de Babylone, in the 7th arrondissement. She was in the heart of Paris, not far from the Eiffel Tower. Laussucq lodged with a sympathetic neighbour, who ran a guesthouse.

The two then moved on to La Creuse in the eastern department of Haute-Saône, and from there to Maidou near Crozant in the Limousin region of central France. On Tuesday, 4 April, 'Diane' sent her first radio message from Maidou to London. They were healthy and safe, she told them, and ready to start work.

At this point, work consisted of organising the 'Heckler' network. This gave Laussucq plenty to do, but left Hall with time on her hands.

She spent it investigating the La Creuse, Cher and Nièvre undergrounds, and training groups of men. For hard-pressed members of the Secret Army, Hall had a particular talent: she could organise guns. Once she'd put in a good word with London, the night skies would blossom with parachutes as containers of arms swung gently down into the eager hands of the Resistance. London trusted Diane. If she asked for guns, she got them.

Hall stayed on the move through April and May. Then she had a message from London to say that one of the SOE's agents had been arrested, and that Hall herself might be compromised. Time to move on once more. She returned briefly to Paris and Rue de Babylone, then shuttled between Paris, the Loire and Burgundy. Finally, a new set of orders arrived. She should proceed to the Haute-Loire.

• • •

Allied military leaders now set about preparing a simple trap. Readers familiar with the game of chess will know about a tactic called a 'fork'. This is a chess position where one piece simultaneously threatens two of the opponent's pieces. If the opponent moves one of his threatened pieces to safety, he loses the other. The role of the Resistance would be to act as an attacking piece in a gigantic military fork.

By the spring of 1944, it was clear that the Allies would soon attempt a landing on the Western European mainland. The Germans expected it to occur around the Pas-de-Calais, the far northwest department of France and the one with easiest access from England: at this point the crossing from Dover to Calais is both short and simple, only 33 kilometres across the English Channel. The Allies did everything in their power to reinforce this idea, with elaborate deceptions involving double agents, dummy wooden aircraft and fake radio traffic; in fact anything they could think of to keep all eyes on the Pas-de-Calais and away from the beaches of Normandy.

From 1942 onwards, the Germans had poured enormous energy and resources into building an 'Atlantic Wall', a line of defence that stretched along the Atlantic coast of Europe from the north of Norway to the Spanish border. When the Allied attack came, the Atlantic Wall was designed to hold the Allies at the beaches until German reinforcements could be wheeled in to throw the invaders back into the sea. So the principal job of the Resistance would be to stop the Germans bringing up their reinforcements. They would be needed to wreck railway lines, block roads, destroy bridges, sabotage airfields, attack barracks, ambush troops on the move—anything to keep the German reinforcements from reaching the front.

The Resistance had an additional role to play. If the occupying forces in, say, the Paris area succeeded in reaching the invasion point, then that would leave Paris as an easy target for a Resistance takeover. Wherever the Germans sent reinforcements forward, the Resistance would swoop on the vacated territory. On the other hand, what if the Germans decided not to reinforce their defences but ordered their troops to instead stay where they were and try to hold on to their territory? Then the Allied invasion force would soon punch a hole in the Atlantic Wall, and the invasion would succeed. So the presence of a powerful, armed Resistance was intended to put the Germans in a no-win fork. Try to reinforce, and you commit yourself to fighting your way across wrecked bridges, blocked roads and through ambushes. Succeed in getting through? Then watch your conquests be taken over by the Resistance filling the vacuum you left behind. Stay where you are? Then watch the Allies pouring in through a hole in the Atlantic Wall, sweeping everything before them.

That was the plan for invasion day. But even before the actual invasion, the Resistance had an important role to play in tying up German forces. A guerrilla army can wreak havoc on its enemies using very limited resources. As an example, during the 'Troubles' in Northern Ireland the British maintained between 9000 and 21,000 troops there; yet they were facing a Provisional IRA that counted its armed and active members in the hundreds rather than thousands. So for the Secret Army in France in 1944, a train derailed here, a 'collaborator' assassinated there, an army patrol ambushed somewhere else—all these meant that the Germans were kept constantly busy, and constantly on the back foot, rather than organising a defence against the inevitable invasion.

It would be nice to write that the Resistance on the Plateau set about the Germans with devastating effect in May of 1944. Nice, but untrue. A list of the actions fought is hardly the stuff of wartime derring-do.

12 May: Theft of 30 kilos of lard, six sausages, four legs of ham and five kilos of butter from a lady farmer in Le Mazet-Saint-Voy. The thieves told the farmer they were STO dodgers living in the forest of Le Meygal, and that if she lodged a complaint they would come back and burn down her farm.

20–21 May: Three young men aged between twenty and 25 staged a series of raids across the Plateau. They stole 1000 francs from a lady farmer at Chomor near Le Chambon; 2300 francs and four sausages from a farmer at Gratte near Le Mazet; 5000 francs and three sausages from a home in Ronsaveaux; and finally a massive 54,925 francs from an unnamed individual, consisting of 4925 francs from community funds and 50,000 francs from the individual himself (or herself).

25 (or 26, the facts are unclear) May: Four men armed with submachine guns broke into the town hall at Le Mazet-Saint-Voy and demanded that the secretary hand over the census records from 1921 to 1930. They then moved to the home of the town hall secretary in Le Chambon and demanded at gunpoint that she hand over the keys. Next they ransacked the town hall looking for census figures.

Having failed to find what they wanted, they took 500 meat ration cards, 500 bread ration cards and 500 assorted other ration cards. They left in a Peugeot car in the direction of Fay-sur-Lignon.

26 May: Four men robbed two farmers: they took 6000 francs, 30 kilos of lard and twelve sausages from the first farmer, and 1700 francs, fifteen kilos of lard and two legs of ham from the second. This time they didn't get away with it completely. One of the thieves was arrested by the gendarmes, along with an accomplice charged with receiving stolen goods.

27 May: The same men who had raided the town hall of Le Chambon on 25 or 26 May returned, heavily armed, and took away the 1925 census information, the register of food ration coupons and other pieces of census information.

It may well be that some of these actions were carried out by the faux maquis, the freelance bands of thieves pretending to be part of the Resistance. But your average rural village thief seldom carries a submachine gun or wants census information. Most of these raids have the fingerprints of the Resistance all over them.

• • •

At some point in the first half of 1944—the date is unclear—Pierre Fayol, head of the armed Resistance in Le Chambon, decided he should move house. Dr Le Forestier had received a tip-off from the gendarmes that the Germans were searching the area using radio-detector cars. They were also looking for someone called 'Rivière', one of Fayol's pseudonyms. He might already be under surveillance. He found new lodgings at Le Riou, near Le Mazet.

On 2 June 1944, what Fayol describes as 'real military operations' began. He was ordered to move some of his Secret Army troops to Mont Mouchet, on the far western edge of the Haute-Loire beyond Le

Puy-en-Velay. There they would be commanded by a Captain Hulot, who had arrived from the Loire, and whose cousin André Kauffman was one of Fayol's troops in Yssingeaux. About eighty men from the Plateau accordingly set off for Mont Mouchet. Meanwhile, Fayol was told he should stay where he was and await further orders. What, he wondered, was going on?

Four days later, at 6.30 am on 6 June, the answer became clear: the invasion began. By that evening, 160,000 Allied troops (including 73,000 Americans, 61,715 British and 21,400 Canadians) had landed on the beaches of Normandy. This was D-Day. The liberation of Western Europe had begun. And so had the Resistance's real fight.

Part V

...

LIBERATION

15

Guns

The first action fought by the maquis of the Plateau broke the most fundamental rule of guerrilla warfare, and failed as a result. Whole books are written about the military theory behind guerrilla actions, so there is something presumptuous about trying to condense it to a few sentences in a single paragraph. Nevertheless, the first principle can be stated fairly simply: hit and run. Don't get dragged into a head-to-head battle with a well-armed and well-trained regular army. You'll lose.

On 9 June the Mont Mouchet battle began. Some 3000 German troops, with air support, set out to rid the area of maquisards once and for all. The Resistance fighters were outnumbered five or six to one by regular Wehrmacht troops, and were not as well armed. The Germans launched their first attack at Venteuges, a few kilometres east of Mont Mouchet. At the same time, a group of well-trained and well-armed maquisards attacked the Germans at the tiny village of La Vachellerie, near Monistrol-d'Allier. Over the next two days the Secret Army fought a series of battles with regular German troops across the area. Predictably, the maquis took a terrible mauling. They lost 260 killed and a further 160 wounded. In addition, the Germans shot 100 civilian hostages. German casualties are unknown, though one Resistance report claimed 1400 German dead and 1700 wounded.

This is transparent nonsense. The outcome was not a defeat for the maquisards, nor was it a victory for the Wehrmacht. The 'Battle of Mont Mouchet' was more a series of inconclusive skirmishes, with neither side able to claim a win. After three days the maquisards were ordered by their officers to disperse, which they did. It was a salutary lesson, ending the dream of finishing off the occupation of the Haute-Loire with a few well-aimed bursts of Sten-gun fire. The Germans were a tougher bunch than that.

Pierre Fayol needed no telling. He could see the folly of a head-on charge. There were better ways to harass the Germans.

• • •

Sometime in the first half of June 1944—there is no record of the exact date—a fearful pounding on his front door woke Pierre Fayol. On the doorstep stood Maurice Lebrat, one of his Resistance fighters. Lebrat told him that one of his men, Sergeant Petit, had some important information which he had to convey to Fayol in person. Petit was waiting by the road outside.

Petit did indeed have some important news. A British agent, a woman, had arrived in Le Chambon and had demanded to meet someone senior from the Secret Army. Together with Petit and Lebrat, Fayol went straight away to meet her. For reasons that would soon become apparent, the meeting took place in a field well away from the village. Fayol found himself in the presence of a tall American woman—not British—who spoke French with what Fayol describes as a 'terrible accent'. She introduced herself as Diane. She was accompanied by a French woman who spoke not a word all night; Fayol never even learned her name.

Diane didn't waste time with pleasantries: she got straight down to business. 'Do you have sites for parachuting?' she demanded.

'Yes,' said Fayol.

'Can you muster up about forty men?'

'Ten times that number if we can arm them,' Fayol responded.

'Are you willing to follow orders?'

'What sort of orders?' Fayol asked.

'Sabotage,' said Diane.

'Yes, anything that isn't against the instructions of my chiefs.'

While all this was going on, Fayol heard an aircraft overhead. For the first time in the Ardèche, it delivered a man instead of arms: Lieutenant-Colonel Vanel, a Canadian, together with his radio, arrived by parachute. Fayol now knew why they had met in the countryside, not in the village. Clearly something important was happening.

Diane had a final question. 'What do you need?'

Fayol had a ready answer. 'Guns and explosives for operations, and some money for the quartermaster.'

Apparently satisfied, Diane told Fayol: 'Come and find me at eight o'clock tomorrow morning. We'll go and look around the area.' She and her French companion then left, while Vanel stayed behind.

A nonplussed Fayol asked Vanel whether he had to obey orders from the American. You bet, said Vanel. Diane was the equivalent of a lieutenant colonel.

The next day, Fayol and Diane, accompanied by Maurice Lebrat, checked some potential parachute sites. The American seemed to like what she saw. Between them, they agreed on some codes. 'The shark has a soft nose' would send the Resistance scurrying to a drop site near Yssingeaux. 'This dark moonlight falls' repeated three times would signal a similar snowstorm of parachutes at Villelonge. Diane then handed Fayol a bag that she said contained 150,000 francs, and abruptly ordered Lebrat to count it.

Lebrat counted carefully, and announced: 'A hundred and fifty-two thousand francs.'

'That's wrong,' said Diane. 'Count it again.'

Lebrat recounted the money. 'A hundred and fifty-two thousand francs,' he repeated.

Diane's tone changed. 'My mistake. I must have confused myself. I didn't use much money on the trip here.'

Both Fayol and Lebrat felt they had passed some kind of test. Diane's next words confirmed this. 'When I get back, I'll have a mission for you,' she said. She also told Fayol he could expect a parachute drop of arms at Cosne-sur-Loire, about 300 kilometres away in the Nièvre, on the night of 15 June. He would hear the code message confirmation on the BBC.

The radio now crackled between London and the Plateau, beginning with what was clearly a strongly favourable report from 'Diane' on both the Plateau and Pierre Fayol. In the message log of the SOE in London is the following entry, dated 18 June 1944:

VIRGINIA HALL:
Reports a group at CHAMBON of 200 well-led men, soon to be increased to 500, and states it would be worth sending 2 officers, a W/T operator and arms to this Maquis.[52] *(It is planned to put her in charge of this Maquis.)*

Meanwhile, Pierre Fayol received some more welcome news. As of 24 June, he was appointed head of the FFI, the Secret Army,[53] in the Yssingeaux sector. He was Jean Bonnissol's successor.

• • •

As we have seen, the Germans did not station troops on the Plateau. They had a group of soldiers convalescing in three hotels in Le Chambon, principally the Hôtel du Lignon; however, these men were unarmed and could never be seen as an occupying force. There are no precise records of what happened to them, but it is thought that around 10 June—four days after the Allied landing in Normandy—the majority of them pulled out of Le Chambon and headed for the nearest Wehrmacht base, in Le Puy-en-Velay, 42 kilometres away. It is also possible that some deserted and joined the Resistance. This would certainly have made sense for any Russians in the group.

The Le Puy force, under the command of Major Schmähling, was in no position to spread its handful of troops across every village and field in the Haute-Loire. So, for the Resistance, the Plateau was there for the taking. 'Capturing' a village consisted of not much more than arranging for a few men to arrive by car with Sten guns slung over their shoulders and announce that they had won. This was generally followed up by 'occupying' the town hall, the post office and anywhere else that looked useful. By that standard, Le Chambon was liberated early. On 14 June, only eight days after D-Day, André Trocmé felt able to return openly from his exile in the Château de Perdyer and resume his work as Le Chambon's pastor.

He did not like everything he saw on his return. Young maquisards strolled the streets, openly carrying weapons. There was talk of revenge. 'Collaborators' went in fear of their lives. As always, Trocmé chose to speak out, in a Sunday sermon at the temple.

The greatest tests for our country, and perhaps for our church as well, are still ahead of us. We have come to know, bit by bit, war in all its forms, and we are now cast into the furnace with the rest of the country. However, our little difficulties are nothing compared with the problems in burnt and bombed cities, and in those places where fighting is still going on.

These coming tests will tell us all what kind of people we are. There will be those who choose the selfish life, who seek to profit from the suffering of others. And there will be those who will instead allow themselves to be swept up by a spirit of enthusiasm, sacrifice and devotion.

The true Christian does not seek an earthly kingdom. He seeks the Kingdom of God. He does not use, in the fight against all forms of evil, the earthly weapons of violence, lies and vengeance. I have been happy to see, from the day of my return, that you have all stayed calm and steady. A spirit of moderation and gentleness should now reign among us.

The message was clear. Keep those weapons of the spirit sharp, but leave it at that—stay away from guns, and revenge. It was entirely consistent with everything Trocmé had said and done in the past. But it was far removed from the spirit of the times.

Édouard Theis returned to the Plateau at about the same time as Trocmé, so there were once again two voices preaching pacifism. But by now nobody was listening.

• • •

In the days immediately following D-Day, the Allies' luck held. Hitler remained convinced that the D-Day landings were some kind of diversion, and that the 'real' invasion would still come via the Pas-de-Calais. So he kept his crack Panzer tank divisions well to the rear, ready to reinforce the Calais area when they were needed. The Atlantic Wall had not done its job of confining the Allies to the Normandy beaches. Now the German reinforcements were not forthcoming, and the Allies were able to consolidate. By 12 June, six days after D-Day, the Allied forces had managed to link up along a huge, solid front across Normandy. Men and arms continued to pour ashore. Allied casualties during the landings were heavy: by 21 June they had lost 5287 killed, 23,079 wounded and 12,183 missing. But there was clearly no stopping them.

In the midst of this, Hitler unleashed his much-vaunted 'secret weapon', the V-1 flying bomb. This was a pilotless jet-propelled aircraft, known in Germany as the *Vergeltungswaffe*, the 'reprisal weapon'. On

14 June, the first of a swarm of V-1 'doodlebugs' crossed the English Channel from a launch site near Calais, and exploded on English soil. The doodlebugs were rightly feared, but they were never going to win a war, or even disrupt the invasion. The Allies continued their advance into France. And the BBC made sure everybody in France knew it.

By the end of June 1944, the situation in Occupied France was pretty close to anarchy. Who was the government? Was it the Pétain administration, still issuing proclamations from Vichy? Or was it the London-based government-in-exile of Charles de Gaulle, now in command of the Secret Army? De Gaulle's forces already controlled large swathes of the French countryside and were allied to the advancing British, American and Canadian forces. Who should a gendarme listen to?

On 8 June, two days after the Allied landing, the various brigades of gendarmes in the Haute-Loire had been ordered to go to the departmental capital, Le Puy, and join their comrades there. This had the effect of splitting the various gendarmeries, as some obeyed orders and moved to Le Puy, while others simply joined the maquis. On 11 June the earlier order was countermanded: the gendarmes were to return to their posts. But when the depleted numbers of gendarmes returned, they found the situation had changed. A report on Resistance activity held in the departmental archives in Le Puy spelled out the new situation.

Cars and motorcycles carrying armed maquisards are moving about in large numbers in the sector around Montfaucon. Moreover, the town of Dunières has been held by maquis forces since the evening of 11 June. They occupy the town hall, the post office, the gendarmerie, and the railway station, and they control the railway line and the roads. These Resistance forces come from the Ardèche, particularly from Saint-Agrève. They issue travel permits and they have detained the mayor, Monsieur Malartre.

The gendarmes' dilemma was well exposed on the night of 27 June. At around 9 pm, eight armed men set about robbing the Guilhot petrol station in Yssingeaux. The local sub-prefect tried to intervene but was brushed aside. The remaining gendarmes arrived and proceeded to open fire, seriously wounding one of the maquisards. The next day a handwritten proclamation was delivered to the police station.

Gendarmes,

I give you until tomorrow 29 June at 6 pm to hand yourselves in, together with your arms and belongings, at Saint-Agrève. If you don't carry out this order, you will all be shot. We will keep some of your families as hostages, and the family of the sub-prefect.

(Signed) The commander, French Armed Partisans 73201, French Forces of the Interior.

The following day at 9 pm, three hours past the deadline, 120 armed men stormed into Yssingeaux from Saint-Agrève. They cut the telephone lines, then descended on the gendarmerie, with the captured sub-prefect at the head of the party. They grabbed no fewer than 40 gendarmes, including the most senior officer, Lieutenant Morel, and a young woman, the daughter of a French government technical adviser. The maquisards announced that they were seeking vengeance for the death of one of their members—the man wounded two evenings earlier had subsequently died.

Somehow, calm prevailed. It was agreed that the dead maquisard should be buried in Yssingeaux, and that all the senior dignitaries of the town should attend the funeral service, including the sub-prefect. The whole thing passed off without further incident. But it was clear that the gendarmes were no longer in control of their turf.

• • •

Three tragedies struck the Plateau in July and August 1944, the first of them on 5 July. The Beau-Soleil guesthouse, which for four years had bustled with refugee children and students from the New Cévenole School, was now reduced to hosting three students. Other rooms were occupied by maquisards, some of them recovering from their mauling in the Battle of Mont Mouchet. Three adolescents were together in the house on the fateful day: Manou Barraud, the fifteen-year-old daughter of Georgette Barraud, the proprietor of Beau-Soleil; Manou's classmate and boyfriend, Jean; and a third youngster.

The trio of teenagers wandered aimlessly around the house. Most of the maquisards had gone into the village of Le Chambon, so their rooms were unoccupied. The three looked idly in cupboards and drawers. In a drawer, Jean found a pistol left behind by one of the maquisards. He picked it up. There was an ammunition clip still in place, so Jean removed it to make the pistol safe—or so he thought. He then began to fiddle with the safety catch, and with the trigger. There was still one bullet in the breech, and Jean accidentally fired it.

The bullet struck Manou in the abdomen, cutting a major artery. She fell instantly. Manou's older sister, Gaby, heard the shot from downstairs. She rushed up to the room. She and Jean did their best to comfort Manou. Then Gaby raced to fetch Dr Le Forestier. He and Gaby returned in his car to find a very weak Manou. Dr Le Forestier examined her, but it was a foregone conclusion. 'She's lost,' he said simply.

The entire village of Le Chambon was immersed in grief. Georgette Barraud was a close friend of André and Magda Trocmé's. Manou was buried in the Trocmé family plot in the Le Chambon municipal graveyard, near the Protestant church.

It was not the end. There was more tragedy to come, this time directly affecting the Trocmé family.

• • •

One of the bloodiest events in the story of the Plateau has been more or less airbrushed from history. It rates a couple of perfunctory sentences in most histories, and facts are hard to come by. Yet the Wehrmacht daily report of 10 July 1944 estimates that '135 terrorists were shot and some 200 killed in battle'. This is clearly a wild exaggeration, but there is general agreement that between 30 and 50 civilians were killed, and there are claims of around 50 German casualties.

The action took place over two days, on 5 and 6 July 1944, in and around the small town of Le Cheylard in the foothills of the Plateau, about 25 kilometres south of Saint-Agrève. Le Cheylard had been a centre for Resistance activity, and the Germans decided to put a stop to it. It may or may not have been a coincidence, but 5 July was a Wednesday, which meant it was market day in Le Cheylard. The streets were crowded at 11 am, when the first of many aircraft arrived overhead and began strafing the town indiscriminately.

At the same time, two columns of German troops now headed for the village. The first column came from the southwest, from the direction of Mézilhac in the Dorne Valley. The 17th Company of the Secret Army ambushed them at the tiny village of Sardiges. With the help of some Polish Resistance fighters, they managed to push the Germans back towards Noirol. One of the heroes of the day was a twelve-year-old boy named Roger Planchon, who had previously acted as a runner for the Resistance. He was awarded the Croix de Guerre for his part in the action,[54] one of the youngest Resistance fighters ever to receive such an honour.

The second German column arrived from the southeast along the Eyrieux valley from the direction of Saint-Barthélemy-le-Miel. There it ran into the 31st Company of the Secret Army. This time the Germans made no mistake. After bloody fighting, they pushed past the Resistance troops and on to Le Cheylard, which was by now in flames. Resistance reinforcements from the FTP (Francs-tireurs et Partisans, roughly 'French gunmen and Partisans') rushed in from Lamastre and managed to catch some Germans, but it was too late. Le Cheylard had been devastated. The Germans now withdrew, leaving the Resistance to bury the dead, including civilians. There are no reliable figures for German casualties, though there are reports of up to 50 killed or wounded. The same sources talk of 'dozens' of French civilians and Resistance fighters killed.

The appalling fate of Le Cheylard led many on the Plateau to wonder if any of their villages were safe. Should the Plateau be evacuated? Some people from the villages took to the forests to avoid being caught in the next aerial attack.

There was a further lesson. For the second time, the Resistance learned that it was too poorly armed to be a match for a well-trained regular army, particularly an army that could call up air support. Hit and run would have to be the policy until the Allies arrived. Or the Germans left.

· · ·

On 11 July 1944 the village of Fay-sur-Lignon 'fell' to the Resistance, the last village on the Plateau to do so. A mere five weeks after D-Day, the Plateau was now entirely in Resistance hands. The same appears to have been true of most of the Haute-Loire. The Germans still occupied the departmental capital of Le Puy-en-Velay, where the Gestapo, the German military police and the Vichy Mobile Reserve Groups were still on the loose. However, they were completely surrounded in Le Puy, and they knew it. On 16 July the local head of the Vichy government's thuggish Milice, wrote in his report: 'The encirclement of Le Puy is complete. Within a very few kilometres from the centre, [the Resistance] are masters of the Haute-Loire.'

Reprisals began on 12 July. Members of the 07.106 Company of the FTP shot two Germans and a Frenchman at Saint-Agrève. They were buried in a mass grave in Astier Wood. To this day, the area is known as the Bois des Allemands, 'the woods of the Germans'.

• • •

By 11 July, Pierre Fayol had begun to worry about the shipment of arms promised by 'Diane' for 15 June. Almost four weeks had passed without the expected coded message from London, and there had been no word from Diane. On 11 July, he sent Jacqueline Decourdemanche to Cosne-sur-Loire to investigate. To her astonishment, Jacqueline found herself face to face with Diane. The drop was that night.

It duly arrived. No fewer than 21 parachutes brought Sten subma-chine guns, Bren machine guns, Remington rifles and machine guns, ordinary hand grenades, Gammon anti-tank grenades, plus ammunition for the various weapons. With each parachute container, there was also a small box of tea marked 'Diane'. The FFI of the Plateau would now be properly armed. And Virginia Hall had some of the comforts of home. Hall also needed somewhere to stay. It needed to be a site with good radio reception, which suggested a hill rather than a valley. At first she lodged with Pierre Fayol and his family, spending a lot of time at the kitchen table coding and decoding messages. However, radio-detector vans were busy trying to track down spies, and it made no sense to put both herself and Fayol at risk at the same time and in the same place. She moved to Panelier, the guesthouse used by Fayol's friend, the writer Albert Camus. It had the advantage of being very isolated. Next, she moved in with the redoubtable Madame Lebrat, who had a farm between Le Chambon and Villelonge. Hall asked if Madame Lebrat would mind if she sent the occasional radio message from the farm. Madame Lebrat was indignant. 'What on earth are you going on about?

A radio transmitter! Yes, I'm very happy with that. But I don't want any guns in the house.'

At first Hall hid her code books and other incriminating material under the ashes in Madame Lebrat's fireplace. Then she found a complicated way of isolating one part of the house's water supply so that she could create a dry chamber. The code books and equipment would be safe there. Earlier, she'd had problems with interruptions to the electricity supply, which meant interruptions to her radio transmissions. So she built a makeshift electricity supply from an old bicycle. She removed the wheels and attached the pedal mechanism to a generator. She could then pedal for dear life while transmitting. For someone with a wooden leg, it cannot have been easy.

She now reported on troop movements and strengths, and kept London up to date on political developments and the mood in France, and particularly in the Haute-Loire. She was also the chief liaison between London and the Resistance in the area. If they needed anything, 'Diane' got it for them.

Hall was nothing if not diligent. The message log of the Special Operations Executive in London records on 18 June: '20 telegrams from this operator.' On 1 July it recorded: '21 telegrams received from this operator.' The 23 July summary for 'V. Hall' reads: 'Has 400 maquis in 5 groups. Awaiting arms for unlimited recruitment.'

In a memorandum dated 27 October 1944—in support of a request to have her awarded a medal for bravery—Lieutenant de Roussy de Sales wrote to his superior officer, Lieutenant-Colonel Paul van der Stricht, head of the Western European section of the Secret Army, describing her activities.

While in the Haute-Loire, Miss Hall made many receptions [Translation: organised many parachute drops], *and with the cooperation of a Jedburgh team she succeeded in organising, arming and training three FFI battalions which were involved in several engagements with the enemy and many sabotages.*

Meanwhile, Pierre Fayol began to play mind games with the increasingly demoralised Germans. He already had a German-speaking propaganda team in the area, consisting of a Russian Jew, Joseph Bass (of Network André), Otto Ernst, Guillaume Dest, and Fayol's wife, Marianne. He set them to work producing a stream of leaflets titled *Deutscher Männer in Waffen—Wahrheiten der Woche* (roughly 'German men at arms—Truths of the week'). The leaflets were widely distributed wherever German soldiers gathered. The 'André' group also produced Товарищи (*Tovarichi* or 'Comrades') for the benefit of Russians who might be induced to desert from the Wehrmacht.

Sometime around the end of July, the promised Jedburgh team arrived by parachute. It consisted of a French officer, Captain Foncroise; a Scottish officer, Captain Hallowes; and a radio operator called Williams. To the delight of one and all, Captain Hallowes arrived wearing a kilt.

London asked Fayol to look at the best way to put the railway out of action between Le Puy and Saint-Étienne. There was also the related business of harassing the Germans as they tried to move about, and in particular preventing them from breaking out of the Haute-Loire and reinforcing those resisting the Allied invasion. All in all, there was plenty to do.

On 1 August, Lieutenant Alfred Morel, the most senior gendarme in Yssingeaux, made an important decision. He could no longer serve the Vichy government. He joined the Resistance. It was a sign of the times.

• • •

Pierre Fayol soon had a plan for blocking the railway line between Le Puy and Saint-Étienne. The railway was single track only, making it a comparatively simple target. Fayol's plan would involve two teams. One would sabotage the track itself at the Chamalières bridge, about twenty kilometres northwest of Yssingeaux, where the railway line crossed the Loire. The other team would then set about derailing the locomotive as it arrived at the bridge. That should leave the line well and truly blocked.

On the night of 2 August they struck. The first team used explosives to rip a huge chunk out of one side of the stone arch bridge, leaving the track unsupported. When the ancient Mikado-type steam locomotive tried to cross the bridge, its massive weight would do the rest.

The second team boarded the train before it reached the bridge. The plan included—at some risk to the maquisards—making sure the French train crew suffered no harm. So the maquisards took over the driver's cabin and prepared to stop the train at the right moment. The crew were one thing: the passengers were another. As far as the maquisards knew, the passengers were Germans. (In fact they were Milice, but that would do as well.) The passengers could take their chances in the subsequent train wreck. When the train came to the bridge, the Resistance team stopped it at the weak point and threw two Gammon anti-tank grenades into the cabin to immobilise the engine, then got themselves and the crew out of the way of the explosion.

The broken locomotive crashed through the weakened bridge and sat jammed in the gap in the arch left by the earlier sabotage work. In Fayol's words, the railway line between Le Puy and Saint-Étienne was now 'indisputably cut'.

Fayol's success did not pass unnoticed. Although he had been appointed head of the Yssingeaux sector on 24 June, the formal letter of appointment must have sat on somebody's desk for over a month. On 8 August, the author of the letter, Lieutenant-Colonel Vanel, the Canadian who had parachuted into the Plateau and who now controlled the Resistance for the Ardèche, had added a handwritten PS at the end: 'Allow me to congratulate you on your successful sabotages in the last few weeks.'

A week later, on 15 August, the regular French Army began its first serious assault on the European mainland. A massive Allied force, mostly French and under French command, landed on the Mediterranean coast of France on a 150-kilometre front from Nice to Marseille. The Americans arrived first, on 15 August, while the Free French forces landed next day. They then pushed north, through Provence. The occupying Germans were now being squeezed from both sides.

• • •

The second tragedy affecting the Plateau began on 4 August. Two Resistance fighters, Jean Mercy and Edmée Debray, had been imprisoned in Le Puy for some three months. In the feverish atmosphere of the time, there was a real risk that the two men might be summarily executed at any moment. Dr Roger Le Forestier decided to go to Le Puy to plead their cause. Everyone advised him against it: Le Puy was the last piece of German-held territory in the entire Haute-Loire, so he would be crossing the 'front line' between the very jumpy Germans and the equally jumpy Resistance. His chances of being shot at by either side were high. Both his wife, Danielle, and André Trocmé begged him not to go. However, Le Forestier was not one to change his mind easily. He prepared a makeshift Red Cross flag, which he draped over the roof of his car to brand it as some sort of ambulance. That would protect him, he believed.

On his way to Le Puy, Le Forestier gave a lift to two maquisards. That in itself was foolhardy, given that they were headed for the local German headquarters. Worse, he failed to ask them if they were armed, or to check them for guns.

Against the odds, the trio arrived safely in Le Puy. At about 3 pm Le Forestier parked his car in the main square, and all three men got out. Their timing could not have been worse. The Resistance had chosen this particular moment to rob a bank in Le Puy, grabbing several million francs. The Feldgendarmerie swooped on the area, sealing it off and searching everything and everybody that moved. When Le Forestier returned to his car, the police had already searched it and found two pistols, carelessly and unforgivably left there by the maquisards. They promptly arrested Le Forestier. Possessing guns was a capital offence. The machinery of tragedy had been set in motion.

On the same day that Le Forestier made his ill-fated trip to Le Puy, the Resistance carried out another execution. Jean Rambaud, a student from Tence, was taken to a disused quarry between Tence and Le Chambon, and shot. He was accused of being an informer.

• • •

Jean-Pierre Trocmé peers out of his photographs as the spitting image of his father. He was the oldest of the three Trocmé brothers, a rather serious young man who was also a good scholar, talented pianist and promising poet. On the evening of Saturday, 12 August, he went to a poetry reading in Le Chambon given by the established French actor Jean Deschamps. The reading included a powerful and haunting rendition of 'Balade des Pendus' ('Ballad of the Hanged Men'), the most famous work by the fifteenth-century poet François Villon.

Villon had been convicted of killing a priest, and he is reputed to have written the poem in prison while awaiting his own execution. In the poem, Villon visualises himself as one of a group of hanged men swaying in the wind.

Now here, then there, as the wind changes
It tosses us around to its pleasure . . .

While he read this, Deschamps swayed back and forth in imitation of a body moving at the whim of the wind. It was a compelling performance. The whole poem is a plea for forgiveness and under-standing. It concludes with the lines:

Prince Jesus, who is Lord of all,
Keep us from the tyranny of hell:
Let the devil have no claim over us.
Men, make no mockery here,
But pray that God absolves us all.

Nobody can say with certainty what led Jean-Pierre to tie a piece of cord around his neck the next day and attach the other end to the toilet tank lever high on the bathroom wall. The most probable explanation is that he wanted to discover for himself what it felt like to have a noose around his neck and to sway in the wind. 'Balade des Pendus' was part of his school curriculum, and he might have been asked to recite it, or comment on it, at any time. Perhaps he could match the power of the Jean Deschamps reading if he knew the feeling at first hand?

Whatever the explanation, André and Magda Trocmé returned from a Sunday afternoon walk to find Jean-Pierre dead, his body suspended in a crouching position above the lavatory, his feet touching the floor, with the noose still in place. They tried to revive him, but it was too late. When Dr Riou examined the body, he was in no doubt as to the cause of death: Jean-Pierre's neck was broken, probably as a result of falling while still wearing the noose. There seems to be little question of suicide: there was no note, no history of depression and the bathroom door was not locked. He had been facing the bathroom mirror, probably studying his efforts to reproduce Deschamps' powerful performance, when he slipped.

The Trocmés were distraught. There is no account of Jean-Pierre's death in Magda's memoirs. She left it to her husband to speak for them both. André Trocmé even lost his faith in God, however briefly.

I could no longer pray because my prayer sometimes bounced against an angry God who told me: 'It is because you went into hiding and because you have been afraid of death. I took your son instead of taking you.' At other times my prayer simply disappeared into nothingness and I stopped praying because I could not have a dialogue with a God who did not say anything, who was elsewhere, in another world.

For the second time in little more than a month, the Plateau was called on to mourn the death of an innocent child. Jean-Pierre was buried alongside Manou Barraud.

• • •

Danielle Le Forestier went to Le Puy in the hope of visiting her husband and perhaps pleading on his behalf. She was refused. She made a second trip, this time accompanied by André Trocmé and Auguste Bohny, the Swiss Red Cross representative on the Plateau. This time she was led to the office of Major Schmähling, the most senior German officer in Le Puy.

To this day there is controversy over what exactly happened, and what was said at the meeting. However, it is uncontroversial to say that Danielle, together with Trocmé and Bohny, was told that a military court had sentenced Roger Le Forestier to death. That sentence had been commuted after Le Forestier had agreed to be deported and to work as a doctor in German factories. He had already left for Germany.

The truth was different. The question is whether Major Schmähling believed his story, or knew it was a lie. In the confusion, chaos and anarchy of France in August 1944, with decisions taken and countermanded on an hourly basis, it is simply impossible to judge what he knew, or even what he believed. But we do know the outcome. Roger

Le Forestier was transferred to Fort Montluc prison in Lyon, and hence into the care of Klaus Barbie, 'the Butcher of Lyon'.

On 20 August, on Barbie's orders, 120 Montluc prisoners, including Le Forestier, were taken to the village of Saint-Genis-Laval on the southwestern outskirts of Lyon. While Barbie himself supervised, the prisoners were marched, two by two, into an empty house. First they filled the upper floor of the house, then the ground floor. When all the prisoners were inside, the Germans systematically machine-gunned them all. They then set the house on fire with petrol and phosphorus so that the bodies could not be identified.

16

Victory

The Allied landing on the Mediterranean coast introduced a new element into the conflict. The Normandy landing had involved mostly American, British and Canadian troops. The Mediterranean landing, for the first time, brought the Free French Army as well as the Americans into the fight for France. Led by General Jean de Lattre de Tassigny, known to his men as 'King John', the Sixth Army Group had already taken the French island of Corsica. Now it marched triumphantly north on the French mainland, absorbing members of the Resistance into its ranks as it advanced. The Germans were now in full retreat.

On the evening of 17 August 1944, two days after the Allied landing, the German forces in the Haute-Loire were told by senior officers in Lyon that their position was, in effect, hopeless. Captain Ernst Coelle, who was in charge of the Russian contingent of Wehrmacht troops in the Haute-Loire, made contact with Lyon for the last time that afternoon. He was told to move his troops out of Le Puy and to head north to join up with the remaining German forces in Lyon. Colonel Metger, the senior German officer based in Saint-Étienne, appears to have been in Le Puy at the time, because the order was repeated to him there. Major Schmähling, who was in command of the Le Puy garrison, discussed the next moves with Metger, his superior officer.

The two men agreed they would move the Le Puy garrison out the next day, to link up with Metger's troops in Saint-Étienne, before moving on to Lyon. A motorised column would set out from Le Puy before dawn to secure the road as far as Bellevue-la-Montagne, about twenty kilometres north of Le Puy. That would open an escape route for the main body of troops, who would set off at midday. This first convoy would consist mostly of German troops, together with some civilians. As Schmähling did not have enough trucks, some of Coelle's Russians would have to wait at the Le Puy barracks until the next day.

• • •

All wars produce strange coincidences, bizarre misunderstandings and chance events. This process was now about to sweep up both the Resistance and the German forces in the Haute-Loire. Pierre Fayol's men had been told that Dr Le Forestier and two members of the Resistance were to be taken in a convoy from Le Puy to Saint-Étienne. Sadly, by then Roger Le Forestier was already in Fort Montluc prison awaiting his fate at the hands of Klaus Barbie, and therefore beyond the reach of Fayol's well-intentioned rescue efforts. However, the Resistance was not to know this. As far as they were concerned, any German convoy leaving Le Puy would very likely include Le Forestier. They would attack it. They could not know that the German convoy leaving Le Puy on 18 August was not a prisoner escort but the beginning of a full-scale retreat of the Germans from the Haute-Loire.

Fayol knew there was only one open route north towards Saint-Étienne out of Le Puy. All other roads were blocked by the Resistance, as was the railway line. The Germans would have to take a narrow departmental road, the D906, through Bellevue-la-Montagne, then probably turn right onto the even narrower and twisting D498 through the mountains to Saint-Étienne. The Resistance set off in a convoy of no fewer than 54 vehicles to set up an ambush. They chose Saint-Geneys, a village on the road north out of Le Puy, about six kilometres short of Bellevue-la-Montagne. Any German convoy setting off for Bellevue would necessarily pass through Saint-Geneys.

The terrain suited Fayol well. Just beyond the northern exit from the village, there was flat land leading to a forest on one side of the road, while on the other side the land was steep but covered with grass. Fayol placed the Y1 Company from Yssingeaux on the edge of the forest, and his own Section on top of the grassy hill. There they waited. Nothing came. After a long wait, one of the officers sent a motorcyclist to scout the village and report. Ominously, the motorcyclist did not return.

Fayol decided to take a look for himself. Two front-wheel-drive Citroëns set off towards the village, with Fayol in the lead. In the car with Fayol was a Dr Grunefeld, who had insisted that he wanted to take part in a military operation. The second car was occupied by three officers, Captain Hulot, Lieutenant Kaufman and Lieutenant Gaudelette. At the edge of the village they came under heavy fire from machine guns and rifles. It is impossible to know whether the fire was coming from the advance party sent off by Schmähling to clear the route as far as Bellevue-la-Montagne, or the main convoy itself, though from other testimony about timing it seems certain that it was the advance party. Either way, Fayol was in trouble. His car was hit. The occupants of both cars decided to make a break for it. Fayol continues:

> When we got out of the car, we were greeted by bursts of machine-gun fire. Dr Grunefeld and I were able to escape to the left of the road. My only thought was to get back to my Section, but this meant crossing 800 metres of steep open fields, keeping well to the left to stay out of the field of fire. I could hear bullets whistling all around me. When I turned round, I saw Dr Grunefeld lying flat in the grass. I thought I'd never see him again. The people in the second car took off on foot in the direction of the small wood very close to

*the other side of the road. In that short distance, Gaudelette was
killed and Hulot wounded.*

*When I got back to the Section, the first person to welcome me
was Abbé Volin, in full uniform. 'Ah, it's you,' he said to me. 'I didn't
know who it was, but I thought: this one's still standing.' I told my
Section to open fire again. We had M16 rifles and a Remington
light machine gun, and we were able to block the convoy for quite
a long time. Then they started firing mortars at us, and they were
getting a bit too accurate! So I gave the order to pull back. When
it was all over, the Germans had to slow right down, with forward
scouts and flank guards in position while they moved. That was
the moment we started harassment operations to sap the morale of
the German troops.*

*A few days later, Dr Grunefeld reappeared amongst us, hale and
hearty. On the day of the battle, he was the only one wearing civilian
clothes. He told us he had lain down in the grass and pretended that
he had been taken by surprise by all the shooting. A French lorry
driver picked him up and brought him to safety.*

Major Schmähling kept a diary, so it is possible to see these events
from the German point of view also. According to his journal, the night
of 17 August had been a busy one in Le Puy. Files had to be destroyed.
Various tradesmen and shopkeepers kept arriving at the barracks,
demanding to be paid. There was also the 'heavy responsibility', as
he put it, of taking with them all the civilians who had been placed
under German protection. This was largely a euphemism for the
various Vichy French *miliciens* and their families, who tagged along
with the Germans because they could expect swift retribution from
the maquisards if they stayed. At midday on 18 August, Schmähling
informed the prefect of the Haute-Loire, André Bousquet, that they
were leaving. However, there were more delays and the convoy did

not get away until 6 pm. When it set off, the convoy was several kilometres long.

There were more interruptions on the way. Vehicles broke down. Some of the convoy appeared to be stuck back in Le Puy, but a scout sent back to find out what was happening did not return. By 9 pm it was getting dark. Schmähling ordered the convoy to stop for the night. In three hours, they had advanced only a miserable five kilometres from Le Puy. Schmähling's diary records their discomfort.

18 August: It was impossible to pass the night in peace. We continually heard explosions, machine-gun fire, and grenades going off.

19 August: Daylight finally came, bringing a morning of bright sunshine. If the situation had not been so serious, it might have been possible to enjoy this adventure. The men and women, still a bit drowsy, got out of their cars. Mothers fed their children. The soldiers had their breakfast by the side of the road. It seemed peaceful everywhere. When the sun started to warm us up, our unscheduled halt didn't seem too bad. We were still there at eleven o'clock, waiting for Coelle and his Russians to join us. Then Lieutenant Heitz arrived. We had sent him to Le Puy to take a look around. He told us what had happened to Coelle: the Russians announced that they had had enough of the sound of guns. They weren't moving. The barracks was probably now in the hands of the Resistance. At this point Colonel Metger gave the order to advance.

By the time they had reached Saint-Paulien, five kilometres short of Saint-Geneys, Schmähling's car began to overheat. They kept moving, slowly. Two kilometres further on, they stopped again. The cars were overloaded. Metger ordered Schmähling to continue with his men on foot. They set off. Every time the column halted, Schmähling had to run 500 metres to the front to see what was going on. When they got close to Bellevue-la-Montagne, they came under fire for the first time. That led to a delay of an hour. By four in the afternoon they made it to the approach to the village of Estables, a few kilometres north of Bellevue-la-Montagne. They were attacked again, and again the column halted.

Schmähling was now ordered to clear his way through the village. He had a few Russians with him, and he chose them to support him. This didn't work out well: the Russians refused to attack, and instead fired their guns aimlessly in the air. Schmähling picked twenty German troops and tried again. They were continuously under fire, without being able to see the enemy. They moved ahead in stages. Schmähling saw the first of his German soldiers fall, screaming, a few steps ahead of him. The soldier had been shot in the stomach and died quickly. They continued as far as the first house in the village, which was taking heavy fire. In the village itself, they linked up with a second group of Germans. Schmähling wrote later: 'I surprised myself with what I could do!'

Meanwhile, Colonel Metger had managed to force the attacking maquisards back. The guns fell silent. Metger ordered the vehicles to reassemble in the village. Everyone should try to get some sleep, he said, while sentries kept the enemy away.

20 August: The day dawned bright and sunny. The village seemed completely dead. Not even a cat appeared on the street. The population had left because of yesterday's fighting.

The convoy prepared to move off, but progress was far from smooth. The vehicles continued to break down, and the convoy did not get moving until around 10 am. When they finally reached the next village, they were told that the road ahead was blocked. The maquis had blown up one of the bridges. The convoy crawled forward, not knowing how far it could continue.

> *In the evening we arrived at a village. A peasant complained that his only horse had been requisitioned without any compensation. I promised him I'd do something.*
>
> *In a house near Usson the Russians smashed all the furniture. The owner complained that a German had taken the only water bucket he owned. Although I was exhausted, I tried to find the bucket, but no luck.*

Progress was equally slow the next day, 21 August. Schmähling decided to reduce the loads on the vehicles in the hope that they would stop overheating. As a fine example of the surreal nature of the journey, the Germans wrapped up non-essential supplies in parcels and took them to the nearest post office, where they posted them on to themselves. There were 200 parcels in all.

> *It was 11 am when we finally got away. A few kilometres further on, we stopped again. Our troops needed to repair a bridge destroyed during the night by the enemy. The maquisards did not let up: they fired at the troops working on the bridge. All day we tried to respond. The road towards Estivareilles [eight kilometres after Usson] was under constant fire. Our column was now completely encircled.*
>
> *We were stuck. I had taken the Estivareilles road twice in the past, so I knew that without the bridge we could not move forward. The Resistance had us trapped.*

• • •

After the ambush at Saint-Geneys, Pierre Fayol returned with his men to the command post at the Château de Vaux, not far from Yssingeaux, to await new orders. Next day, 19 August, he discussed the situation with Captain Perre from the Lafayette group of the Resistance. Perre told him they had already attacked the German barracks in Le Puy, but his small group was on its own and it had proved too much for them. Could Fayol help? Fayol was willing, but he was still awaiting orders.

However, André Gévolde, one of the senior Resistance figures, returned soon after from Estivareilles to announce that the fight to the northwest was practically over. Fayol was free to take whatever action he thought fit.

Fayol quickly assembled his troops and headed for Le Puy to join the Lafayette group. It did not take him long to realise that the position of the remaining German troops—mostly Russians anyway, and all of them trapped inside Le Puy's Romeuf barracks—was hopeless. He decided to head down to the prefecture to see what was happening there. He wandered around the deserted corridors until he found the prefect's office, and installed himself in the prefect's chair.

He did not have to wait long. A group of Germans arrived in the form of a delegation. Fayol received them in the office, flanked by Commander Montagnon from the André network of the Resistance and two officers from the Lafayette group. The Germans had a request. Would Fayol agree to a ceasefire while they collected their wounded? Fayol wasn't having it. The Germans had fifteen minutes to surrender unconditionally, or face the consequences. Fayol assured them that they would be treated as prisoners of war in accordance with the Geneva Rules.

On the button of fifteen minutes, Captain Coelle, accompanied by a French-speaking German nun, Sister Elze Pelse, emerged from the barracks and surrendered on behalf of his remaining troops. The Resistance now had 170 prisoners of war: seven German officers and 163 other soldiers. They also had their guns, and their ammunition. With Schmähling's column now camped in the neighbouring French department of the Loire, the whole of the Haute-Loire was officially in Resistance hands.

• • •

Major Schmähling, still stuck on the Estivareilles road, had no difficulty assessing his position. There was no way out. He sent a messenger to Colonel Metger to tell him that a maquisard prisoner had assured them that if they surrendered they would be treated properly in accordance with the rules of war. At 7 pm Metger asked Schmähling to join him to discuss the situation with a French Member of Parliament who had arrived on the scene. The Frenchman was accompanied by Sister Elze Pelse, who could act as interpreter and who could also vouch for the facts. The Frenchman informed them that Captain Coelle had been taken prisoner in Le Puy, and that he and his soldiers had been correctly treated. The Frenchman offered them a time and place to meet to discuss their surrender.

The Germans had a serious problem. Clearly they would be correctly treated themselves, but what about the 'civilians' in the convoy? These were mostly French Milice and their families, and there was little love lost between the Milice and the Resistance. Might the maquisards want to settle a few old scores? That would have to be discussed as part of any surrender deal. 'Half an hour later,' continues Schmähling,

Colonel Metger and Captain Neukirchen[55] went with me to a farm-house, where we found a captain and some officers. The captain explained the situation very kindly, humanely and sensibly: all the hills around us were occupied. It would be impossible for us to get out of the valley. Some 1200 men were ready to attack our column. He was well informed about our situation: we could not count on the morale of the Russians, and we had civilian women and children with us, as well as the sick.

Colonel Metger asked for time to think it over—until ten o'clock the next morning. The Frenchman insisted: for a reason which he was not able to give us, serious consequences would follow if the surrender was not completed by eleven o'clock that night. The implication was clear: they would use bomber aircraft against us.

Our principal condition was that they should treat the civilians, the miliciens and their families, and the men and women who had put their faith in us, in the same way that they treated us. We asked that they would not hold it against the miliciens in general and they would take action against only miliciens who had committed acts that were against the law, and that this would be judged by a proper court.

The French captain agreed, and offered to send the miliciens to Montbrison, where the atmosphere was calmer.

Metger asked for a little more time, until eleven thirty, so that he could talk to his officers and the civilians. The French agreed. The German officers now sat down to assess their situation. They had a mere 80 combat-ready German soldiers, and most of these were needed to drive the vehicles. True, they also had some Russians, but they were likely to refuse to fight. They had twenty badly wounded German soldiers, a further twenty seriously ill Russians, plus 50 women and children to protect. They also had precious medical supplies like X-ray machines, surgical instruments and medicines, which they were reluctant to abandon. It was theoretically possible for the 80 fit Germans to try to make a break for it, but with 1200 maquisards raining fire down on them, the odds did not look good.

Metger then talked to the leaders of the milice, *and to some representatives of the civilians. He explained the situation to them, underlining the fact that the surrender would not go ahead without their approval. Following a discussion, they agreed that they would go along with Metger. He then took the decision.*

Sometime around midnight on 21 August, Metger surrendered. In the final battle, the Germans had lost seventeen men killed, while Resistance losses were seven dead. It was as inexpensive a result as either side could have hoped for.

For Pierre Fayol, the job was not yet done. His orders included ensuring that some sort of civil government filled the gap left by the departing Germans. Clément Charbonnier had already been appointed prefect-in-waiting for the Haute-Loire. Fayol went to Charbonnier's house and told him his time had come. Fayol says simply: 'I escorted him to the prefecture, and installed him.'

• • •

General de Lattre de Tassigny's Free French Army forces wasted no time. They had landed on the Mediterranean coast of France, 200 kilometres south of Le Chambon, on 16 August, a day after the first American forces. On 31 August a young Swiss volunteer, Hans-Reudi Weber, was making his way from a Bible class in Le Chambon to his home at the guesthouse Faïdoli. To his astonishment, he found a solitary French tank parked at the side of the road. The tank commander was waiting for a radio message from an overflying plane. The message would give him his next destination. Meanwhile, he was the first Free French regular soldier on the Plateau.

On 3 September, five years to the day since the outbreak of war, General de Lattre de Tassigny's main force reached Saint-Agrève and drove on to Tence, by way of Le Chambon-sur-Lignon. Contemporary photographs show scenes of wild rejoicing, with French tricolour flags flying from every building, crowds lining the streets cheering and waving, and soldiers in Free French Army uniforms waving back at them from trucks and tanks. The Plateau was now in the hands of not just the Resistance but the government of General de Gaulle. The German occupiers, and their Vichy French stooges, were no more. The next day, 4 September, the Free French Minister for the Interior, André Philip, spoke to the people of Le Chambon from the steps of the war memorial. His wife, Mireille, who had been one of the leading Resistance figures in Le Chambon, and had stayed there through most of the Occupation, stood in the crowd. Now they were reunited, and the Plateau was free. It was a great day.

For the Jews, mostly children, still in Le Chambon, it was not such a joyful time, however. A week earlier, on 27 August, the Russians had led the world's press into Maidanek camp in Poland. This was the first of the Nazi death factories to be liberated. What had previously been a terrible rumour had become an even more terrible fact: the Nazis had been systematically murdering people on an industrial scale. Not hundreds, not thousands, but millions. Here was the proof: a stunned and horrified press inspected gas chambers and crematoria inside an electrified barbed-wire fence and guarded by fourteen machine-gun towers. The handful of survivors told stories of bodies stripped then burned to ashes.

The raiding gendarmes had told the hostel managers in Le Chambon that the Jews were being 'transferred' to Poland where they could 'live in peace', and the children still on the Plateau had clung to a dream of being reunited with their families after the war. Now many of them would have to face the fact that their parents and grandparents, older brothers and sisters, uncles, aunts, all of those packed off in trains heading 'east', might have been murdered. Would they ever see their families again?

• • •

On 9 September Hitler unleashed his second 'secret weapon', the fifteen-ton V-2 rocket. It was bigger and deadlier than the V-1 'doodlebug' flying bomb, and it began its destructive career by falling into the London suburb of Chiswick. The V-2 was another fearsome weapon, but it was never going to win the war. The Germans were well and truly on the run all over Europe.

When the Germans surrendered at Le Puy and Estivareilles, the FFI found itself with 120 German prisoners on its hands. They were handed over to the French police, who were told they should be treated as prisoners of war. The police housed them in the Château du Pont-de-Mars, a few kilometres south of Le Chambon. Although it was closer to the village of Mars, the chateau was still in the parish of Le Chambon-sur-Lignon.

André Trocmé was never other than consistent. In the Weapons of the Spirit sermon, he had said: 'To love, to forgive, to show kindness to our enemies, that is our duty.' Now he proceeded to live up to his word. He went to the chateau and asked to speak to the most senior German officer. This turned out to be Julius Schmähling, whom he had met when pleading for the release of Roger Le Forestier. Major Schmähling was polite to the point of being obsequious. According to Trocmé: 'He saluted me and clicked his heels and called me *Herr Pfarrer* [Mr Pastor].' However, Schmähling was not yet ready to admit total defeat. 'The fortune of war will change,' he told Trocmé. 'Our Führer has more than one trick up his sleeve. For now, strategic retreat. Then, one of those offensives—and he knows their secret—that throws everybody back into the sea. Like at Dunkirk! Haha!' This was not the point of the visit, so Trocmé changed the subject. Would the major like Trocmé to conduct Protestant services for the prisoners? Schmähling could see no reason why not. 'Excellent,' he told Trocmé. 'I'm a Catholic, but I will give the orders and everyone will come along.'

So Trocmé began a regular routine. He would conduct his usual service in the church at Le Chambon on Sunday morning, then repeat the service in the afternoon at the chateau. He would even use the same sermon in both places, spoken in French in the morning and in German in the afternoon. The German prisoners packed the services, although that was probably attributable more to being ordered to turn up than to any burning desire to hear messages of peace and reconciliation.

Trocmé's actions went down badly with both the Germans and the people of the Plateau. On the French side, the mood of the time was vengeful. All over France, 'collaborators' were attacked, even killed. Women accused of fraternising with the Germans had their hair shaved off, or worse. German prisoners made easy targets. In the popular view, Trocmé's actions were tantamount to aiding the enemy.

On the German side, the soldiers listening to Trocmé's message were dismissive. The French would be sorry. The Germans had been fighting communism. The day was fast coming when the Germans would not be around to protect them any longer from Stalin's hordes.

The Germans were also unhappy about their food. While they had been running the country, they ate well. Now they complained that they were being starved, although in fact they were receiving the same rations as the civilian population of France. Nevertheless, Trocmé decided a little relief work might be in order. It was September, and in France the grape harvest was looming. Trocmé managed to lay his hands on a crate of grapes from the Midi, which he distributed among the German prisoners. This went down particularly badly with his parishioners. 'The "tourists" started muttering again that, after all, I was a "Boche",' Trocmé wrote subsequently.

• • •

Paris fell to the French 2nd Armoured Division on 25 August 1944. By the beginning of September, nearly all of France had been cleared of Germans, and the Allies were pushing on into Belgium. By 9 September they had taken Brussels and were closing in on Germany itself. However, there was an oddity: a handful of German enclaves clung on in France.

The Germans had well-defended submarine bases in the French ports of Lorient (on the south Brittany coast), at Saint-Nazaire (at the mouth of the River Loire), and at La Rochelle, on the Atlantic coast of France north of Bordeaux. The German garrisons in all three ports decided to hang on, and the Allies simply bypassed them. All three clung to their positions until the last day of the war, 8 May 1945, and then surrendered without a fight.

The island of Oléron, where I live, guards the entrance to the port of La Rochelle. The Germans hung on here, too. I have the front page of *Le Monde* dated Thursday, 3 May 1945, framed and hanging over my desk. The splash headline says *HITLER EST MORT* ('Hitler is dead'). Down below, but still on the front page, a headline reads: *L'île d'Oléron entièrement libérée* ('The island of Oléron totally liberated'). The story reads:

> *On the island of Oléron, the strongest resistance was met in Saint-Pierre from the SS. From Tuesday evening the whole island has been in the hands of our soldiers. 1,500 prisoners were taken, including the commander of the garrison. Our losses were small. The local people suffered very little.*

So my home, in Saint-Pierre, must have been within earshot of what may have been the last battle on French soil of World War II. Happily, my neighbours appear to have escaped unscathed.

• • •

Virginia Hall's movements after the liberation of the Plateau are not easy to trace (not surprisingly; spies tend not to leave a forwarding address). However, we know that on 25 September 1944 she asked to retire from the US Office of Strategic Services, the OSS, saying that her mission was now completed. A note in the files shows that on

28 September her resignation was accepted. Not for long, though: a second note, written the same day, suggests that she be·rehired. Hall replied by reminding them that her six languages—English, Spanish, Russian, Italian, French and German—must surely come in handy somewhere; if ever the US government wanted to create some sort of central intelligence agency to replace the OSS, she would be happy to serve with it in some overseas post. The CIA was yet to be established, but it had at least one talented volunteer waiting in the wings.

Virginia Hall's sense that her mission was over was understandable. For the people of the Plateau, there was still work to be done. As always, there is maddeningly little information available about the fate of those refugees still left there and who were now theoretically free to go. What is certainly true is that they could emerge, blinking, into the sunlight. They could use their real names and real identities. There was no longer any need to fear the knock on the door in the night. Secrets could be revealed: 'Mademoiselle Grabowska' and 'Jean-Claude Plunne' could meet openly as Mira Rosowsky and her son Oscar; Madame Berthe could acknowledge Egon. However welcome that change must have been, it still did not mark the end of their problems.

There cannot have been more than a few hundred refugees left on the Plateau after the Liberation. Of the Jews who had found shelter there, many were German, Austrian and Polish, so there was no possibility of returning to their homes, or even to their countries, in September 1944. For them, the war was still going on. So they remained on the Plateau, awaiting developments.

For French Jews, it was a different story. Although their homes may have been vandalised and their possessions stolen, very often the apartment or house was empty and waiting for them. Technically, they were able to return to their homes. Yet there was no quick exodus. People hesitated to move until the war had been finally and definitively won.

The children still sheltering on the Plateau faced the biggest problem. In many cases their parents had been 'deported' to the camps, so the odds were high that they had been murdered. In general, the children stayed on with their adopted families until the end of the war and often beyond. An enormous international operation set about discovering the fate of all those sent off to the camps. There were survivors from the camps, but the task of matching them with surviving children in another country was daunting, to say the least. Meanwhile, the children still on the Plateau had to be supported, which required money. Happily, the money could now arrive openly from the United States or Switzerland. It no longer had to travel in unmarked suitcases.

Oscar Rosowsky fell seriously ill at about the time of the liberation of the Plateau. He contracted typhoid, and for fifteen days lay in a semi-coma, with high fever. Russian doctors in Le Puy treated him successfully, and within three months he was back on his feet. He worked briefly as a journalist on the newspaper *Lyon Libre*, but his real ambition never changed: he still wanted to be a doctor.

Like many members of the Resistance, Pierre Fayol was quickly absorbed into the regular army, the Forces Françaises de l'Intérieur or FFI. He became second-in-command for the Haute-Loire. Fayol was a trained soldier, but some of the Resistance were not. Many of those who lacked formal training were now sent off to French military schools. Their new military careers would not involve quite as much action as they had seen in their maquisard days. General de Gaulle's government planned quite a different future for them. France would soon need a strong army of well-trained and disciplined soldiers . . . to occupy Germany.

• • •

When the European war ended on 8 May 1945, the exodus of refugees from the Plateau began in earnest, and continued until well into 1946.

Some were able to return home. Dr Mautner, who had borrowed the Trocmés' clothes boiler so often, returned with his wife to his native Vienna, and resumed practice as a doctor. Many of his old patients returned to him. Hilde Hoefert, the language teacher from Vienna who has some claim to being the Plateau's first Jewish refugee, also returned home, where she continued working as a teacher.

The Austrian Jews may have returned home but it was notable that, as far as anyone can recall, not a single German Jew returned to Germany from the Plateau. For them, the United States, Israel and South America were the popular destinations. They had enough of Germany, and they also had enough of Europe.

Dr Jean Meyer, who had fled with his wife and daughters from Paris in June 1942, had joined the maquisards and headed Pierre Fayol's team of doctors in the Ardèche. His two daughters, Ariane and Lise-Hélène, stayed in the Tante-Soly guesthouse in Le Chambon. Two of Dr Meyer's sons, Bernard and Francis, had also joined the Resistance. Francis was killed fighting the Germans in the Alsace. The rest of the family returned to Paris, to their old apartment. Dr Meyer resumed practice as a doctor.

Rudi Appel, who had lit Hanukkah candles with such pleasure, was reunited with his mother, who had hidden in Grenoble. They moved to the United States in 1946, where they joined Rudi's father and brother.

Alexander Grothendieck, a young German friend of Rudi's at The Wasps' Nest, appears to have been one of the first to leave Le Chambon. He had passed his baccalauréat at the New Cévenole School, and is generally thought to have moved to Montpelier in late 1944, with his mother. He went on to become one of the world's great mathematicians.

Nathalie Stern was thirteen years old when she moved into The Shelter, in July 1942. She waited three years for a letter from her parents, and thought they had abandoned her. But her parents had hidden themselves successfully in Agen, and called for her in May 1945, when they were certain the war was over.

Louis Claude Milgram was only three years old when his Jewish Parisian parents agreed to place him with the Ollivier family at La Bâtie de Cheyne, just outside Le Chambon. Knowing that circumcision was a sure giveaway, the Olliviers stopped using the name Louis and switched to Claude, or Claudie, and brought Louis up as a girl, treating him as their own child. He was reunited with his family in 1946, and had real difficulty adjusting to his new situation.

And so it went. For many of the Jews who had sheltered on the Plateau, their strongest wish was to obliterate the memory of years of fear and misery. They set about making a clean break with the past by changing countries. For many, the habit of keeping their Jewishness to themselves was hard to break. When the war ended, the Sauvage family—Léo, Barbara and Pierre—moved to New York, where Léo worked as a foreign correspondent for the French newspaper *Le Figaro*. Pierre, who had been born in Saint-Agrève hospital in March 1944, attended the French Lycée (high school) in New York, and lived a contented bilingual life in his family's adopted country. At the age of eighteen, in that very Jewish city of New York, he found out for the very first time that he was a Jew.

CONCLUSION

So how many were saved? As with everything to do with this story, accurate figures are hard to come by. Estimates range from a high mark of 8000 down to a modest 'more than 1000', but the most commonly quoted figure is 5000. The numbers game began with a plaque erected in Le Chambon in 1979, which saluted the courage of the people of Le Chambon and surrounding country who 'hid and protected thousands of the persecuted' against the Nazis. The plaque was signed by 'the Jewish refugees in Le Chambon and in the neighbouring communities', so it was generally taken that the 'thousands' who were sheltered were Jews.

Oscar Rosowsky was a member of the committee which organised the plaque. Two years later, in 1981, he was more specific about the numbers. In a paper published by the Historial Society of the Mountain, he wrote: 'I estimate at more than 5000 the number of refugees, more than two-thirds of them Jews, who passed through the region and were saved.' So we can take 'more than two-thirds of more than 5000' as Oscar Rosowsky's first detailed estimate of the number of Jews saved. Let's call that number 3500.

He has stuck consistently to the overall number 5000 ever since. He based this estimate on the number of false papers he and Sammy

Charles produced in their twenty-month forgery careers. However, in an interview given in 1982 for the 1989 documentary *Weapons of the Spirit* he said without qualification that 5000 *Jews* were sheltered on the Plateau. As we shall shortly see, this increase from 3500 to 5000 led to one of the more enduring myths of the Plateau story. Then in 1990 in his contribution to the symposium held in Le Chambon to examine the history of the rescue operation, he reverted to the old number, telling the audience the figure of 5000 should be broken down into 3500 Jews with the remaining 1500 coming from a mixture of *réfractaires*—young men dodging the STO—and members of the Resistance.

There are other numbers to take into account. Rosowsky and his team were not the only forgers on the Plateau: Roger Darcissac, Édouard Theis and Mireille Philip were all busy running up fake documents for Jews and others. To complicate things still further, not all the Jews sheltering on the Plateau had false papers. Some of them kept their own identity, despite the risks. And not all of Rosowsky's papers necessarily went to the Plateau. So estimates based on numbers of the Rosowsky bureau's forged papers are not the whole story.

The next tally comes from André Trocmé, who chose the middle ground. The author Philip Hallie quotes him as estimating the number of Jews saved at 2500. Hallie thought this estimate was too low: he was inclined to agree with the estimate of 5000. When the new Lieu de Mémoire (literally 'Place of Memory', but 'Memorial Museum' might be a better English description) opened in Le Chambon in June 2013, the catalogue was extremely conservative. It said simply: 'Around 800 Jews were officially registered on the Plateau, to which must be added the numerous *clandestines*. So it is impossible to know exactly how many were saved, but we know the names of more than 1000, and new witnesses are coming forward all the time.' In other words, the official estimate is a hesitant 'more than 1000 Jews, and rising'. So there we have the choice: Oscar Rosowsky, about 3500 Jews rescued (twice); then Oscar Rosowsky, 5000; Philip Hallie, 5000; André Trocmé, 2500; and the Lieu de Mémoire, 'more than 1000'.

There is a statistic commonly bandied about which is nonsense and should be disposed of straight away. It was given its most prominent recent airing by Barack Obama in a speech in Washington on 23 April 2009, Holocaust Remembrance Day. Obama said: 'We also remember the number 5000—the number of Jews rescued by the villagers of Le Chambon, France—one life saved for each of its 5000 residents.' Obama's version is more inaccurate than most. The usual formula requires that '5000 Jews were sheltered by 5000 Protestants, one for every man, woman and child in the community.'

These numbers are simply wrong on one count, and open to challenge on another. We can dispose of the 5000 Protestants straight away. There were not 5000 Protestant 'villagers of Le Chambon'. There were 2378. And there were not 5000 Protestants on the Plateau Vivarais-Lignon. There were 9000. The '5000 Jews' is more problematic, and still the subject of heated argument. Oscar Rosowsky now says that when he spoke about 5000 Jews in *Weapons of the Spirit*, he was merely repeating a joke doing the rounds towards the end of the war, that there were more Jews than Protestants on the Plateau. The numbers behind that particular joke are even more baseless. Not even the wildest optimists have suggested that more than 9000 Jews owe their lives to the generosity of 9000 Protestants.

The second error is to suggest that *at any one time* there were 3000, or 5000, or 7000 (the highest estimate I have come across) refugees on the Plateau. There were those who came to the Plateau simply because it was the starting point for the 'pipeline' to Switzerland. These refugees may have stayed there for a mere few days, just long enough to collect their false papers and Boy Scout hat before setting off for the Swiss or Spanish border. Others came to the Plateau to escape immediate danger; these people were usually from a large city like Paris or Lyon, where raids and round-ups were frequent and vicious. Having acquired a new identity, and new papers to go with it, they moved on to another part of France, usually in the countryside, where the dangers were less acute. The Italian-occupied zone was popular, as was the Cévennes area.

The numbers who stayed long term on the Plateau are hard to establish. The various children's homes supported by organisations like the Cimade and the OSE had a capacity of not much more than 200 at any one time. However, that does not take into account those in guesthouses like Tante-Soly and Beau-Soleil, and there were plenty; nor does it take into account those like Hanne Hirsch, who moved on to Switzerland after a comparatively long time on the Plateau. André Trocmé estimated that in the summer of 1942 there were 150 Jews spread around the various outlying farms and villages. That number would have soared after the German occupation of the whole of France, but again there is no way of knowing by how many.

So where does all that leave the question of numbers? Reduce Oscar Rosowsky's numbers to allow for some of his papers leaving the Plateau. Add some back in to allow for all the extra forgeries carried out by Roger Darcissac, Édouard Theis, Mireille Phliip and others. Keep in mind the comparatively small capacity of the various children's homes. Now allow for those who didn't bother with fake papers and false identities. Where does all that leave us? Taking all the possibilities and all the variations into account, I will stick my neck out and say Oscar Rosowsky's repeated figure of 3500 Jews rescued is probably about right. But the reader's guess is as good as mine.

• • •

What of the other Jews in France? The best figures available include some suspiciously precise numbers, but the consensus is that there were something like 350,120 Jews living there, of whom about 150,000 had French citizenship. That leaves about 200,000 'foreign' Jews in France, more than half the total, who were liable to deportation to the camps. Even among those with French citizenship, some 30,000 had been naturalised in the 1930s, and under Vichy law were vulnerable to having their recent citizenship taken away at any time.

Of the original 350,000 Jews in France, some 272,800 survived the war, about 78 per cent. The remaining 77,320 were murdered in the camps. The number of murders is, of course, shocking. Nevertheless, France had by far the highest Jewish survival rate of any occupied country. In Poland only nine per cent survived, while other occupied countries fared almost as badly: Greece, thirteen per cent; Holland, nineteen per cent; Yugoslavia, nineteen per cent; Slovakia, twenty per cent; and so on. So what was different in France?

There was a fascinating exhibition held at the National Archive in Paris from 28 September to 26 December 2011. Entitled simply *Fichés* (Records[56]), it dealt with the various identity documents used in France from 1848 to the 1960s. A section of the exhibition focused on the Vichy years. In that period, the traditionally officious French bureaucrats had gone into overdrive, creating a paper and cardboard blizzard of official means of identification: identity cards for French citizens, for foreigners, for public servants; employment permits; residence permits; provisional residence permits; travel permits; exit visas; transit visas; safe conduct visas; demobilisation certificates; internment camp release papers; special passports for STO workers; and more.

The various French departments rather than the central government issued many of these documents. So the papers and cards could differ in size, colour and wording from department to department and region to region. It was a forger's paradise. No fewer than 141 different specialist forgery teams were active all over France, supported by 124 delivery networks. Many Jews in France owed their survival to the work of these forgers.[57]

Some Jews escaped from France to Spain—the commonly accepted number is about 25,000. A total of 30,000 Jews escaped to Switzerland, mostly from Germany but also from France.[58] A smaller number escaped from France to the United States. So a significant number of Jews living in France in 1940 survived either by assuming another identity or by escaping to another country.

But that cannot be the whole story. Clearly an enormous number of Jews didn't leave France and didn't live under an assumed name. They could not have made it without the goodwill and blind eye of their non-Jewish French friends and neighbours. Jews were ignored or tolerated, and sometimes actively hidden, all over France. There was no overall conspiracy to protect Jews, nor any strong popular feeling that something should be done about their plight. These were isolated acts of kindness, but there were many of them.

So where does that leave the Plateau? The answer, surely, is that while there were individual acts of courage and humanity all over France, and throughout Europe for that matter, the sheer scale of the Plateau operation dwarfs all others. That is what makes the Plateau's story special. Much of the Plateau rescue operation was uncoordinated and spontaneous. Much of it was not. It involved a sophisticated money smuggling operation, the creation of a series of institutions to house refugee children, and a forgery bureau that was second to none. By way of comparison, Oskar Schindler saved about 1200 Jews; the Plateau saved about three times that number. The Plateau worked openly, then clandestinely, but always effectively.

• • •

Anyone looking into the story of the Plateau inevitably faces a further question. Surely, common sense dictates, someone in authority must have been turning a blind eye to what was going on there. Otherwise, how did the people of the Plateau get away with it for so long? The two most popular candidates for secret protectors are the prefect Robert Bach, and the German commander Major Julius Schmähling.

The case for Schmähling is interesting. He had been a history teacher back in Germany, at Aschaffenburg in Bavaria, so he may have had liberal instincts. He served in the German Army in World War I and remained in the Army Reserve afterwards. He joined the Nazi Party on 1 May 1937. When war broke out, he was called up from the Reserves. He was comparatively old for a middle-ranking German officer: when he took command of the Le Puy garrison in December 1942 with the rank of major, he was 58. So he was no young hothead. It is a matter of record that during this period the synagogue in Le Puy remained open, and Jews were able to attend school openly. We also have the testimony of a young French Jew, Serge Klarsfeld,[59] who fled with his mother and sister from Nice to Le Puy in September 1943. They had been told that Jews were safe there because 'the German commander isn't interested in them'. When Serge and his mother arrived in Le Puy, they met a rabbi named Poliatchek who told them that up until then the German commander had not mounted any operations against the Jews. It is also claimed, by those who propose Major Schmähling as the protector, that only thirteen per cent of Jews in the Haute-Loire were arrested and deported, compared with 22 per cent in France as a whole.

The same thirteen per cent statistic is invoked in support of Robert Bach. The case for Prefect Bach really comes down to whether he deliberately set out to deceive his Vichy government masters with a series of letters and reports claiming that the Jews had left the Plateau, or whether he was covering for his own failure to seize them, or, finally, whether he actually believed what he wrote. Having ploughed my way through endless manila folders of Bach's letters and directives, held in the Haute-Loire departmental archive in Le Puy, I have no sense of a man on a rescue mission. His style is rather that of a middle-ranking public servant doing and saying what he thought he had to do and say to keep his job. If that was the plan, it didn't work. The Vichy government sacked him in October 1943.

My strong feeling is that nobody in authority—not Robert Bach and not Julius Schmähling—sustained the rescue mission on the Plateau. I think the major force protecting the Plateau was geography. If Schmähling had had 30,000 men under his command, and if Prefect Bach had had 10,000 gendarmes willing to do his bidding, then between them they might have been able to station enough people on the Plateau to control it. But with the sparse numbers available to them, they had no chance. So whatever their views, if they wanted to impose their will on the Plateau, resources and geography were against them.

However, the Haute-Loire should probably be grateful to Schmähling for not being worse. I don't believe he was an active protector of Jews, but I'm sure he could have made their lives worse than he did. After the war, Schmähling made two trips back to Le Puy. On the second trip, in September 1967, he was welcomed at the town hall and generally well received. As this was at the height of Franco–German rapprochement while they jointly ran what was then called the Common Market, it was certainly in keeping with the spirit of the times.

• • •

There was a revealing incident in Le Chambon on the evening of Sunday, 2 June 2013. The brand-new Memorial Museum was due to open its doors the next day. As part of the lead-up to the opening, in the tiny cinema opposite the Le Chambon railway station, Pierre Sauvage showed publicly for the first time the remastered version of his documentary *Weapons of the Spirit*. At the end of the screening, which was warmly applauded by the audience, Pierre and a group of local historians fielded questions.

Suddenly a middle-aged man stood up from the audience and began denouncing the whole Memorial project, saying it was a waste of public money and that it made the perennial mistake of giving all the credit to Le Chambon and not enough to the surrounding villages or to the Plateau as a whole. The very fact that the Memorial was situated in Le Chambon was an example of this distortion of history. There was a rumble of disagreement from the cinema audience and the odd suggestion that the angry man either sit down or shut up, or preferably both. In the end, he stormed out.

It is only fair to say that he spoke for a lot of people. I have struggled in the preceding pages to avoid this very trap. Yet the facts cannot be escaped. Yad Vashem, the Israeli-based organisation charged with the task of singling out those who gave outstanding help to Jews during the Holocaust, has created an award called 'Righteous Among the Nations'. To qualify for this award, a person must be non-Jewish and have saved 'one or several' threatened Jews, at risk to his or her own life and safety or the lives and safety of his or her family, without seeking or receiving any reward. In 1990 Yad Vashem declared that 'the residents of Le Chambon-sur-Lignon and neighbouring communes' should be recognised as Righteous Among the Nations. Le Chambon is the only French village so honoured, and one of only two villages in the world to join the list of the Righteous. The other is Nieuwlande in Holland.

By 1 January 2001, Yad Vashem had recognised 67 individuals from the Plateau as Righteous Among the Nations. Of these, seven came from Le Mazet-Saint-Voy, four from Fay-sur-Lignon, three from Tence, two from Saint-Agrève, and one from Freycenet. The remaining 50 came from Le Chambon. So it is hard to tell the story of the Plateau without singling out the village and referring to it continually.

André Trocmé presents a similar problem. What exactly was his importance? The first thing to say is that his trip to Marseille was surely the beginning of the large-scale rescue operation on the Plateau. Yes, there were refugees in Le Chambon before, but until Trocmé's meeting with Burns Chalmers and the Quakers in Marseille, the Plateau was giving shelter to a mere handful of individuals who had found their way there largely by chance. By the middle of 1941 there were funded homes ready to accept children 'transferred' from the camps, and a well-organised system for moving them to the Plateau. That would not have happened without Trocmé's drive and initiative. Myriad others across the Plateau and elsewhere were important too: Auguste Bohny, Édouard Theis, Mireille Philip, Madeleine Barot and Georgette Barraud, to list some of the more obvious names. But André Trocmé's energy and intellectual gifts played a special role. It is true that the rescue operation continued unchecked when Trocmé went into hiding, but it was his involvement at the beginning that set everything else in motion.

That brings us to Charles Guillon, the forgotten man of the Plateau saga. As we have seen, he moved to Geneva straight after the Armistice in June 1940, and was based there for the rest of the war. Some extravagant claims are made on Guillon's behalf, including the suggestion that he organised teams of saboteurs to wreak havoc in factories supplying the Germans. He is also credited with organising teams of spies in French ports, within the French railway system and among French pilots, to report on German movements and activities. All of this may or may not be true. What is beyond doubt is that, from his base in Geneva, 'Uncle Charles' was a key figure keeping the funds flowing into the Plateau and thereby sustaining the rescue efforts of the Quakers and the Cimade. He made repeated trips himself from Geneva into Occupied France, almost certainly carrying money with him. He was on a Gestapo wanted list, but that did not deter him from risking his life crossing the frontier.

According to the admirable and reliable Plateau historian Gérard Bollon, Uncle Charles worked with the Resistance network 'Gilbert' and its leader Colonel Groussard, feeding information to British intelligence. His sabotage efforts were conducted in partnership with an old friend, Fred Harrison, a Paris couturier, who in turn organised volunteers from the Boy Scouts and the UCJG. Asked about it after the war, Guillon said: 'Thanks to the extreme caution of Harrison, we didn't lose a single man, to my knowledge.' Details are scarce on all of this.

There are those who would diminish Guillon's efforts by saying, in effect, that he led a comfortable life in Geneva, with plenty of food, while those who stayed behind on the Plateau suffered all sorts of dangers and deprivations. However, there is good evidence that this was not a view widely shared by the voters of the commune of Le Chambon-sur-Lignon. On 19 May 1945, Guillon was again elected mayor of Le Chambon, a job he held until 1959. He seems to have gained the respect of the whole of the Haute-Loire as well: in 1945 he was also elected President of the General Council of the Haute-Loire, and remained in office for four years. He continued to commute between Geneva and the Haute-Loire for his work running the world secretariat of the YMCA and YWCA.

• • •

In general, victory in war goes to the side that outdoes the other in violence. World War II was no exception. André Trocmé was a pacifist. I am not. André Trocmé believed that men can always be persuaded away from evil. I do not. In particular, I do not believe that the likes of Klaus Barbie can be persuaded to mend their ways by talk alone. Ultimately, they will be deterred only by a superior show of force.

That is not to say that Trocmé's pacifism was a failure. On the contrary, it must have saved innumerable lives. If the Plateau had resorted to violence in 1941 or 1942, it would have attracted a violent response from the Vichy government or from the Germans. That, in turn, would have spelled the end of the rescue operation. So the pacifism preached by André Trocmé and Édouard Theis played a significant part in keeping the rescue effort going, particularly in the early years. When the emphasis switched from protecting refugees to expelling the Germans, then it became a contest in violence, and pacifism was bound to be sidelined.

I have often wondered what André Trocmé made of his years after the war. He was not the complaining or self-pitying sort, so he kept his thoughts to himself. He visited the United States in 1945, largely to raise funds for the New Cévenole School, and while he was there agreed to work part-time for the MIR, the International Movement for Reconciliation, as its European secretary. At this point he was quite an international figure. The European MIR had its main office in Paris, so he was able to return to Le Chambon and continue part-time as pastor.

However, the Regional Council of the Reformed Church eased him out of the Le Chambon job as senior pastor, and even out of his home in the presbytery, in 1948. They claimed they needed a full-time pastor, who would need somewhere to live. The Trocmés moved to a long-empty rented house in Le Chambon village, near the railway station. This must have been a miserable and humiliating experience for Trocmé, and may have revived memories of his early years as an outsider. Could this be the reappearance of Trocmé the troublemaker, the André Trocmé who couldn't be found a parish? Trocmé hurled himself into fund-raising for the school, as well as his MIR work, but it was evidently not enough to satisfy him. After four years, he left Le Chambon for good, and agreed to work full-time with Magda as co-secretaries of the European MIR. Together they travelled widely, including attending an audience with Pope Pius XII in the Vatican, and taking part in a peace conference in India which led to a meeting between Magda and Indira Gandhi. In 1958, André attended a second papal audience, this time with the newly elected Pope John XXIII.

Throughout all this, the Trocmés must have faced a problem which is long forgotten today but which overshadowed all peace movements in the 1950s and 1960s. There were prominent and independent-minded peace activists and pacifists aplenty in Europe and the United States at the time, including world figures like the British philosopher Bertrand Russell. But the issue that dominated all talk of peace in the 1950s and 1960s was nuclear disarmament.

Quite simply, the Soviet Union was a late starter in the nuclear arms race. Britain and the United States had first tested an atom bomb in July 1945. The Soviet Union carried out its first nuclear test four years later, in 1949. By 1950 the Cold War was well and truly under way. The Soviet Union, four years behind in the arms race, set about discrediting the nuclear arms program of the west. Somehow 'peace' and 'nuclear disarmament' became irretrievably bound up together, and Russian-led communists often succeeded in hijacking the word 'peace' for their own purposes.[60]

For André Trocmé, a long-standing and principled supporter of peace, it must have been a nightmare. Every time he spoke, he risked being seen as a communist dupe. Here was a man whose pacifist beliefs had literally been tested under fire and found not wanting. He should have been a world figure, not someone sidelined as a bit of a crank. How he must have hated it.

• • •

According to the latest numbers from the United Nations High Commission for Refugees, there are over 11 million refugees in the world today, fleeing from an alphabet of troubled countries from

Afghanistan to Zimbabwe. At the time of writing, the country hosting the largest number of refugees is Pakistan, with 1.6 million people having crossed the border from Afghanistan. The Iranians have over 800,000 Afghan refugees as well. Next comes Jordan, with over 600,000 refugees, mostly from Syria, and Lebanon, with just under 600,000, again mostly Syrian. Kenya has some 550,000 refugees from Somalia.

You might expect that this would lead to a wave of sympathy and compassion around the world, with people lining up to comfort the oppressed and give shelter to the homeless. Not so. Around the world, political parties compete to see who can be 'toughest' handling desperate refugees. They are shipped off to remote islands or locked up in desert camps, in baking heat, and held there in appalling conditions, sometimes for years. In general, being 'tough' means being as inhuman as possible, in the hope of discouraging more refugees from arriving, or perhaps encouraging them to choose some other destination before they even begin their journey.

It would be nice to report that the world learned lessons from World War II, that the universal relief at the end of the fighting and the defeat of Nazism led the world to say 'never again', and mean it. Yet among leaders all over the world today there are strutting buffoons who steal and cheat and lie and torture, and get away with it. The mighty still oppress the weak. There are millions of blameless people denied dignity, security and basic human rights in Syria, in Zimbabwe, in Palestine, in North Korea, in far too many countries and regions around the globe.

I would hope that anyone who has read this book would approve of the actions of the people of the Plateau. If yes, then that leads to the question of whether there is anything any of us can do today to match their sheer decency and courage. Their story offers a ready alternative to selfish indifference, to the pitiless mantra of nothing-to-do-with-me. For those of us lucky enough to live in a liberal democracy, we can vote.

If we followed the example of the people of the Plateau and vowed to be part of the resistance against injustice, we could do it. How? A vote against 'toughness', and a vote for anybody with a credible policy for let's-do-something, would be a start.

WHATEVER HAPPENED TO . . . ?

Rudi Appel was reunited with his mother after the war, in Grenoble in France. In 1946 they migrated to the United States, where they joined Rudi's father and brother in Philadelphia. Rudi changed his name to the more American 'Rudy' and went to work as a furrier. Not content to remain an employee, he started his own successful company in New York. He still works. The company sells air-conditioning equipment, and some of its best customers are in Saudi Arabia. 'They're the ones with the money,' Rudy says philosophically.

Catherine Cambessédès Colburn enrolled at the Sorbonne after the war, then won a scholarship to Mills College, California, where she studied American Civilization and Anthropology. In California she met her husband, David, with whom she had two sons and a daughter. She taught French privately at home, then at Stanford University. She is still funny and pert and good company. At the end of 2013 she wrote to me: 'I live near San Francisco, but haven't forgotten Le Chambon. For all that California sunshine is wonderful indeed, but so are the steady, sturdy people of Le Chambon.'

Roger Darcissac continued as headmaster of the primary school in Le Chambon after the war ended. He became a rather austere figure, much admired but not always loved. He was inclined to dismiss the events on the Plateau as unremarkable: the people of Le Chambon had simply followed the dictates of their consciences, and that was that. He died in 1982. In 1988 he was recognised by Yad Vashem as one of the Righteous Among the Nations.

Pierre Fayol was absorbed into the regular French Army, the FFI, and became a career army officer. After a brief period as deputy head of the FFI in the Haute-Loire, he was sent to join the occupation forces in Germany, first to Baden-Baden, then to Berlin. Fayol was an engineer by training, and at the end of 1946 he moved to Morocco, where he remained until 1957. He died in 1994.

Charles Guillon was re-elected mayor of Le Chambon when the war ended, and served as president of the General Council of the Haute-Loire from 1945 to 1949. He rose in the hierarchy of the YMCA and YWCA until he was world secretary. He continued to divide his time between the Plateau and Geneva until his death in 1965. He was late to receive recognition for his wartime work, but in 1991 Yad Vashem declared him one of the Righteous Among the Nations.

Virginia Hall returned briefly to the United States when the war was officially over. However, she was quickly back at work. From 1945 to 1947 she worked for Voice of America, but as soon as the CIA was set up she joined, and worked in Paris as a political analyst. In 1950 she married a Franco–American former OSS agent, Paul Goillot, whom she had met during the war. She left the CIA in 1966 and retired to the small village of Barnesville, Maryland, not far from Baltimore, where she tended her beloved garden. After the war she received the American Distinguished Service Cross, the only one awarded to a civilian woman in World War II, as well as the French Croix de Guerre with palm, and the British civilian award the MBE (Member of the British Empire). She died on 18 July 1982. Right up till her death she refused all requests from authors and journalists to interview her about her exploits. 'Too many of my friends were killed because they talked too much,' she would reply.

Hanne Hirsch was reunited with Max Liebmann (see below) very soon after her arrival in Switzerland in February 1943. At first they both helped to run refugee camps there. They were married in Geneva on 14 April 1945, and Hanne gave birth to a daughter in March 1946. After the war, she learned that her mother had died in Auschwitz. The Liebmann family moved to the United States in 1948, with only $70 to build a new life. They succeeded. She and Max now live in comfortable retirement in a suburb of New York and keep in regular contact with friends from Le Chambon.

Max Liebmann learned after the war that both his parents had died in Auschwitz. Living in Geneva, and with a small child, he and his wife, Hanne Hirsch (see above), decided to look for a better life in the United States. There they quickly prospered. Max found work straight away. Later he went to business school to learn accounting, and made even more rapid progress. He retired as vice-president of his company, but that was not his only vice-presidency. At the time of writing he was senior vice-president of the American Gathering of Holocaust Survivors.

Pierre Piton disappeared from view after the war, and I have had real difficulty establishing what happened to him. When he first came to the Plateau and the New Cévenole School, he had intended to train as a missionary. He appears to have at least partly fulfilled this ambition: he left for Africa after the war, where he is thought to have helped to set up businesses in local communities. He did this, not as a colonial entrepreneur, but as a kind of one-man Peace Corps. If anyone reading this knows more, please write to me care of the publishers of this book, and I will expand this entry in future editions.

Oscar Rosowsky's story has one of the happiest endings of all those who took part in the Plateau adventure. When the war was over, he fulfilled his lifelong ambition to become a doctor. He went on to become president of the General Medical Council of France. He lives with his Italian wife just south of Paris, not far from Orly airport. One room of his apartment is devoted to his medical books and equipment, while another contains memorabilia of his career as a forger. He is still funny, mischievous and a joy to know.

Pierre Sauvage, born in the Saint-Agrève hospital on the Plateau in 1944, moved with his family to New York in 1948. He returned to France, where he fell in love with film at the Cinémathèque Française in Paris. The director Otto Preminger brought him back to New York as a story editor. His most important work involved returning to Le Chambon with a camera crew, as a result of which he wrote, produced, directed and appeared in his remarkable documentary telling the Plateau story. In the course of his research, he discovered the original of Trocmé and Theis's 23 June 1940 joint declaration, which led to the documentary's title, *Weapons of the Spirit*. Released in 1989, it won numerous awards, notably the DuPont-Columbia Award in Broadcast Journalism (sharing it with Ken Burns's series *The Civil War*). After its release, Pierre continued to fight for recognition of the Plateau's World War II rescue activities. For five years he ran a memorial exhibition in the heart of the village of Le Chambon, *Expo du Carrefour* (Crossroads

Exhibition). He argued (ultimately successfully) for the creation of a proper museum and Place of Remembrance. In 1982 he set up the Chambon Foundation, based in Los Angeles, and later the Varian Fry Institute. He lives in Los Angeles with his entertainment lawyer wife, Barbara M. Rubin, and continues to make documentaries; *Three Righteous Christians*, to be released in 2014, is the source of the quotes from Abbé Glasberg (p. 77) and Madeleine Barot (p. 78).

Édouard Theis remained headmaster of the New Cévenole School until his retirement in 1963. He is another of the forgotten men of this saga. He was overshadowed by André Trocmé (literally—Trocmé was slightly taller) and seldom receives the credit he deserves. Yet he was an active forger, he and his wife, Mildred, hid refugees in their own house, and he was an important *passeur*, working with the Cimade to smuggle refugees into Switzerland. He tended to be reserved—it is completely in character that he told nobody how or where he hid himself when he left Le Chambon in 1943. He died in 1984. Both Édouard and Mildred Theis were recognised by Yad Vashem in 1981 as Righteous Among the Nations.

André Trocmé, as we have seen, must have regarded the years after the war as something of an anticlimax. His intellectual skills were never in doubt, but his political skills were sometimes lacking. His confrontational style ensured there was no shortage of enemies in high places, particularly ecclesiastical high places in France. Nevertheless, he had friends: he was twice nominated (by the Quakers) for the Nobel Peace Prize. He was quite an international figure, travelling widely, including attending the 1958 Hiroshima and Nagasaki Conference to oppose the development of the H-bomb. He was also a very public opponent of the Algerian war. He retired from the MIR at the end of 1959, and in May 1960 took up work as a pastor in Geneva, with his own parish of Saint-Gervais. Again, his furious energy kicked in, and he raised funds for, set up and managed the Saint-Gervais-Philippeville Diesel School, which taught local Algerians to repair and service diesel engines. He retired from Saint-Gervais in 1968, and died on 5 June 1971. Shortly before his death, he was named as one of the Righteous Among the Nations by Yad Vashem. He refused to accept the medal unless it was awarded to the whole village and not to him alone. It was not his only distinction: he also received the *Rosette de la Résistance*, awarded for 'remarkable acts of courage that contributed to the resistance of the French people against the enemy'. He must surely be the only high-profile pacifist ever to receive it.

Magda Trocmé worked alongside her husband through their years as joint secretaries of the MIR in Europe. When they moved to Geneva, she taught Italian at the University of Geneva School of Interpreters, and at the high school in Annemasse, just across the border in France. After André's death, Magda stayed on in Geneva for a year, then moved back to France, to Paris. She was much in demand internationally as a speaker, travelling in Europe as well as the United States and Israel. In 1981 she was awarded an honorary PhD from Haverford College, Pennsylvania, sharing the platform with Rosa Parks, hero of the American civil rights movement. In this period, she devoted herself to putting her husband's memoirs into some sort of order, as well as making a start on her own. In 1986 she was named as one of the Righteous Among the Nations, receiving the award at the Israeli embassy in Paris. She died in October 1996.

Nelly Trocmé Hewett came to the United States in early 1947 as an *au pair* for a Quaker family in Pennsylvania. She attended Earlham College and graduated with a degree in English and French. In 1951 she married an American, with whom she had three children. They moved to Minneapolis-Saint Paul, Minnesota, in 1953, where Nelly now lives. At first Nelly tutored French privately, then in the mid-1950s began teaching French in college-prep schools. She retired from teaching in the 1980s and has three grown grandchildren. She is a tireless communicator, and maintains regular contact with innumerable survivors of the Plateau, as well as taking a lively interest in Plateau affairs.

Appendix 1

HUGUENOTS

The preceding chapters tell the story of what happened on the Plateau Vivarais-Lignon between 1940 and 1944. This appendix deals with the whole history of the Plateau and its Huguenot character. It is an attempt to uncover an answer to the most puzzling question of all: why did the Huguenots of the Plateau risk their own lives to save Jews?

For the better part of 2500 years, the Plateau Vivarais-Lignon stayed out of trouble by being off the beaten track. After the Stone Age, the first known inhabitants were four tribes of Celts calling themselves Vellaves (roughly 'mountain people') in the west, Ségusaves in the north, Helviens in the east, and Gabales in the south. They seem to have coexisted peacefully, an early example of the tradition of neighbourly live-and-let-live on the Plateau. The Celts and their prehistoric predecessors left very little behind: a couple of stone monuments known as *dolmen* and a scattering of basin-like sacrificial stones. Compared with the prehistoric treasure troves elsewhere in France, such as Brittany and the Dordogne, the Plateau is bare.

There are a few villages with telltale '-ac' placenames, suggesting that Caesar's Roman legions included the Plateau in their conquest of Gaul. There is Chavagnac near Saint-Agrève, Champagnac near Fay-sur-Lignon, Arnissac and Bronac between Le Chambon and

Yssingeaux, and more. However, other than these names and a couple of stretches of characteristically straight Roman road, the Romans also left no traces behind. There is no triumphal Roman arch, no amphitheatre and no bathhouse. The Romans left the Plateau pretty much as they found it.

As in so many parts of Europe, Christianity followed in Roman footsteps. The first Christian evangelists arrived on the Plateau sometime around the third century AD, and by 290 the town of Le Puy had its own bishop. But the Christians proved to be slow starters. Although Christian parishes were established on the Plateau sometime around the seventh and eighth centuries, the first known church buildings did not begin to spring up until around the ninth or tenth centuries, more than half a millennium after the first evangelists had arrived. This tardiness is more evidence of the Plateau's remoteness and inaccessibility.

In general, skirmishers and invaders kept their distance. The Muslim Saracens, for example, began an invasion of France in 718 AD, sweeping up from the south along the Rhône Valley, and by 725 AD had fought their way as far north as Autun, about 300 kilometres beyond the Plateau; however, they left the Plateau to itself. It was too remote, too steep, too easy to defend . . . and there was very little to loot or pillage once you had conquered it.

By the end of the first millennium AD, the Plateau was functioning more or less indistinguishably from the rest of Europe. Agriculture continued to dominate the European economy, so wealth and land went together. The Roman Church, with the Pope at its head, was God's earthly agent. It is not clear which ecclesiastical orders dominated the Plateau in the first millennium, though there are records of Benedictines from about the seventh century. In the second millennium, records show that the mysterious order of military monks known as the Knights

Templar[61] set up shop in Devesset and gradually expanded their parish borders through the twelfth and thirteenth centuries.

The first 300 years of the second millennium were a time of intellectual and political turmoil all over Europe. Crusaders went off to the Crusades, inquisitors tortured and burned alive supposed heretics, a succession of popes squabbled with a multitude of kings over who was in charge on earth, and King John of England had his wings clipped by his barons, who pressed him into signing the Magna Carta in 1215. Kingships changed hands, either by succession or conquest, and the latter often led to a new set of lords and landowners in the conquered territories.

The fifteenth century marked the beginnings of the Renaissance, when art and science flourished for the first time throughout Europe. Leonardo da Vinci had yet to paint the *Mona Lisa* (or invent the helicopter), but a spirit of intellectual curiosity began to eat away at the bleak superstitions of the Dark Ages and the Middle Ages.

This situation remained undisturbed for both church and state until 31 October 1517. On the eve of All Saints' Day a 33-year-old German monk called Martin Luther nailed his 95 Theses to the door of the Castle Church in Wittenberg, Germany. His specific target was the decision of Pope Leo X to sell 'indulgences'—bits of paper that absolved the purchaser of his sins, without repentance or even confession—to pay for the rebuilding of St Peter's Basilica in Rome.

In the language of today's computer world, Luther's scandalous attack on church greed and corruption went viral. It was part of the church's bad luck that the printing press had recently been invented in Germany, in time to spread Luther's accusations to the wider world. Within months, all Europe knew about the young monk's anger and disgust. In his lifetime, his books became international bestsellers, with hundreds of thousands of copies printed and sold. Luther's attack resonated throughout Europe, and led to the creation of breakaway churches—generally known as Protestant or Reformed churches—which did not accept the Pope's authority, and whose priests and monks displayed an unprecedented interest in simplicity, honesty and modesty. The new church movement quickly took root.

However, the new teachings of Luther did not take serious hold in the Vivarais-Lignon until sometime after 1528, when a certain Étienne Machipolis preached the Reformation message in Annonay, on the far northeast edge of the Plateau. Machipolis, so it was said, had heard Luther himself preaching in Saxony, so his message came straight from the source.

It was not all plain sailing. The next year a local priest called Laurent Chazot was burned at the stake, as a heretic, in what is now called the Place du Martouret (Place of Martyrs) in Le Puy. He was accused of preaching support for Luther's ideas. He seems to have been the victim of a bizarre miscarriage of justice, springing from a case of mistaken identity: he was accused of coming from 'Le Chambon *vers* Dunières', meaning a village in the direction of Dunières, which is fifteen kilometres north of Le Chambon and not at all in the same direction. In the similar-sounding Dernières, two noble families and a priest were known to be ardent followers of Luther. In fact, Chazot was quite a different priest, and not from either Dunières or Dernières. However, the local inquisitors were in no mood to be distracted by petty details, and carted him off to the stake anyway. He has some claim to being the Plateau's first post-Reformation martyr.

In 1554 a young theology student named Pierre Bourgeois de Beaux set off from Tence on the Plateau for Geneva, in Switzerland, to continue his studies. He arrived on 15 October. A second theology student, Claude Riou de l'Aulagnier-Grand, followed him, arriving on 8 August 1559. These two students opened up the strong religious and political connection between the Plateau and Geneva, while bringing back to the Plateau the most rigid and fundamentalist forms of Protestantism, as taught by Jean (in English usually rendered as 'John') Calvin. What neither the students nor the anti-Semitic Calvin could have predicted was that 400 years later, their brand of Protestantism and the Geneva connection would become vital factors in saving the lives of thousands of Jews.

• • •

The word 'Huguenot' is the French nickname for a Calvinist. Calvin was born in Picardy in northern France in 1509. He broke with the Catholic Church in 1530 and fled to Geneva, where he continued to teach and preach. There is no record of where or how the word Huguenot first appeared, though it was certainly in use by 1560. It is a slightly derogatory term, originally used in the same way an Englishman today might call an Irishman a 'Paddy', or an Australian might call an Englishman a 'Pom'.

The exact derivation of the word is still a matter of controversy. There are three main contenders. The simplest is that it is formed from the Flemish term *huis genooten*, meaning 'housemates', and refers to the fact that the early Protestants met in each other's houses rather than in churches. A rival suggestion looks to an early sixteenth-century Swiss religious leader called Besançon Hugues. Although Hugues died in 1532, he was regarded as the inspiration for the Amboise Plot of 1560, a French Protestant attempt to usurp the power of the French House of Guise and thereby bring about closer ties with Switzerland. As the Amboise plotters were about as popular in France as Guy Fawkes and the Roman Catholic Gunpowder Plotters are to this day in England, to be called a Huguenot (follower of Hugues) was not the obvious first step to winning friends and influencing people. The final—and only flattering—possible explanation is that a long-dead King of France named Hugues Capet was noted for his fairness and respect for the dignity of others. According to this version, the word

Huguenot simply means 'little Hugues' or 'those who follow Hugues'. I leave it to the reader to make up his or her own mind. I'd put my money on Besançon Hugues.

Although the Reformed Church grew rapidly, particularly in northern Europe, Protestants remained a comparatively small minority in countries like France. By the middle of the sixteenth century there were perhaps 2000 Protestant congregations, with 1.5 million adherents, in a total French population of around 15 million. However, the new religion proved very attractive to the French nobility in particular, so its strength and influence went well beyond its limited numbers. By 1570, Huguenots had their own castles, garrisoned towns, even ports, as well as their own schools and churches.

Understandably, the Catholic Church decided it could not simply sit back and let the Protestants get away with their impudent rebellion. They regarded Luther personally and his followers as heretics, to be hunted down and destroyed where possible. Thus began the Wars of Religion of the sixteenth and seventeenth centuries. These were fought with the kind of bitterness and cruelty that is made possible to this day when both sides in a conflict are convinced God is with them.

This time the Plateau did not escape the violence. The Protestants led the charge. In 1567 a Protestant force, recruited from the Vivarais lowlands, laid siege to Catholic defences, first capturing the town of Saint-Agrève, then seizing the Catholic commander in Devesset. They continued their rampage well into the following year. It was a rare military win for the rebels. Elsewhere in France, the Catholics had both the numbers and the military might, and they continued to dominate.

In 1570 Catherine de Medici, the wife of King Henry II of France, offered the Protestants some respite with the Peace of Saint-Germain, which, in one of its many provisions, specifically named Saint-Agrève on the Plateau as a place of Protestant refuge. The peace did not last. On 23 August 1572 Catholics set about massacring Protestants all over France in what has come to be known as the St Bartholomew's Day Massacre.[62] The bloodbath began at a Protestant royal wedding in Paris and rapidly spread to the provinces, with some 3000 Protestants killed[63] in the space of a few days. It is still remembered with bitterness by Huguenots all over the world. The plot had the full support of the French king, Charles IX.

The Plateau survived the massacre more or less unscathed. Whether as part of the plot or merely by coincidence, the Catholic governor of Le Puy had issued a decree a few days earlier that all non-Catholic church services were to end, and all citizens should take themselves off to mass. The Protestant citizenry in the lowlands around Le Puy decided that discretion was the better part of valour, and responded by either going along with the order or else scattering, some to the comparative safety of the Plateau and some to exile in other countries. This avoided an immediate catastrophe.

However, St Bartholomew's Day proved to be the beginning of a Catholic counter-offensive in the area. In 1574 the Catholics burned down the church in Tence and set about massacring any Protestants they could find. Four Protestant ministers from Le Velay were hanged under the orders of the governor of Le Puy. Under this pressure, the Huguenots of the Haute-Loire continued to split three ways: some simply capitulated, some moved out of France altogether and a third group retreated deeper into the Plateau, where the local population hid them. Legend has it that when the hanging governor of Le Puy finally arrived on the Plateau to see for himself what was going on, he found the population prostrate on the Catholic church's flagstones, singing canticles, while the Catholic priests calmly conducted a mass. It may not have been heroic, but it was highly effective. The Huguenots lived to fight again.

Religion and politics continued to mingle in France. By law, all French kings were required to be Catholics. In 1589, the Protestant

Henri de Navarre was due to succeed Charles IX then Henri III and be crowned King Henri IV of France. He was told he had to convert to Catholicism. This he did, famously declaring: 'Paris is well worth a mass.' However, he continued to look kindly on Protestants, and in 1598 he issued the Edict of Nantes, which, while affirming Catholicism as the state religion of France, nevertheless gave the Huguenots more or less equal rights of worship with Catholics. The edict was intended to end the Wars of Religion, and it certainly brought about a lull that lasted beyond Henri IV's assassination in 1610.

With Henri IV's departure, the tide turned. Henri's son Louis XIII was only nine years old when he became king, and he had for his regent the redoubtable Cardinal Richelieu, who set about breaking the power of the French nobility by razing their castles, and attacked Huguenots at all levels and at every opportunity. This was not a happy time to be a Protestant, even on the Plateau. Although Saint-Agrève was nominally a place of refuge, it had been put to the torch in 1580, and its protective walls had been knocked down. The battle raged up and down the Plateau: the Protestants would destroy a castle; the Catholics would sack a town.

Between 1622 and 1627, Richelieu triggered off no fewer than three Huguenot wars, ending in 1629, after the fall in 1628 of La Rochelle, whose siege the Cardinal personally commanded. Louis XIII's successor, Louis XIV (known as the Sun King), took things further, proclaiming that France should have 'one king, one law, and one religion'.

For the next 50 years, the French state did what it could to ensure the repression and destruction of the Huguenots. Meetings of Protestants were banned, and Protestant church services were declared illegal. By 1683, the Huguenots of the Plateau had had enough. Armed rebellion looked like the only answer. Led by Jacques Molle, a cavalry officer from Le Chambon, they prepared to fight.

The story of Cadet Molle (in French, *cadet* usually means the younger of two brothers, but it can also mean a young gentleman destined for military service, and in this case both meanings probably apply) is still part of Plateau legend. Molle was an enthusiastic Protestant but also a clever organiser. The Plateau was awash with spies at the time, and the authorities quickly got to hear about Molle and his plans. In March 1683, he was charged with 'rebellion against justice and disobedience to the orders of the king'. A party of archers was dispatched to Le Chambon to arrest him and bring him to trial. With a few friends, Molle barricaded himself in his house. The group, who were armed with pistols and maybe muskets, promptly killed one archer and wounded another. The surviving archers stood their ground and began shouting at Molle to give himself up, to which Molle responded by shouting equally loudly that the people of the town were on their way to rescue him, and the archers had better watch out. Molle proved to be right. According to the Provost in charge of the archers, what looked like the entire population of the town came charging towards them, roaring with fury. The arresting party beat a prudent retreat.

Next, on the orders of the Provost Marshal of Le Puy, a party of nine archers arrived in Le Chambon in April 1683. They were under orders to disperse the Protestant assemblies in Le Chambon and Saint-Voy and arrest the chief mutineer, Molle. This time Molle barricaded himself in a farmhouse, and again killed one archer and wounded another. No sooner had Molle wreaked this new havoc than two or three hundred irate townspeople, all armed, arrived at the farmhouse and began shouting: 'Courage! Courage! Courage!' The townsfolk then killed a second archer, and dragged the bodies of the two dead archers off and burned them. At this point the task of arresting Molle lost all its appeal, and the survivors from the arresting party fled. Molle was seen parading in the streets of Le Chambon later that day, two pistols jammed in his belt and looking very pleased with himself.

Despite small victories like Molle's, the pressure on Huguenots was now intolerable. Their churches and schools were closed down all over France; adults were imprisoned and their children packed off to orphanages. The king even chose his roughest dragoon soldiers, under a policy known as *dragonnades*, for the unlikely role of missionaries. The dragoons were forcibly billeted with Huguenot families (at the expense of the host family) and left to 'persuade' the Huguenots to renounce their faith. As a result, Huguenots fled in huge numbers to Holland, Belgium, Germany, Switzerland, Britain, America, and even to far-off South Africa. The numbers are hard to come by, but it's estimated that around 550,000 Huguenots converted to Catholicism and remained in France, while a further 250,000 left the country. This exodus was France's loss: in general, the Huguenots were from the wealthier, better-educated and most skilled section of the population. They were merchants and entrepreneurs, professionals and artisans. They took with them their money, their talent and their crafts, particularly lace-making, silk weaving, clockmaking and optometry, and often became among the most successful citizens in their new countries.

When the dragoons finally arrived on the remote Plateau, they set about their work with all the subtlety and courtesy traditionally displayed by occupying forces throughout history. There are plenty of records of 'tough times', including the abrupt commandeering of animal feed, or grain, or simply money, from local farmers. There were rapes of wives and daughters, together with arbitrary arrests and punishments. Contemporary records tell of some of the individual acts of brutality and cruelty. One party of dragoons was billeted with a farmer called Matthieu Riou. After generally maltreating him, they told him it was time he took himself off to mass. He refused, saying he would rather die. The dragoons then obligingly tied him to a horse and dragged him through the streets, leaving him for dead outside the church. Happily, he survived and was able to escape to Switzerland.

The importance of these stories, whether of the swashbuckling Jacques Molle or the almost-martyred Matthieu Riou, is that they have survived as part of the folklore of the Plateau. As with similar tales in Ireland or the Basque Country, these stories are told and retold, embellished and distorted, set to music, turned into fiction, exaggerated and immortalised. Streets are named after the heroes, and statues put up in their honour. In testimony given in 1990, Oscar Rosowsky remembered from his time on the Plateau 'the feats of arms which were recalled over and over during long winter evenings when the farms were cut off by snow'. These legends form the bedrock of the Plateau's stubbornness, its individuality and its courage.

• • •

By 1685 Louis XIV was convinced he had finally rid France of the Huguenots, and revoked the Edict of Nantes. The Revocation, in effect, declared an open season on France's remaining Protestants. Churches were destroyed, and Protestant ministers were given fifteen days to leave France or face execution. This was the beginning of the period known in Huguenot folklore as 'the Desert'. The church simply went underground. Services were held in private homes, in barns, in forests, in caves. Some of these Desert hideouts remained on standby literally for centuries, and were used by refugees on the Plateau during World War II.

The period of the Wars of Religion was surely the defining era for the Huguenots of the Plateau. They now knew what it felt like to be a persecuted minority. In the course of 150 years of religious wars, they also learned survival skills: how to keep their heads down, their eyes and ears open, and their mouths shut. Above all, they learned to stick together. Dumas's famous slogan for *The Three Musketeers*, 'one for all, and all for one', might have been created for the Huguenots of the Plateau Vivarais-Lignon.

From 1700 onwards, a period of relative calm prevailed on the Plateau. The worst of the *dragonnades* ended. The Catholic and civil establishment, both centred in Le Puy, continued to grumble about the presence of large (and illegal) Protestant communities in the hills beyond them. They made desultory semi-military efforts to drag the Plateau into line, but never sent a large enough force to do anything effective. There were occasional arrests, and some general harassment, but no major campaign—no final solution, if you like, to the Huguenot problem. Tackling the remote Plateau always seemed more trouble than it was worth. Meanwhile, the Protestants tried to keep themselves to themselves. They were aided by the minority Catholic population of the Plateau, who generally regarded their Protestant neighbours with a tolerant eye.

In 1787 Louis XVI—who deserves better than to be remembered only for marrying Marie Antoinette, obsessively mending clocks and parting company with his head—passed the Edict of Tolerance, which officially ended the persecution of Protestants. For the first time in the nearly 200 years since the original Edict of Nantes, events were moving in the right direction for France's Huguenots.

Then came 1789, the year that changed everything. The French Revolution received a warm welcome on the Plateau. The consensus was that if the French kings and their hangers-on, who had harassed and persecuted the Huguenots for 250 years, were now going to get their comeuppance from the revolutionaries, what wasn't to like about that? This optimism was certainly justified by the Declaration of the Rights of Man, proclaimed by the revolutionary government in 1789, which gave equal rights to all French citizens, including Protestants. The next year a new law granted a right of return to all those (and their descendants) who had fled France to escape religious persecution,[64] singling out the Huguenots for special mention. This was surely a time of optimism on the Plateau.

As with most revolutions, the initial optimism was short-lived. The revolution degenerated into chaos, then terror. Catholics briefly found themselves on the receiving end of revolutionary disapproval, as the French state turned its back on religion and the religious establishment. The church was seen as part of the Old Order. Some recalcitrant priests sought shelter from their former Protestant enemies on the Plateau, and were willingly taken in. The wheel had come full circle.

With the arrival of Napoleon in 1804 and a new civil order throughout France, the entire Plateau benefited. Even the Napoleonic Wars left the Plateau largely undisturbed. As far as the Huguenots were concerned, peace had arrived, and, left to its own devices, the Plateau prospered. In the course of the nineteenth century, new churches sprang up, both Protestant and Catholic, all over the Plateau. The Wars of Religion were over. Peaceful coexistence was the order of the day.

• • •

In the nineteenth century, two major innovations on the Plateau, one cultural and one political, had far-reaching implications.

While the Plateau remains to this day a largely agricultural community, breeding sheep and cattle and growing grain crops, a new industry took strong root in the nineteenth century: hospitality. As the industrial revolution brought new ugliness and grime to the larger towns and cities of Europe, the rising middle class of city-dwellers sought an escape. The seaside was the most popular answer, of course, but mountains had their advantages: they offered clean air, and a unique, idyllic charm. They were great places to hike, play tennis, ride horses, swim in a clean river, enjoy a picnic, ride a bicycle and pitch a tent. They offered a chance to relax outdoors that no smoky city could match.

In the first instance, Saint-Agrève was the major beneficiary. It was (and is) attractive, and at the time it was the largest village on the Plateau. So hotels and guesthouses appeared, and the wealthy restored or built gracious second homes there. Tourism was largely a summer trade: people came to the mountains to escape the heat, crowds and pollution of the cities. The bourgeoisie of Lyon, Saint-Étienne and even Paris decamped to the Plateau, mostly to Saint-Agrève, in promising numbers.

However, this began to change in the late nineteenth century. In 1886 the private railway company CFD (Chemins de Fer Départementaux, roughly 'Regional Railways') started building a substantial rail network on the Plateau. On 21 September 1902, with much ceremony, the line opened as far as Saint-Agrève. But to get to Saint-Agrève, passengers first passed through Dunières, Tence and Le Chambon. Quite simply, they got off the train at the earlier stops, and Le Chambon-sur-Lignon was the principal beneficiary. As a result, in the early twentieth century the majority of the tourist business on the Plateau shifted to Le Chambon.

Tourism was so important that in 1910 the town set up a tourist office, known as a *syndicat d'initiatives*, to try to draw in more people. They were hugely successful: richer families would spend up to three months at a time on the Plateau, and come back for more the following year. One family came from as far away as North Africa, and stayed for a month every year. The posters and brochures are fascinating; some even hark back to old battles. 'Protestants, take your holidays in Le Chambon-sur-Lignon,' one undated old poster advises, over an idyllic drawing of a village dominated by a Protestant church and nestling in picturesque hills. Charles Guillon took a similar and primly moralistic line. In his capacity as mayor, he wrote in a tourist brochure: 'Le Chambon is above all a place for families: it is an ideal holiday venue for children and teenagers. They can lead a perfectly free life here among the mountains and the pine woods, because our air is pure, and so is our mountain lifestyle.'

It all worked. People poured off the little narrow-gauge train, 'The Clog', into Le Chambon, Tence, Saint-Agrève and the rest of the Plateau, anxious to breathe in the clean mountain air, swim in the clear (if chilly) waters of the River Lignon, and generally refresh themselves away from smoky cities, grimy factories and terrible mines. The numbers are impressive. In 1934 the village of Le Chambon had a permanent population of around 900, but in July this number rose to about 4500, swelling to 6000 in August, then dropping back to 4000 in September. The people of the Plateau welcomed these strangers not simply as a source of extra money (though that must have been handy in a poor agricultural community) but also as an act of charity. They *knew* their visitors would be healthier and happier as a result of their time on the Plateau. So they encouraged them to come, to stay and to come back again. It helped everybody.

The other important development on the Plateau in the nineteenth century was purely political. The Huguenots of the Plateau had embraced enthusiastically the notion of equal rights for everybody as set out in the Declaration of the Rights of Man; after all, this simple idea had transformed their lives. So they remained loyally republican, a position that became increasingly identified with the political left.

France had a bumpy ride in the nineteenth century. Napoleon had brought stability in the wake of the French Revolution, then glory as he conquered most of Europe. After Napoleon's defeat and departure in 1812, France toyed with a restored monarchy (Louis XVIII), a restored republic (the Second Republic), a restored Emperor (Charles Louis Napoleon Bonaparte, Napoleon's nephew, who became Napoleon III), and finally settled on a Third Republic, which lasted until the arrival of the Vichy government in 1940. Throughout this period the Huguenots of the Plateau remained doggedly on the side of the republican left. Indeed, their voting record is almost suspiciously solid. Between 1876 and 1936 in Le Chambon and Le Mazet, the combined vote for moderate left-wing republicans, a few radicals and the odd hard-line socialist never fell below 90 per cent of the total. In 1914 the voters of Le Mazet set some kind of democratic record for a non-rigged ballot by voting 100 per cent for the candidates of the left. The left's worst showing was in the second round of voting in 1932, when a mere 81.2 per cent of the voters of Le Chambon chose the left-wing ticket. This dismal result was well and truly compensated for in the same round in Le Mazet: 98.8 per cent turned *à gauche*.[65]

In the 1930s, the politics of France, and indeed the whole of Europe, were deeply polarised between the far left and the far right. In a world still scarred by World War I and the Great Depression, there seemed little choice: either you were a socialist or you were a fascist. Russia led the way for the left. Germany, Italy and Spain led the way for the right. The towering figures in Europe were Stalin, Hitler, Mussolini and Franco. The Plateau wanted no part of any of this. It was in favour of the rights of man, as set out in the Declaration of 1789, and the political parties of the left seemed to respect this ideal more wholeheartedly than the parties of the right. Otherwise, there was not much to pick between them.

So we have a picture of the Plateau up to the outbreak of World War II. Its people had a proud tradition of resistance, and of sticking together. Their history and folklore told them what it was like to be persecuted, hounded and victimised. It also taught them that their best hope of salvation lay in solidarity, in trust between neighbours and in keeping a low profile. If they could manage these things, they could withstand anything the world threw at them.

Beyond that, they had developed a tradition of hospitality, which continues to this day. There were guesthouses aplenty on the Plateau, and hotels, hostels and campsites. The people of the Plateau had formed the habit of welcoming strangers into their houses. Without all of this, and without the courage and leadership of some remarkable men and women, the extraordinary events of 1940 to 1944 might never have happened.

Appendix 2

THE WEAPONS OF THE SPIRIT

This is the full text of the joint declaration by André Trocmé and Édouard Theis. On Sunday, 23 June 1940, the day after the Armistice was signed, Trocmé read it as a sermon from the pulpit in the Protestant church of Le Chambon-sur-Lignon, while Édouard Theis sat in full pastor's robes just below him. Although it was read by Trocmé alone, it is clear from the first sentence that it was intended as a joint statement by the two pastors. Translating it is no easy task. For instance, in the first paragraph, the declaration quotes Marc Boegner's 'appelle à l'Église protestante de France à l'humiliation', which translates literally as a 'call to the Protestant church of France to humiliation'; however, in French, words like 'humiliation' carry a different weight and meaning than the same word in English, although the dictionary would have you believe otherwise. I have translated this as a call to the French Protestant Church 'to humble itself', while later in the sermon I have translated it as 'to hang its head in shame', which is probably what an English speaker would have said in the same circumstances. So while what follows sticks very closely to the original, it is not a word-for-word match. My major concern has been to preserve the rhythm, power and defiance of Theis and Trocmé's words, which might otherwise have been, as they say, lost in translation.

—PG

Brothers and sisters,

The President of the Protestant Federation yesterday gave a radio talk, to which we would like to add our voice. In his talk, Monsieur Boegner called on the Protestant Church of France to humble itself for the mistakes that led our people to our present state.

Just as the Israelites of the Old Testament suffered, so we have come to our moment of suffering and humiliation.

Therefore let us all be humble, and be ready to carry our own share of responsibility for the general catastrophe. Let us hang our heads in shame for the sins we have committed, and for others' sins that we failed to prevent; for letting things drift; for our lack of courage; for all of these failings that made it impossible for us to stand firm as storms approached; for our lack of love when faced with others' suffering; for our lack of faith in God, and our worship of wealth and power; for all the feelings unworthy of Christ which we have tolerated or kept alive in our hearts: in a word, for the sins we all share, which are the real and only cause of all the unimaginable tragedies that befall us.

Let us hang our heads in shame before God, each one of us, as individuals, as leaders or members of a family, as citizens and as Christians, as pastors and church elders, as youth leaders, as members of youth groups, as Church worshippers. We beg God to forgive us for our own sins and for the sins of our people, for the sins of humanity today and of the Church today. In this we are united. It is to God alone that we must look for relief from our suffering. However, we must guard against some forms of humility that would be disobedience of God.

First, let us be on our guard against confusing humility with hopelessness, and from believing and spreading the word that all is lost. It is not true that all is lost. Gospel truth is not lost, and it will be proclaimed loud and clear in our church from this pulpit, and during our pastoral visits. The word of God is not lost, and that is where you will find all the promises and all the possibilities of a recovery for all of us, for our people, and for the Church. Faith is not lost: real humility doesn't weaken faith; it leads to a deeper faith in God, a more powerful desire to serve.

Second, we must guard against humbling ourselves not for our own sins but for the sins of others, in a spirit of bitterness and rancour. In recent days, during pastoral visits, we have heard many complaints: from soldiers against their officers, and from officers against their soldiers; from bosses against their workers, and from workers against their bosses; from rich against poor, and from poor against rich; from pacifists against patriots, and from patriots against pacifists; from believers against non-believers, and from non-believers against believers. Each accuses the other, each tries to dodge his or her own responsibilities and pass the blame on to their fellow citizens, or foreign nations, forgetting that only God can judge and measure the guilt of each of us. We do not believe that this kind of humility leads us on the proper road to recovery for our country, and for the Church.

Third, in our shame, let us not lose our faith and our convictions, based on the Gospel. We may not have made proper use of the freedom that was given to us, but let us not give up that freedom, under the cover of humility, and turn ourselves into slaves; let us not give in without a struggle to the new ideologies. Have no illusions: the events of recent days mean that the totalitarian doctrine of violence now enjoys formidable prestige in the eyes of the world because it has, from the human point of view, been impressively successful.

So, yes, let us hang our heads in shame, but let us not bow down to such a doctrine. We are convinced that the power of this totalitarianism is like the authority of the Beast of the Apocalypse, described in chapter 18 of the Book of Revelation. It is nothing other than anti-Christianity. For us it is a matter of conscience to spread that message today, as yesterday. We know well that the sons and daughters of our church gave their lives to fight this totalitarian doctrine. So humbly admit to your sins, yes, but don't give in to a new heathenism. It is by giving our lives to Jesus Christ, according to his Gospel, to his universal Church, that we keep our faith and show true humility.

In this call to Christian humility, brothers and sisters, we would like to add a few exhortations addressed to you in the name of our Lord Jesus Christ. First, let us abandon today all divisions among Christians, and all squabbles among the French people. Let us stop labelling ourselves and others, because that is the language of scorn: let us abandon right and left, peasants, workers, intellectuals, proletarians and plutocrats, all the terms we use to accuse each other of some wrongdoing or other. Let us learn to trust each other again, to receive each other, to welcome each other, reminding ourselves that every time we come together, like the early Christians, we are brothers and sisters in Christ.

Then, having abandoned these suspicions and hatreds, and the political passions that go with them, let us gather resolutely around Jesus Christ, the head of the universal Church, and embrace his Gospel, and only his Gospel, as our source of inspiration, obedience and action.

Finally, understand that the return to obedience obliges us to make some breaks: breaks with the world, and breaks with ways of living that we have accepted so far. We face powerful heathen pressures on ourselves and on our families, pressures to force us to cave in to this totalitarian ideology. If this ideology cannot immediately subjugate our souls, it will try, at the very least, to make us cave in with our bodies. The duty of Christians is to resist the violence directed at our consciences with the weapons of the spirit. We appeal to all our brothers in Christ to refuse to agree with or cooperate in violence, especially in the coming days when that violence is directed against the English people.

To love, to forgive, to show kindness to our enemies, that is our duty. But we must do our duty without conceding defeat, without servility, without cowardice. We will resist when our enemies demand that we act in ways that go against the teachings of the Gospel. We will resist without fear, without pride, and without hatred. But this moral resistance is not possible without a clean break from the selfishness that, for a long time, has ruled our lives. We face a period of suffering, perhaps even shortages of food. We have all more or less worshipped Mammon; we have all basked in the selfish comforts of our close family, in easy pleasure, in idle drinking. We will now be made to do without many things. We will be tempted to play our own selfish game, to cling on to what we have, to be better off than our brothers. Let us abandon, brothers and sisters, our pride and our egotism, our love of money and our faith in material possessions, and learn to trust God in Heaven, both today and tomorrow, to bring us our daily bread, and to share that bread with our brothers and sisters.

May God free us from both worry and complacency. May he give us his peace, which nothing and nobody can take away from his children. May he comfort us in our sorrows and in all our trials. May he see fit to make each of us humble and faithful members of the Church of Jesus Christ, of the body of Christ, waiting for his kingdom of justice and love, where his will shall be done on earth as it is in heaven.

ACKNOWLEDGEMENTS

Writing is supposed to be a lonely business, but the writing of a book like this is impossible without the continual, massive and totally unrewarded support of a multitude of experts and participants, and others who simply take an interest and want to help.

My first thanks must go to those eyewitnesses who gave generously of their time. When I was starting out on my research, I conducted long interviews with Oscar Rosowsky, Max and Hanne Liebmann, Rudy Appel, Nelly Trocmé Hewett, Catherine Cambessédès and Pierre Sauvage. Their contribution did not end with the interviews: afterwards I bombarded them with emails and phone calls demanding impossible acts of recall. What was the *exact* date when this or that happened? *How much* money was in the suitcase? Perhaps as an act of self-defence, some of them read the manuscript when it was still a work in progress, and made myriad helpful suggestions and corrections. I am deeply grateful to them all.

Nelly Trocmé Hewett needs special mention. She more than any other suffered from my endless emails and queries. She generously and unhesitatingly introduced me to her extraordinary network of friends from the Plateau. She is a retired schoolteacher, and her habit of correcting pupils' homework has happily survived into her retirement.

If the accents on French words like Cévenole and Saint-Agrève now face the right way in the preceding text, readers can thank Nelly and her eagle eye. As well as saving my stumbling French from many a spelling or grammatical howler, Nelly was also a remarkable fact checker. Any mistakes in this book are mine and mine alone, and there would have been more of them without Nelly's help. *Merci*, Nelly.

Catherine Cambessédès, another retired French teacher, also did her bit correcting my homework. At one point she sent me 27 pages of handwritten notes, many of them adding revealing little details to the story she first related to me when I interviewed her back in May 2012. *Merci*, Catherine.

My thanks to Dr Wendy Chmielewski for permission to quote from the André Trocmé and Magda Trocmé papers, part of the Swarthmore College Peace Collection, Swarthmore, Pennsylvania. Roger Darcissac was a keen photographer (he took the stunning photograph of his son Marco that appears on the cover of this book) and his family donated his photographs and albums to the village of Le Chambon-sur-Lignon. My thanks to Aziza Gril-Mariotte, the *chef de projet* of the Lieu de Mémoire's collection of photographs and papers, for permission to use them in this book. Others who contributed have been acknowledged in the text.

As will be clear from the bibliography, the historian Gérard Bollon is a prolific writer on Plateau topics. He was one of my first interviewees, and he took me on a conducted tour of the Plateau while I photographed the House of Rocks, The Wasps' Nest, The Flowery Hill, Tante-Soly's, the New Cévenole School and other landmarks. He patiently answered endless email queries written in my beginner's French, and for more than two years generously steered me in right directions.

Nelly Trocmé Hewett's friend Joann Cierniak, who writes about music, theatre and the performing arts, came to my rescue when I was getting bogged down in the research. She read parts of the book as a work in progress, and her encouraging response reassured me and kept me going.

Nobody can tackle a subject like this without taking advantage of the research already done by other authors and historians. My first need when I began my research was an accurate chronology: step forward François Boulet, author of the excellent *Histoire de la Montagne-refuge*; step forward also Léon Chave, who prepared a very full chronology as his contribution to the 1990 symposium *Le Plateau Vivarais-Lignon: Accueil et Résistance 1939–1944* (The Plateau Vivarais-Lignon: Welcome and Resistance 1939–1944).

That symposium occupied a central place in my research. There is endless controversy over the events on the Plateau. Who did what? Who mattered? Who didn't? A lot of the uproar was triggered by the publication of Philip Hallie's 1979 book *Lest Innocent Blood Be Shed*, the first attempt to tell the Plateau story. The book was translated into French and published as *Le sang des innocents* (*The Blood of Innocents*). It was widely and disapprovingly read by some French survivors from the Plateau. Hallie was a moral philosopher, not a historian or a journalist, and he got a lot wrong. (He got a lot right, too, let it be said!) The symposium set out to put the record straight. The beauty of it, from my point of view, was that everybody who took part had to stand up in front of their contemporaries and fellow survivors from the Plateau to tell their story. If they strayed from the path of truth or righteousness, there were people on hand to pull them up. So in general I preferred to accept the version of events set out in the symposium, simply because each story in there had survived the scrutiny of an army of live fact-checkers.

Pierre Sauvage's documentary *Weapons of the Spirit* had an important role in the creation of this book. My friend Winton Higgins lectures in, among other things, genocide prevention, at the University of Technology, Sydney. His work led him to Pierre's film and to the

Plateau's story. Winton in turn suggested the subject to me. So Pierre's documentary began the chain of events that led to this book. I must have watched the documentary 50 times or more. Again, it was crucial to my research, because it contains interviews with Magda Trocmé, Édouard Theis, Pierre Fayol, Henri and Emma Héritier, Madeleine Barot, Georgette Barraud, Roger Darcissac and others who appear in the preceding pages. It enabled me to visualise them as people, not just as names. Further thanks to Pierre for patiently answering my endless requests for information and sometimes for reassurance. We don't always agree, particularly on rescue numbers, but he has been an important and generous ally in the creation of this book.

The staff at the departmental archive of the Haute-Loire were tirelessly helpful as I ploughed through police reports, departmental directives, pleading letters, arrest warrants and all the other trivia that adds up to collective repression. It makes for sorry reading.

The staff at the Mémorial de la Shoah (Holocaust Museum) in Paris were equally helpful, digging out old press cuttings and pointing me in the direction of helpful books and articles. I spent some time in the National Archive in Paris where the staff were, again, endlessly helpful. It was wonderful to read old issues of *Combat*, the Resistance newspaper edited by Albert Camus.

My wife Roslyn's French is fluent, unlike mine, and I could not have conducted the original interviews with Oscar Rosowsky and Gérard Bollon without her help.

That leads me to thank my two French teachers, Alain Bohée and Christelle Dubois. With Alain, I practised storytelling and dialogue in French. Christelle set about drumming the complexities of French grammar into me. A lot of this book was written as part of my French homework for Christelle: I translated from French, and Christelle (who normally teaches English, not French) checked my translation. Such infelicities and inaccuracies as survived this process are all my own work, and Christelle shall remain totally blameless.

I received a lot of encouragement from the engaging mayor of Le Chambon, Eliane Wauquiez-Motte. Her fluent English made communication simple, and her warmth and generosity are outstanding. The people of Le Chambon are lucky to have her. Her son Laurent is a deputy in the French National Assembly and was Minister for Employment in the government of Nicolas Sarkozy. He is spoken of as a future leader of the Gaullist UMP. We shall see.

My thanks to those who gave me a place to rest my head while I was conducting this research. Nelly Trocmé Hewett took my wife and me in for two nights in Saint Paul, Minnesota, a city I'd never visited before but would certainly go to again. Further thanks to an old friend, the writer Cyra McFadden, who kept us dry externally (but not internally) in her Sausalito houseboat while I was researching in the San Francisco area.

My friend Tom Keneally, who has some experience in these matters (he is the author of the remarkable *Schindler's Ark*, filmed by Steven Spielberg as *Schindler's List*) gave me a lot of advice on post-publication problems. Tom's words of wisdom remain untested at the time of writing, and will remain so until the book is actually out there, but I am the better armed for having received them.

Clara Finlay did an extraordinary job copy-editing the manuscript. As well as her excellent trimming of my wayward prose, she submitted no fewer than 1003 entirely sensible queries (Microsoft Word counts them), and the whole book is much the better for her painstaking fact-checking and incisive questioning. My regular editor, Angela Handley, has done her usual stylish job of converting my word mountains into a book. Richard Walsh agreed to read the early chapters as a work-in-progress, a request which all publishers sensibly resist, and was a vital source of encouragement when the burden of the research threatened to overwhelm me.

My final thanks must go to the people of the Plateau Vivarais-Lignon, whose unfailing decency and sheer courage give hope that the human race might be capable of good as well as evil. When I began researching this book, I often asked myself whether the people of the Plateau would behave the same way today. In the years 1939 to 1944 they were a community of farmers, living simple lives in rural isolation. Now they have television and broadband to bring the outside world into their homes. Might this new sophistication mean that those old values have gone, squeezed out by the secular embrace of the global village? If they were asked to do it all again today, could they?

Let me tell a story. On the night of the preview screening of the remastered version of *Weapons of the Spirit* in Le Chambon in June 2013, I found myself seated next to an old woman from the village, a total stranger, perhaps in her eighties. She asked me over and over when the film would start, and each time I did my best to explain to her. Finally, her daughter leaned across her and apologised to me, saying that her mother was a bit forgetful these days and had a habit of asking questions again and again. I murmured that it was no problem, and we waited. The film finally began. At several points in the film, a community group of villagers sings an old Protestant hymn, 'La Cévenole'. The old lady sang along with them, in a clear voice, remembering every word. It occurred to me then that the old values were still alive, and would be passed on. So if the question is: 'Could they do it again?' I would answer yes, they can.

NOTES

1   France has undergone so many currency changes since 1942, beginning with a string of devaluations between 1945 and 1959, then a switch from old francs to new francs in January 1960, then a further switch from the franc to the euro in 1999, that it is a mind-numbing task to try to come up with an accurate reflection of this sum in contemporary money. One 'authority' put it at as high as US$3600 in today's money, but that makes no sense at all. At the time, a dirt-cheap room could be rented for 500 francs a month, so 100 francs is less than a week's rent at peppercorn rates.

2   Most English–French dictionaries translate the English word 'church' as *église*. However, this is not strictly accurate. An *église* is the term for a Catholic church; a Protestant church is a *temple*. In the same way, a Catholic clergyman is a *prêtre* (priest), while a Protestant clergyman is a *pasteur* (pastor). In most French towns you will find somewhere a *Rue du Temple*—in other words, the street of the Protestant church.

3   This quote is absolutely irresistible to me. I live on the Île d'Oléron, only a few kilometres from Domino. I wonder what André Trocmé would make of the island today, with its two discreet nude beaches, topless women spending their summer stretched out in the sun, and some very tempting bars and restaurants not far from Domino.

4   In French, the word *bled* means something like 'remote place'. It is a pejorative term, implying that the remote place is also a bit of a dump. André was headed for the Sahara Desert region of southern Morocco.

5   The Cévennes, a mountainous area of southern France near the town of Nîmes, is important in Huguenot history. In 1702 a group of Cévennes Protestants known as Camisards rose up against the French king Louis XIV (the Sun King). Fighting continued until 1710, and there was no official peace until

315

1715. The word Cévenole, meaning 'of the Cévennes', thus invokes memories of Huguenot courage and stubborn resistance, as well as of their persecution.

6 In France, a *commune* is simply a rural local government area, centred around a town or village. The head of the commune is the *maire* (mayor).

7 The full history of the Plateau is dealt with in some detail in Appendix 1. Any reader who cares to read the appendix now rather than later will have a fuller understanding of what follows. The main body of the book tells the story of what happened and when in the mid-twentieth century. I would hope that the appendix goes some way towards answering the much more difficult question: why?

8 *Les genêts d'or* refers to the golden-flowered plant usually called Scotch broom. The local peasants regularly tied *genêts* together and used them as brooms of the sweeping variety. They referred to both the plants and the homemade brooms by the regular French word *balai*.

9 Les Barandons still exists. It is now a public campsite, trading under the slightly more impressive name Chalet des Barandons.

10 In France today, a *papeterie* is generally a stationery shop. This is an older usage of the word.

11 The full text of the declaration is reproduced in Appendix 2.

12 There is a curious resonance between this declaration by Boegner and Pétain's belief that France needed to cleanse itself. The mood of the time in France was certainly self-critical. And, at this point, Boegner was generally supportive of the marshal.

13 The whole world has reason to be grateful to Bingham and Varian Fry. Among the rescued were the artists Marc Chagall, Max Ernst, André Breton and Marcel Duchamp, together with the historian and philosopher Hannah Arendt. It was Arendt who, reporting on the trial of her tormentor Adolf Eichmann in Israel 40 years later, came up with the haunting phrase 'the banality of evil'.

14 The Fellowship of Reconciliation was an international and interdenominational organisation based in the United States and dedicated to promoting peace.

15 In her memoir, Magda names the official as Charles Guillon, the former mayor. Although Guillon had already resigned and moved to Geneva, he made repeated trips to Le Chambon between August 1940 and April 1941, and continued to preside over council meetings. So it is theoretically possible that Magda is correct. However, Magda's account is so much at odds with everything we know about Guillon, that it seems more likely that she talked to somebody else.

16 Richard H. Weisberg, *Vichy Law and the Holocaust in France*, New York University Press, New York, 1996, p. 38.

17 Magda recalls his words as: *Matam' la lessifeusse, s'il fous plait*? Dr Mautner's accented version of: *Madame, la lessiveuse s'il vous plait*?

18 This fatuous and paranoid piece of legislation seems to have survived the war and stayed on the statute books at least until the 1960s. I vividly remember the procedure for checking into French hotels at that time. As well as registering in the usual way, you filled in a little green card with name, passport number and so on. I was told the hotel passed this card on to the local prefecture.

19 It was also known as Ça File Doucement (roughly 'The Slow Goer'), which became the name of the student newspaper at the New Cévenole School.

20 *Faïdoli* is a nice-sounding nonsense word, the first word of a popular Swiss folk song. It's a bit like 'fiddle-de-dee'. There is no translation.

21 The stories are utterly charming, rather biblical in tone, and always with a moral. They are available in a collection, *Angels and Donkeys*, translated by Nelly Trocmé Hewett (Good Books, Intercourse, Pennsylvania 17534, 1998).

22 The Pearl Harbor attack took place on the morning of 7 December 1941, Honolulu time. Because of the position of the International Date Line, this was 8 December in Europe.

23 Laval returned to high office in April 1942, as President of the Council (prime minister) in the Vichy government, and continued in power until August 1944. After the war he was tried for high treason, found guilty and shot.

24 Gurs and the town of Oloron-Sainte-Marie are about nineteen kilometres apart.

25 Max and Hanne presumably spoke to each other in German at the time. However, the quotes above are from an interview conducted in English, and both Max and Hanne used the English phrase 'round-up'. This needs explanation. The big fear of Jews in France was of *rafles*. The French word *rafle* can be translated as either a police 'raid' or 'round-up'. It comes from the French verb *rafler*, meaning to 'snatch' or 'snaffle'. I have retained 'round-up' here because in English a raid usually takes place at a single location while a round-up implies a sweep of an area. The events in Lyon and elsewhere were clearly round-ups.

26 The report author's arithmetic clearly left something to be desired.

27 Italy occupied the southeast corner of France, including Provence and the important cities of Nice, Grenoble and Toulon. So the whole of France was occupied, but not all of it by Germany. There were differences between the two occupying powers. In the early part of the Occupation, the Italians showed exemplary courage in refusing to hand over Jews from their territory to the Germans, to the point where the German foreign minister Ribbentrop complained to Mussolini: 'Italian military circles lack a proper understanding of the Jewish question.' But Mussolini's long-term Jewish mistress Margherita Sarfatti had helped Mussolini to launch his Fascist Party in Italy, and the party accepted Jews as members. Mussolini was not about to be browbeaten.

28 This was, of course, well and truly offset by the arrival of the Germans with their tried and tested apparatus of repression, notably the Gestapo and the SS. If the French bureaucrats were running at half-throttle, the Germans had their heavy boots flat to the floor.

29 *La Peste* is generally regarded as the book that clinched the Nobel Prize for Camus in 1957.

30 The Armée Secrète (Secret Army) was the widely used name for the merged forces of armed French resistance led by Jean Moulin. It first appeared in 1943 after the merger of Combat, Libération-Sud (Liberation South) and Franc-Tireur (roughly 'French Gunman').

31 The word *maquis* is frequently used by English speakers as though it had no meaning other than armed resistance fighter. But in French it is simply the word for scrub or undergrowth. So the maquis were those who went off into the bushes to hide. Of course, many of the STO-dodging maquis quickly joined the armed Resistance, while those members of the Resistance who lived in hiding in forests and in the countryside may properly be called a maquis.

32 As indicated in the Prologue, there are endless problems converting 1943 francs to modern currency. However, if 500 francs was the going cheap rate for a month's room rental, then five francs was surely a trivial sum.

33 Hard grains from a local plant mostly used as animal food. The grains had to be boiled for hours before eating.

34 Author's note: Magda was nothing if not a born storyteller.

35 Le Forestier's slightly confusing reference is to André Trocmé, pastor of a parish with 1200 members and father of four children; Édouard Theis, headmaster of a school with 400 students and father of eight children; and Roger Darcissac, who was also headmaster of a school and father of three children.

36 Société d'Histoire de la Montagne, *Les Résistances sur le Plateau Vivarais-Lignon, 1938–1945*, Éditions du Roure, Polignac, 2005, p 81.

37 Jeanne Merle d'Aubigne, Emile C. Fabre, Violette Mouchon, *Les clandestins de Dieu: Cimade 1939–1945* ('God's Underground: Cimade 1939–1945'), Labor and Fides, Geneva, 1968.

38 I was in the Boy Scouts and we spent a lot of time learning to make bush shelters from trees using only string and an axe, learning to light fires without matches, and learning about using a map and compass to find our way around the Australian bush. We learned to leave secret signs on the ground to mark out a trail, and we could do a bit of first aid. I don't think this was Lord Baden-Powell's intention when he set up the Boy Scouts, but the skills we learned certainly would have made us better-than-average people smugglers.

French Boy Scouts (*éclaireurs*) were curiously divided along religious lines. There were *éclaireurs unionistes* (Protestant scouts), *éclaireurs israélites* (Jews) and *Scouts de France* (Roman Catholics). This religious division seems to have made not a jot of difference to the Plateau rescue mission, though the sheer demographics of the situation meant that Protestant and Jewish scouts did most of the guiding work.

39 Author's note: I doubt this.

40 Piton's exact words were *passaient en manteaux de cuir et chapeau mou parmi une foule monstre*, which translates literally as men who 'went about in leather coats and soft hats in a massive crowd'. 'Men in leather jackets and felt hats' was French slang for the Gestapo.

41 Abbé Folliet was, of course, a Catholic priest. In Annecy and the surrounding area, which had a largely Catholic population, Catholic priests and not just Protestant ministers carried out much of this underground pipeline work.

42 'Noël' is, of course, 'Léon' spelled backwards. It's fair to say that the Resistance often lacked sophistication in the early days.

43 Daniel Trocmé had lived and worked in Switzerland for seven months, then in Austria for five months. He was completely fluent in German.

44 Throughout this account, Magda refers to the Germans as Gestapo, but that should not be taken as proof.

45 Fresnes was used by the Germans during World War II to hold captured SOE agents and members of the Resistance. Royallieu-Compiègne held mostly Jews but also some Resistance fighters. Some 40,000 inmates of Royallieu-Compiègne were deported, mostly to Auschwitz.

46 These BBC messages are a study in themselves. They were broadcast by the BBC French Service (*BBC Londres*) alongside the evening news and were referred to as *messages personnels*. An SOE agent in Occupied France would radio a request, heavily coded, for supplies. The message would include map coordinates for the drop field, a recognition code consisting of a single letter of the alphabet to be flashed in morse code to the arriving pilot, and a *message personnel* to be broadcast on the night of the drop. Most drops took place in good weather with clear moonlight.

47 The *Milice Française* (French Militia) was a paramilitary force created by the Vichy government in January 1943 to fight the Resistance. Known as *miliciens*, they were a bunch of brown-shirted right-wing thugs recruited initially from pre-war far-right movements. The Resistance feared them more than the Gestapo because they spoke fluent French and were generally well informed about local activities.

48 Indeed he does still own it. He showed me the battered box when I interviewed him in January 2012.

49 808 was another plastic explosive, properly called Nobel 808. It looked like green plasticine, and smelled distinctly of almonds.

50 Although Italy had changed sides and declared war on Germany, German troops remained in Italy, now as an occupying force.

51 Artemis was, of course, the Greek goddess of the hunt. The counterpart Roman goddess was Diana. So the Germans weren't far off with their code name for 'Diane'.

52 This type of force—two officers and a radio operator—was known as a Jedburgh team, named after a small town on the Scottish borders. Jedburgh teams wore military uniform, so they could not be classed as spies and shot out of hand if they were caught. They had the job of organising overt rather than clandestine activity.

53 The expression Secret Army typically refers to armed French Resistance fighters operating *inside* metropolitan France during the Occupation. As France was liberated, the armed Resistance was absorbed into the more official *Forces Françaises de l'Intérieure* (French Forces of the Interior), usually abbreviated to FFI. The FFI is not to be confused with Free French Forces, those remnants of the French Army, Navy and Air Force who chose to stick with General de Gaulle and fight alongside the Allies. In general, until the Liberation, Free French Forces fought *outside* metropolitan France, mostly in the Middle East, North Africa and Indo-China.

54 Planchon went on to become one of France's most distinguished film and stage directors.

55 There have been suggestions that Neukirchen was a Gestapo officer rather than a regular soldier. That is incorrect: he was from the Feldgendarmerie, the German military police.

56 For French grammarians: *fichés* is, of course, the past participle plural of the French verb *ficher*, to file. But the literal translation 'fileds' is too horrible to contemplate.

57 Anybody reading this book and involved in modern law enforcement can take some comfort from an email Oscar Rosowsky sent me in November 2013. He wrote that the forgery results he achieved during World War II would be impossible in the digital age. 'Each French citizen has a 13-digit identification number,' he told me, 'and within the almost infinite combination of numbers there is an almost infinite combination of characteristics. It is possible to extract instantly the information needed [to identify somebody] from this number.'

58 Lest the Swiss get too pleased with themselves over this performance, it should also be pointed out that they turned away slightly more refugees than they sheltered.

59 Serge Klarsfeld went on to become one of the most important historians of the Holocaust in France, as well as a doughty Nazi-hunter. So his testimony in favour of Schmähling carries a lot of weight.

60 As joint-editor in 1961 (with Richard Walsh, the publisher of this book) of the University of Sydney student newspaper *honi soit*, I can remember making very sure that any student peace organisations we supported were not

communist fronts. During this time, anyone calling for 'peace' risked being lumped in with 'fellow travellers' (inadvertent or unconscious communist supporters), or even regarded as one of Stalin's 'useful idiots'.

61 The Knights Templar enjoyed a certain recent notoriety after the 2003 publication of Dan Brown's international blockbuster *The Da Vinci Code*. Anyone interested in a more historically accurate and less far-fetched account of their story would do better to read Clive Lindley's novel *Templar Knights: Their secret history—The end of an epoch 1307–1314*, published in June 2012 as an ebook and available through Amazon.

62 The fact that St Bartholomew's Day falls on 24 August every year is one of those little mysteries of history.

63 Some sources put the number at as high as 20,000, but 3000 is the most commonly quoted figure.

64 The French Nationality Law of 1889 laid down the same rules. It reaffirmed the right of return of those driven out of France for religious reasons, a right which extended to their descendants. The law continued in force until 19 October 1945, when the first postwar French government revoked it.

65 For the record, this solidarity has slipped a little in the twenty-first century. In the second round of the 2012 French presidential election, Le Chambon voted 56.5% for François Hollande, the Socialist candidate and eventual winner, against 43.5% for Nicolas Sarkozy, the centre-right Gaullist incumbent. In the first round, 183 Chambonnais (11.2%) even voted for Marine Le Pen, the candidate of the far-right National Front. In the election for the National Assembly held in June 2012, in the second round the UMP (Gaullist centre-right) candidate Laurent Wauquiez (son of the current mayor of Le Chambon) collected 59.3% of the vote, defeating the Socialist Party's Guy Vocanson (40.7%).

BIBLIOGRAPHY

Books

English language

Camus, A. (trans. R. Buss), *The Plague*, Allen Lane The Penguin Press, London, 2001

DeSaix, D.D. and Ruelle, K.G., *Hidden on the Mountain: Stories of children sheltered from the Nazis in Le Chambon*, Holiday House, New York, 2007

Hallie, P., *Lest Innocent Blood Be Shed*, Harper & Rowe, New York, 1979

Henry, P., *We Only Know Men: The rescue of Jews in France during the Holocaust*, Catholic University of America Press, Washington DC, 2007

Lecomte, F., *I Will Never Be 14 Years Old*, Beach Lloyd Publishers, Wayne, PA, 2009

Mercer, D. (editor-in-chief), *Chronicle of the 20th Century*, Longman, London, 1989

Roberts, A., *The Storm of War: A new history of the Second World War*, Allen Lane, London, and HarperCollins, New York, 2009

Trocmé, A. (trans. N. Trocmé Hewett), *Angels and Donkeys: Tales for Christmas and other times*, Good Books, Intercourse, PA, 1998

Unsworth, R.P., *A Portrait of Pacifists*, Syracuse University Press, Syracuse, NY, 2012

Verity, H., *We Landed by Moonlight: The secret RAF landings in France 1940–1944*, Ian Allen Limited, London, 1978; revised edition, Crécy Publishing Limited, Manchester, 2000

Weisberg, R.H., *Vichy Law and the Holocaust in France*, New York University Press, New York, 1996

French language

Boismorand, P., *Magda et André Trocmé: Figures de resistances*, Les Éditions du Cerf, Paris, 2007

Bolle, P. (ed.), *Le Plateau Vivarais-Lignon: Accueil et résistance 1939–1944*, Société d'Histoire de la Montagne, Le Chambon-sur-Lignon, 1992

Bollon, G., *Le Chambon-sur-Lignon d'hier & d'aujourd'hui*, Éditions Dolmazon, Le Cheylard, 1999

——*Les villages sur la Montagne: Entre Ardèche et Haute-Loire, le Plateau, terre d'accueil et de refuge*, Éditions Dolmazon, Le Cheylard, 2004

Bollon, G. and Flaud, A., *Paroles de réfugiés, Paroles de justes*, Éditions Dolmazon, Le Cheylard, 2009

Boulet, François F., *Histoire de la Montagne-refuge*, Les Éditions du Roure, Polignac, 2008

Cabanel, P., Joutard, P., Sémelin, J. and Wieviorka, A. (eds), *La Montagne refuge: Accueil et sauvetage des juifs autour du Chambon-sur-Lignon*, Albin Michel, Paris, 2013

D'Aubigne, J.M., Fabre, E.C., Mouchon, V., *Les clandestins de Dieu: Cimade 1939–1945*, Labor and Fides, Geneva, 1968

Fayol, P., *Le Chambon-sur-Lignon sous l'occupation: Les résistances locales, l'aide interalliée, l'action de Virginia Hall (O.S.S.)*, Édition L'Harmattan, Paris, 1990

Gril-Mariotte, A. (ed.), *Lieu de mémoire au Chambon/Lignon: Le Plateau, terre d'accueil et de refuge*, Éditions Dolmazon, Le Cheylard, 2013

Henry, P.G., *La montagne des justes: Le Chambon-sur-Lignon, 1940–1944*, Éditions Privat, Toulouse, 2010

Société d'Histoire de la Montagne, *Les résistances sur le Plateau Vivarais-Lignon, 1938–1945, Témoins, témoignages et lieux de mémoire, Les oubliés de l'Histoire parlent*, Éditions du Roure, Polignac, 2005

Film and television documentaries

The Nazis: A warning from history, Laurence Rees and Tilman Remme (directors), BBC TV, 1997

Shoah, Claude Lanzmann (director), Historia, Les Films Aleph, Ministère de la Culture de la République Française, 1985

The Sorrow and the Pity, Marcel Ophuls (director), Télévision Rencontre, Norddeutscher Rundfunk, Télévision Suisse-Romande, 1969

Three Righteous Christians, Pierre Sauvage (director), Chambon Foundation, 2014

Weapons of the Spirit, Pierre Sauvage (director), Chambon Foundation, 1989, re-mastered 2014

INDEX OF PROPER NAMES

Index of Proper Names